RESEARCH AND REFORM

Research and Reform

W.P. Thompson at the University of Saskatchewan

RICHARD A. REMPEL

McGill-Queen's University Press
Montreal & Kingston • London • Ithaca

ISBN 978-0-7735-4174-0 (cloth)
ISBN 978-0-7735-8890-5 (ePDF)
ISBN 978-0-7735-8891-2 (ePUB)

Legal deposit third quarter 2013
Bibliothèque nationale du Québec

Printed in Canada on acid-free paper that is 100% ancient forest free (100% post-consumer recycled), processed chlorine free

This book has been published with the help of a grant from the Office of the President at the University of Saskatchewan.

McGill-Queen's University Press acknowledges the support of the Canada Council for the Arts for our publishing program. We also acknowledge the financial support of the Government of Canada through the Canada Book Fund for our publishing activities.

Library and Archives Canada Cataloguing in Publication

Rempel, Richard A.
Research and reform: W.P. Thompson at the University of Saskatchewan / Richard A. Rempel.

Includes bibliographical references and index.
ISBN 978-0-7735-4174-0. – ISBN 978-0-7735-8890-5 (ePDF).
ISBN 978-0-7735-8891-2 (ePUB).

1. Thompson, Walter Palmer, 1889–1970. 2. University of Saskatchewan – Presidents – Biography. 3. College presidents – Canada – Biography. 4. University of Saskatchewan – History. 5. Geneticists – Canada – Biography. 6. Botanists – Canada – Biography. I. Title.

LE3.S717T56 2013 378.0092 C2013-901848-4

This book was typeset by Interscript in 10.5/13 Sabon.

Contents

Acknowledgments

Throughout the research and writing of this book, I have benefitted from the generous assistance of many people. Foremost among them is archivist Cheryl Avery of the University of Saskatchewan Archives. During all phases of the research, from the initial draft to the revisions to the final manuscript, she has been invaluable as a source of information about important sets of relevant documents, a uniformly constructive critic of various drafts, and a cheerful supporter of this project. I also thank Patrick Hayes from these same archives for his pertinent ideas and assistance in sleuthing out the relevant documents. The director of the archives, Tim Hutchinson, has been a steady supporter despite his many other responsibilities. Three of my former classmates from our undergraduate times together in the late 1950s, Shirley and Duff Spafford and Don Kerr, have read the entire manuscript and contributed, to my benefit, their knowledge of the university, and the history of the province of Saskatchewan. All three hosted me frequently, as well as Don's wife Mildred, a former classmate, who also recalled significant events of the Thompson era. Audrey Brandt also provided welcome hospitality and engaged in many stimulating conversations about the university. I warmly thank Dean and Marg Botham for their warm welcome in Saskatoon. Dean, a former University of Saskatchewan assistant vice-president (Operational Budget), provided important insights about the university administration. President emeritus Peter MacKinnon was always a sustaining, intelligent, and encouraging advocate of this biography, to the extent of providing some financial subventions to allow me to visit the archives frequently. In the president's office, Karen Taylor was an excellent liaison. Professor Eli Bornstein, emeritus chair of

Fine Arts at the University of Saskatchewan, devoted many hours of conversation about the world of President Thompson.

On the difficult issues of describing and assessing Dr Thompson's work and success in genetics, I have had the steady assistance of Dr Margaret Steeves, a paleobotanist, who read the entire manuscript twice, and corrected both the scientific errors and stylistic infelicities, while the geneticist Professor Maureen Rever-DuWors taught me about the history of Thompson's academic field. I thank the fine secretary of the Biology Department at the University of Saskatchewan, Deidre Wasyliw, who was always kind and expeditious in handling my requests to the biology department. I also thank Arlene Duncan, secretary of the Bertrand Russell Research Centre at McMaster University, for assisting me with formatting questions. The late Professor Doug Knott was a knowledgeable source of Thompson's scientific achievements. I thank Professor Michael Hayden, professor emeritus of history, University of Saskatchewan, who both spoke with me and granted me a taped interview about WPT and the University of Saskatchewan. Of great significance to me too was professor emeritus of genetics, Jack Pasternak, of the University of Waterloo, who read over my scientific writing carefully and enabled me to write clearly and accurately the parts of the manuscript dealing with Dr Thompson's scientific research. I certainly came to realize why Dr Pasternak is a noted scientist, a talented writer, and a gifted teacher. My tributes extend to the Hon. Walter Smishek, the last living member of the Advisory Planning Committee on Medicare, for his memories of Dr Thompson. The distinguished economist, Dr Edward Safarian, professor emeritus at the University of Toronto, my last living university professor, gave me his insights concerning teaching at the University of Saskatchewan during Dr Thompson's era. There were useful conversations with Ray Procwat, instructional assistant in the McMaster University biology department. The historian Dr Helen Hatton, of the University of Toronto, cast a close and constructive eye on the manuscript, pointing out numerous style and organizational problems. My long-time friend, and former American colleague, the historian Kendrick Clements, was particularly astute in his reading of the manuscript. I owe thanks to my good friend from high school and university, Garry Beatty. A former deputy minister of finance under Allan Blakeney, Garry taught me much about the New Democratic Party in power in Saskatchewan. I thank my oldest friend Donald Park and his wife Mavis for their kindness in hosting me on my visits to Calgary, where Don explained Dean Arthur Porter's role in upgrading the quality of the College of Engineering in the late 1950s.

Dr Margaret Thompson, professor emerita of genetics at the University of Toronto, talked with me during many afternoons at her home in Toronto about her late father-in-law, Dr W.P. Thompson. Often her son, Gordon, (now deceased) would join in the reminiscing. I also appreciate the kind assistance of Dr Thompson's other son, Bruce, and his wife, Denise. Denise invited me to their home to view photographs of Dr W.P. Thompson and to scrutinize books that had once been part of the late president's private library. Dr W.P. Thompson's two granddaughters, Lucy Smith and Marcia Mayo, made significant contributions to the research and writing of this biography. Marcia and her husband Mike spent a number of days in Raleigh, North Carolina unearthing family letters from storage boxes. These invaluable letters were then sent to me to use in the biography and are preserved in the University of Saskatchewan Archives. They include numerous letters between Marcia and Lucy's mother, the late Mary Thompson Smith, and her parents, Marjory and W.P. Thompson. Both granddaughters also read the manuscript in draft and offered some important suggestions. My wife and I visited the Mayos and Lucy Smith and her husband Lon in New York, to discuss their personal memories of their grandparents.

In Winnipeg, Isabel Auld related her stories about working as a student with Dr Thompson. She also sent letters telling me of other gifted students of Thompson's, who became active researchers at the Winnipeg Dominion Rust Research Laboratory, notably the distinguished plant breeder Margaret Newton. Isabel's husband, Murray Auld, also passed on photographs of Thompson's early career at the university. Murray was the son of the late Hedley Auld, chancellor at the University of Saskatchewan throughout Thompson's presidency. I learned much about Thompson's consideration for undergraduate students from Avis Williamson, his secretary from 1939 to 1945, during Thompson's first six years as dean of Arts and Science. The former executive secretary of the board of governors at Carleton University, the late Donald McEown, the son of Dr Thompson's executive assistant, Colb McEown, spoke with me a number of times and related his own and his father's memories of the Thompson presidency, and read my entire manuscript. Lynn Arnason Friesen recalled her memories of her father's long association with Dr Thompson.

Lynn is a daughter of the late Dr Thomas Arnason, who had been hired by Dr Thompson, and was a much appreciated teacher of biology at the University of Saskatchewan. Elizabeth Seitz, Archives assistant at the University of Regina, was also helpful. I appreciate the thoughtfulness of Steven Leclair and Sarah Marleau at the National Research Council of Canada Archives. I thank Jessica Howarth, editorial assistant at McGill-Queen's University Press. Much appreciation is extended to Ryan Van Huijstee, managing editor at McGill-Queen's, for his careful scrutiny of my manuscript and his kind assistance. My copy editor, Gillian Scobie, demonstrated a distinguished understanding of the art of editing. Caitlin Dyer assisted me in organizing the bibliography. All members of MQUP who worked on this book deserve my generous praise. Dr Andrew Bone, my excellent colleague and senior research associate at the Bertrand Russell Centre, carefully compiled the index for this book. Arlene Duncan, the gifted photocompositor and secretary of the Bertrand Russell Centre, also deserves my praise. She often came to my aid, after my retirement in 2000 as director of the Centre, when I needed rapid secretarial advice. Amy Back was essential in formatting the endnotes and bibliography and possessed a keen eye on matters of style.

Mark Abley of McGill-Queen's University Press was the most gifted, encouraging and responsive editor that I could possibly have had. I thank my daughter Dr Rachel Rempel and my son Robert Rempel for their continued support and encouragement throughout the writing of this biography. The following individuals have also helped me: Christina Bornstein was a kind hostess, well informed on university matters. Ruth Horlick introduced me to Dr Margaret Thompson. Harold R. Baker explained how he broadened University Extension. I value Herb Pinder's description of the congenial "town and gown" Saturday luncheon club gatherings at the Bessborough Hotel.

I dedicate this book to two people, my wife and my late father. My wife Ann has been a consistently patient and constructive reader of various drafts of this project. My father, Professor J.G. Rempel, was long ago both a student of Dr Thompson and later, as an entomologist, a young colleague. He was instrumental in urging Dr Thompson to write an account of his professional life.

I am solely responsible for any errors of fact or interpretation.

Preface

When he joined the University of Saskatchewan in September 1913 as professor and head of biology, Walter Palmer Thompson entered an institution that had taken in its first students only four years earlier. Thompson had never before even been in the province, and, though he had a cursory knowledge of Batoche and Louis Riel, knew little else about the Canadian West. He had not yet met the university president, Walter Murray, who had hired him, nor was he acquainted with any of his new colleagues.

In 1959, Thompson retired, as president. He had spent forty-six years of his life at the University of Saskatchewan. He had raised his daughter and son in Saskatoon, spurned other job opportunities, developed into a world-class researcher in the genetics of wheat chromosomes, and played a dominant role in the development of the university, his innovations still recognizable today. Moreover, he had made many significant contributions to the province as a whole and, indeed, to Canada, notably his role in helping to bring medicare to Saskatchewan. The young man who had known almost nothing about Saskatchewan in 1913 had become a leading provincial and national university policy-maker and a devoted citizen of the province.

This biography traces the life and career of a gifted scientist and administrator. At the University of Saskatchewan, W.P. Thompson became a botanist of international renown. In his prime research years, from 1914 to roughly 1939, he was among the leading wheat chromosome geneticists in North America. Before 1934, he was already known as a distinguished teacher and supervisor. When he became an administrator in 1934, he turned his imagination and organizational abilities to transforming the university. Thompson restructured the college of arts and science curriculum, and led the drive to establish the College of Graduate Studies. He took the lead in amending the 1907 University Act, added new departments, played a key role in the establishment of a medical college, and assisted in the hiring of gifted new faculty. Thompson also directed the beginnings of significant and sustained international outreach for students at the University of Saskatchewan. During his presidency, student academic and leadership initiatives were encouraged and student freedoms both extended and codified by his pronouncements and actions.

During the early years of his retirement, roughly from 1959 to 1965, Thompson continued to serve provincial interests. Although Co-operative Commonwealth Federation (CCF) leader T.C. Douglas and his NDP successor Woodrow Lloyd were the prime fathers of Saskatchewan's medicare plan, Thompson also deserves significant credit. He had the difficult work of managing discordant members of an advisory planning group for Premier Douglas, and guiding the writing and presentation of the report that became the heart of the medicare legislation implemented in the summer of 1962. This legislation was also the precedent for Prime Minister Lester Pearson to promote a national system of medicare in 1966. Thompson continued to work and write on medicare issues until 1965, and published a history of the University of Saskatchewan just before his death on 30 March 1970.

Thompson grew up in the last decade of Victorian Canada and aspects of Victorian values along the lines of the progressive liberalism of John Stuart Mill remained central elements of his character and were present in many of his policies. Thompson had transcended the limited cultural opportunities of his early rural life and demonstrated an ability to excel in university and political life. All his life he retained some of the constructive aspects of the Victorian liberal legacies, notably a firm commitment to high standards and academic freedom, whether in scientific pursuits or personal conduct. Thompson's progressivism was reinforced by the Victorian liberalism of his mentor and friend, Walter Murray, whom he came to admire above all others. Thompson prized independent thinking and had a warm regard for those who had a capacity for arriving at thoughtful, if not always popular, decisions. Such values reflected his well-anchored sense of self-reliance. This respect for firmness was matched by clarity and directness in his dealings with others. He believed in discussing and debating contentious issues in a courteous, rational manner. The Victorian gospel of hard work and self-improvement was integral to his beliefs and actions.

Thompson was an inherent reformer, whose purposefulness was evident in his work on medicare and in his policies to render organizations and systems more efficient, less burdensome, and more rational. He was always, however, an academic and never a politician. Nevertheless, he became a believer in social democracy. His respect and admiration for progressive political leaders, such as the Social Gospel politician J.S. Woodsworth, and the CCF leaders T.C. Douglas and Woodrow Lloyd, place him securely in the company of the pioneers of the Canadian Left. He particularly admired the ideas and social activism of the poet, legal scholar, and civil libertarian, F.R. (Frank) Scott. Thompson's progressivism must be set against his distrust of, indeed repugnance for, the conservative ideas and policies espoused by some Canadians, especially John Diefenbaker, and Americans, such as Richard Nixon, Robert Taft, and Barry Goldwater.

However, Thompson never embodied one of the dominant Victorian beliefs, devotion to religion. Instead, he embraced the antithetical minority cause of religious scepticism and rationalism. Like some distinguished Victorians, notably John Stuart Mill and George Eliot, Thompson was a rationalist all his life. Though he was obliged as a boy to attend the local Methodist church on Sundays, he was a religious sceptic who even from his earliest years was never concerned with any concept of a "spiritual world" or ever involved in any public religious debates. As a boy, Thompson enjoyed the church picnics at Hoover Point on Lake Erie, but only as holiday outings. He did share one central characteristic of the Victorians: the conviction that, however many interpretations of a problem existed, truth could be discovered through rigorous thought and debate. Post-modernist conceptions of the variability of truth never occurred to him.

A useful source for this biography was Thompson's unpublished memoir, *An Academic's Progress*, written in 1969–70, the last year of his life. It is the first and only account Thompson wrote, even briefly, of his boyhood in rural Ontario, and of his years at the University of Toronto and Harvard. Most of the memoir deals with his career as a scientist and administrator at the University of

Saskatchewan and omits almost entirely his personal life. Thompson may have taken this approach because a number of his former biology department colleagues urged him to give an account of his professional career. His writing style is that of a scientist – succinct and unadorned. Thompson focused the memoir almost exclusively on his own academic life, his views on the nature of universities, and his perception of their changing roles. He was a man of his time in regard to his respect for privacy and his acceptance of a male-dominated world, although he was noteworthy, in fact exemplary, in promoting the education of women, both at the graduate and undergraduate levels, and in assisting women in administrative positions to advance. He saw no need to write about his personal family life once he arrived at the University of Toronto in 1906.

Three themes dominate this biography. First, as an experienced teacher, scientist, and administrator, Thompson had firm ideas about what the practical and philosophical goals of universities ought to be. He thought about the issues of who should attend, who ought to teach, and how universities should be governed to best develop mature, well-educated students; to advance research; and to promote the common good. Thompson posed an important theoretical question on university governance: where should authority in the institution reside? During his presidency, some of the issues that he debated related to the diverse ways in which faculty and students aspired to become involved in university governance alongside the senior administration and the board of governors. Moreover, the role of the provincial government in university affairs was an evolving preoccupation in Saskatchewan before, during, and immediately following his presidency. Thompson helped to define these once inchoate roles.

Thompson left no single document outlining his philosophy of education. Yet, in many speeches, both formal and in those written for student receptions and other such passing events, he emphasized the necessity of a liberal education, not just for arts students but also for those pursuing science. These speeches, his liberal and humane policies toward students, and his establishment of new departments, both in the social sciences and the fine arts, best illustrate his philosophy of education. Thompson's introduction of the survey courses, two science courses for all arts students and two arts courses for science specialists, reflect his educational ideal of fostering a coherent liberal education for students. These ideals are evident in his many achievements as president: his introduction of the four year honours program; his insistence on maintaining, rather than splintering, the College of Arts and Sciences; his emphasis on faculty research and establishment and development of a College of Graduate Studies; his introduction in 1952 of student academic counselling; and his commitment to devoting many university policies to the good of the people of the province. Thompson's belief in these policies and their implementation all reflect well and coherently his personal philosophy of higher education as implemented at the University of Saskatchewan. His ideas on university governance are probably best developed in the policies advocated in the Survey Committee document that arose from the committee that he chaired through 1945 and early 1946.

The second theme explores his conviction that universities must nurture science, the social sciences, and the humanities by facilitating faculty and graduate student research. Thompson contended that, without provision for the intense development of the sciences, any contemporary university would be isolated from the modern world and never become first-rate. The university's presidents before Thompson, Walter Murray and J.S. Thomson, had been from the humanities; their specialties were philosophy and theology, respectively. Both men, especially Murray, had understood the need to develop the sciences, particularly for the practical assistance that research in agriculture could offer the province. Both revered the humanities, although J.S. Thomson regretted the lack of imaginative research in the humanities during his presidency. Though W.P. Thompson was self-educated in the literary and social science canon, and respectful of it, he was often critical of faculty work in the humanities and social sciences, especially during his decanal years, and believed that some members of those faculties were inadequate researchers of subjects that were less important to him than the natural sciences. The scholarly achievements of many faculty members in the humanities and social sciences during his presidency dissipated many of Thompson's earlier pessimistic concerns about the inadequacy of scholarship in these fields.

The third theme addresses Thompson's ideas on service. By service, he meant commitment, not only to the university, but also the province, the country, and some international educational centres. He may have been influenced in this by the work of the university's founding president, Walter Murray, but Thompson focused less on the direct and practical role of university extension work than Murray, and more, ultimately, on the "educated imagination." Thompson's ideas on the value of the university to the individual and society are captured in a speech he delivered to students in the College of Arts and Science in the spring of 1943:

> In other words, society needs a body of men with the type of training given in the college of liberal arts and sciences. The college is the best institution for training persons who can recognize changed conditions and new problems, and who can analyze them and plan new policies needed to forward human welfare ... The social objective of the University does not interfere with the individual need for useful training. In reality the university renders its service to society *through* its service to the individual. Properly it does not serve the individual, but through the individual serves the whole of society. In securing the development of a mature environment and developing the individual mind it makes its students efficient instruments for the utilization of learning by society. And the individual needs the broad learning which he may not be able to apply in his business. [This learning is essential] for the full private life, for the durable satisfactions he needs to have the learning and training which the society needs him to have.[1]

Harvard Hockey Club (1911), W.P. Thompson third from left. J.W. Estey (on WPT's immediate left) became a Justice of the Supreme Court of Canada. Courtesy of the Thompson family

WPT in 1912, posing with typical Welwitschia in German South-West Africa (now Namibia). University of Saskatchewan Archives, A-3367

WPT on veranda of hotel, Cape Town, South Africa, 1912. Table Mountain in background. Courtesy of the Thompson family

Playing tennis on the University of Saskatchewan campus tennis courts, c. 1914–15. University of Saskatchewan Archives, A-6784

WPT, Bobbie, and their children Mary and Jimmy in Saskatoon, 1920. Courtesy of the Thompson family

Peter Grant, the much beloved technician in the Department of Biology, University of Saskatchewan, 1925. Courtesy of the Thompson family

WPT's son James (Jimmy) Scott, 1939.
Courtesy of the Thompson family

WPT and Mary at her convocation from the University of Saskatchewan, 1942.
Courtesy of the Thompson family

Biology faculty and students, University of Saskatchewan, 1946. WPT is seated in front, fourth from left; J.G. Rempel, second row, first from left; Jimmy Thompson is in the back row, third from left. Courtesy of the Thompson family

WPT and granddaughter, Lucy Thompson Smith, picking raspberries on the grounds of the President's Residence, University of Saskatchewan, 1948. Courtesy of the Thompson family

WPT, c. 1949–50. First year as university president. University of Saskatchewan Archives, A-3361

"Town and Gown" Saturday luncheon club at the Bessborough Hotel, Saskatoon, c. 1956. WPT third from left. Courtesy of the Thompson family

WPT and Bobbie in the President's Residence, University of Saskatchewan, 1958. Courtesy of the Thompson family

Eleventh International Entomological Congress in Vienna, 1960. Left to right: Elizabeth Rempel; J.G. Rempel; Greta Rempel; WPT. Courtesy of the Thompson family

Formal opening of the W.P. Thompson Biology Building, 1960, with the mosaics of chromosomes in the background. Left to right: Mary; Bobbie; WPT; Peggy and Jimmy Thompson. Courtesy of the Thompson family

WPT and Bobbie in retirement, early 1960s, Hawaii. Courtesy of the Thompson family

Investiture of W.P. Thompson as a Companion of the Order of Canada, 22 October 1968. Left to right: Mrs Michener; Governor-General Roland Michener; Hilda Neatby; WPT; Mrs Spinks; and University of Saskatchewan President J.W.T. Spinks. Courtesy of the Thompson family

RESEARCH AND REFORM

1

Formative Years

Walter Palmer Thompson was born on 3 April 1889 on a farm close to the village of Decewsville in Haldimand County, Ontario, a few miles north of Lake Erie. This hamlet had been founded in the 1830s. The family farm consisted of 100 acres, similar to most farms in the area. It lay very close to the Talbot Road, 5,000 acres settled by Colonel Thomas Talbot, secretary to John Graves Simcoe, the first lieutenant governor of Upper Canada. The original settlement, of ex-soldiers, was intended to protect against a potential American invasion.

The Thompson family was eminently respectable, yet in no way distinguished. Thompson had little or no guidance from his severe, remote, and inordinately religious father. Thompson barely knew him and could scarcely recall him, for his father died in 1896 when Thompson was seven-years-old. In contrast, he was devoted to his mother, who, although not intellectually inclined or interested in reading – Thompson "never saw a book in her hand" – encouraged him in his schoolwork and was proud of his academic successes. All her children felt a deep attachment to her. She died of pneumonia in 1909 when he was only twenty. Thompson remembered his mother with affection, even adoration.

> My mother was very different from my father. She was of average height, plump, with jet black hair and black eyes. She was gay, full of fun, very affectionate. She was adored by all her children. My greatest delight was to be with her alone on such occasions as picking raspberries which grew in great abundance along the stump fences which separated the fields, or while I was

> operating the old plunger type cylindrical churn. I have a very vivid recollection of her going with me after I received my first pair of skates at Christmas to the little pond 200 yards from the house, and helping me put them on and learn to skate. I can't decide now precisely what she did or what it was about her which made us enjoy such occasions so much.[1]

He also cared deeply for his maternal grandfather, James Biggar, whose warmth and sense of fun were so different from Thompson's father. Thompson obviously felt able to express his wry sense of humour with his grandfather. Although the name "Biggar" originated in north Lancashire and on the Scottish border, Thompson's family background on his mother's side was Irish Quaker. Young Thompson may have absorbed some anti-English sentiment from his Irish grandfather.[2] Despite being immersed in English literature and British parliamentary traditions, Thompson's sense of personal identity was not anchored in idealizing, much less deferring to, British ideas of society. He certainly had no patience with anglophilia: he was critical of British royalty, dismissive of the aristocracy, and impatient with British class distinctions. On a number of occasions, from his childhood to his mature years, Thompson wrote sceptically of imperialist sentiment. He recalled one of his school teachers demonstrating the widespread credulity of Canadians who believed the extravagant British propaganda spread by the "jingo" press during the South African War of 1899–1902. This teacher harangued his students about what he believed was a moral crusade against the Boers and their leader, Paul Kruger. Thompson distanced himself from what was then an integral part of Anglophone Canada. He did not embrace the "Canadian identity, prior to the 1960s, that was a subset of British identity, and ... was, whatever its uniqueness, unmistakable in its attachment to empire and to understandings of colonizing superiorities."[3] Thompson remained indifferent and sometimes outright hostile to British royalty, imperial propaganda, and aristocratic class distinctions and pretensions throughout his life. If anything, this attitude deepened as he grew older. Writing to his daughter Mary on 14 October 1951, Thompson was dismissive of the soon-to-be Queen Elizabeth and her husband: "I suppose you hear something of the visit of Princess Elizabeth and her husband. We are hearing too much, particularly of the sugary, slushy kind. They are both very ordinary persons but the easterners are making a terrific fuss of them. I find it hard to take, but mustn't say anything like that outside the house. They are to stop 4 minutes at the university two weeks from today."[4] Later, in 1954, he grumbled again to Mary that he had to go to Kingston "for a meeting of the Executive of the Association of the Universities of the British Commonwealth ... I must be there, although there will be a lot of hooey which I detest about the empire."[5]

His dismissal of British royalty and the country's aristocracy did not reflect any personal insecurity. He was remarkably stable, emotionally secure, even-tempered and, most of all, a rationalist, tending to value people and institutions by their individual merits and their usefulness to society. One had to earn distinction, not inherit it or have it bestowed by outmoded tradition. Thompson would have identified with the political sentiments of the British Liberal Radical, Joseph Chamberlain, who in 1883 attacked the Tory leader, Lord Salisbury, as "the spokesman of a class ... 'who toil not, neither do they spin,' ... whose fortunes have originated ... for such services as courtiers render kings."[6]

Thompson grew up with three brothers and one sister. Wellington, the eldest brother, was twelve years older; Sam two years older, and Jim one year younger. Wellington took over the farm after the death of their father, Sam became a barber, and Jim an engraver and jeweller. Jim was "a close chum," unfortunately plagued by scoliosis. There was also his sister Lily, who was five years older. Though Thompson appears to have seen little of his three brothers after he graduated from the University of Toronto in 1910, he kept in touch with Lily well into his old age.

As a youth, Thompson endured the monotonous toil of farm work. Although he once publicly suggested his "dislike" of farm life,[7] he later described aspects of his youthful work around the family farm and town with something more akin to pride:

> at high school I worked for pay during the summer and as much as possible at other times. In the first summer I was hired man on the farm of Mr Wm. Williamson one mile east of Jarvis. They used me very kindly and I became like one of the family ... In fact all through high school and university I visited and stayed with them at every opportunity. I was a particular favourite of Mrs Williamson. [Mr Williamson] was an excellent farmer and I learned much about farming. He gave me much responsibility.

> During the remaining summers at high school I worked for Mr Axel Anderson, a contractor in Hagersville for $2.00 a day. He kept a considerable gang of men busy building houses. My work was mixing concrete and mortar and toting it for foundations and brick walls, carrying bricks in a hod up a ladder for chimneys etc. After a time he taught me plastering and I became quite expert and spent much time at that. In my last year he obtained a contract from the town for an extensive system of sidewalks. After the first day he took me off the job of mixing concrete and toting it in wheelbarrows, and put me at building the frame for the sidewalk ahead of the gang. This consisted of driving in 2 rows of stakes at the proper distance apart and nailing to them the boards which kept the concrete in place. Mr Andersen was a very fine man though quite uneducated. I became very fond of him and him of me. He often asked me to figure out the costs of his various jobs.[8]

The predictability of daily life was occasionally alleviated by itinerant showmen. Thompson recalled that, as a boy, "about the only form of entertainment which visited our village was travelling shows. These usually consisted of two persons, one of whom gave a magic lantern show to attract the crowd (it was long before the movies). When that was over the real purpose became evident when the other man gave his spiel and started to sell patent medicines."[9]

But most of all, Thompson developed through his independent reading and athletic activities. Sports in particular offered a personally satisfying recreation. Thompson possessed outstanding skills as a baseball pitcher and a hockey player. Men on the local baseball team would often enlist him to pitch for them in games against teams from nearby towns. As Thompson remembered those events, he "acquired a good reputation as a pitcher throughout the region and earned considerable money at $10 or $15 a game playing as a "ringer" for other towns in critical games, especially near the end of the season."[10] The older players respected the fact that he was underage and were considerate enough to refrain from going to beer parlours after the games. Thompson was so successful as a pitcher he was able to earn money for university by pitching for a baseball team in southern Ontario,[11] and considered trying out for a professional team.

In his early days in Saskatoon, Thompson demonstrated the same athletic prowess. At his retirement, the university mentioned in a press release that Thompson and John Bracken[12] sparked the faculty hockey team. Though he seems never to have played hockey while at the University of Toronto, there is a picture of him as a member of the Harvard hockey team, sometime in the winter months from 1910 to 1911.[13]

Like many young boys and girls growing up in the late nineteenth century on the margins of the British Empire, Thompson went to schools, especially at the elementary level, that possessed few or no books. Moreover, a number of his teachers were inadequate intellectually and, often, personally. Some reflected the "flotsam and jetsam" of the profession. They had failed elsewhere, or could not get – or keep – a teaching position in the cities and large towns.[14]

Thompson and his younger brother Jim walked regularly to the nearby village of Clanbrassil (about five kilometers away) to borrow books from the Mechanics' Institute. These visits reveal the roots of Thompson's literacy. The Clanbrassil Institute was not distinctive in Ontario, although the fact that Scots settled the village shows why this educational site developed where it did. The "institute concept," after all, had originated in Glasgow in 1820 with George Birkbeck, who inspired mechanics to establish an institute for men and a number of women to study scientific and literary subjects. Birkbeck then pursued this initiative in London in 1823, creating the first permanent Mechanics' Institute. Then several businessmen, politicians, and teachers began forming similar institutes throughout Britain to teach the leading members of the emerging working classes – the artisans or mechanics – scientific knowledge, especially about developing kinds of machinery. Many workmen increasingly used the Institutes to listen to lectures and to improve their literacy in the reading rooms provided. From the 1830s on, Mechanics' Institutes spread from Britain to North America and Australia. Although British Mechanics' Institutes were conceived of as exclusively urban, in North America they were urban or rural. Few other institutions illustrate so clearly the Victorian gospel of self-improvement and honest labour.

Thompson and his younger brother must have developed on their own the initiative and the intellectual curiosity, to seek out this institute, and to do so while still in elementary school when they were about eleven years old. As Thompson recalled, "there was no library or books of any kind" in either of the two rooms of his school. Nor did he receive any intellectual direction from his family or teachers.

He was not, apparently, influenced – like some other literate people in "Upper Canada" – by sermon literature.[15] Yet by the age of eleven he had read some of the central authors in the English literary canon, notably Charles Dickens, William Makepeace Thackeray, and Shakespeare, as well as the boyhood adventure stories of such writers as G.A. Henty. Mark Twain's *Tom Sawyer* also made a lasting impression. Thompson continued his literary explorations in Hagersville (about eleven kilometers from Decewsville). He couldn't carry these investigations out at the high school, for it had no books. Instead, he haunted the public library, which used to be the town's Mechanics' Institute. There he "read all the standard authors and nearly everything they wrote and some obscure ones."[16] Thompson was especially absorbed by Tennyson's poetry, Macaulay's essays, Shakespeare's plays, and the writings of the American psychologist and philosopher, William James.

Thompson's literary pursuits were coupled with explorations of nature. The curiosity and resourcefulness he demonstrated in his boyhood geological explorations and his growing interest in wild flowers is testament to his early intellectual inquisitiveness.

> All around the forest, in clearings, and on the face of the escarpment many kinds of herbaceous flowers were growing. At an early age I became interested in them and made extensive collections. This was probably an extension of my habit of collecting fossils. I still remember the thrill of finding a book with illustrations, descriptions, and names of plants. I have no idea how I learned to press them. But my interest in them supplanted my interest in fossils, probably because I could make some progress with them.[17]

While in high school, he and a pal made an "enormous collection and identified nearly all the plants of the region," thereby developing his earlier interest from his farm experiences. As he reflected later, "probably the self-education in plant taxonomy was the best thing that could have happened to me."[18] Thompson thus became an emerging botanist who sustained this passion all his life. From the late 1930s until just before his death, his letters to his daughter and granddaughters almost invariably mentioned how various flowers were growing in his garden or expressed his longings for the growing season.

Thompson's trips to the Mechanics' Institute and his botanical explorations reveal his investigative and independent mind. However, Thompson had not yet thought of proceeding past elementary school. When the school inspector, "a man named Moses,"[19] urged him to go on to high school, Thompson demurred at first, thinking that he would be obliged to stay and work on the farm. But Moses persuaded the Thompson family that young Thompson possessed such distinctive abilities that his mother sold the farm to her eldest son, Wellington, and moved the younger children to Hagersville in 1900 to allow Thompson to attend high school. As Thompson noted later, he was the only one from his school who advanced beyond the elementary grades, for the world of his youth was one that praised practical accomplishments and self-reliance while tending to be scornful of academic pursuits. He recalled the occasion "when the first youth from our farming community went away to agricultural college and the talk among the neighbours about the silly highfalutin ideas he would bring back and which would ruin his father."[20]

When the Thompson family moved to Hagersville, they must have taken themselves and their belongings by horse-drawn wagon. Although Decewsville was bounded on the north by the Wabash Railroad, rented by 1897 from the Grand Trunk Western Railway to shorten the time taken on the Detroit-Windsor-Buffalo passenger journey, Thompson gives no indication that he ever took the train. Nor does he give any indication of ever travelling by automobile. Indeed, the first automobile only arrived in Canada in 1898 when a wealthy Hamilton textile manufacturer introduced it. By 1903, when the Hamilton and Toronto Automobile Club were established, there were only 178 cars in Canada, used almost exclusively by the wealthy for social and racing purposes in an era where there were still no paved roads, few gas stations or mechanics, and no garages. The Thompson family, with its modest income, could scarcely have had access to an automobile. Thompson did not even purchase his first new automobile until 1929.

Thompson finally found a consistent mentor in the university-educated principal of the high school, George Jones, and was simultaneously exposed to the excellent teaching of a man named Kaiser. Jones, who was a University of Toronto graduate, was instrumental in convincing young Thompson to go to university. Thompson seems to have been the only person from the Decewsville area to have taken that path, and was certainly the only member of his immediate family to do so. Thompson's brother James, his companion when "haunting" libraries, "a great reader with keen intellectual interests," and the one Thompson considered the cleverest person in the family, never went to high school, much less university, perhaps due in part to his severe scoliosis. Regardless of an individual's intellectual ability, the idea of an extended education beyond the elementary level was then far from generally accepted. The rather extraordinary measures that Thompson's mother took enabled him to continue his early education, and the encouragement he later received set Thompson apart.

When Thompson entered the University of Toronto in 1906, it was probably the first time he had been in the city. His memoir shows that his entire life up to that time had been spent in an area bounded by a few small towns – Decewsville, Hagersville, Caledonia, Clanbrassil, and Cayuga – all of which were within approximately twenty to twenty-five kilometers of the family farm. In writing his memoirs in his old age, Thompson made no mention of any impact his arrival in a big city had on his consciousness and he wrote almost nothing about his urban life during the four years he spent in Toronto.

Thompson arrived at Victoria College when the population of Toronto was about 300,000 and increasing rapidly; by 1912, it had grown to more than 400,000. The city was a bastion of Anglo-Saxons and Anglo-Celts; fewer than 25,000 were from non-English-speaking countries. The vast majority were of English, Scottish, and Irish descent, with the last group divided almost equally between Protestants and Catholics. Religious animosity was rampant. Historians depicted Toronto just before Thompson arrived as "if anything more like Belfast than Belfast itself: 'the capital of evangelical Christianity and Orangeism, a grand duchy of prohibitionism and anti-Catholicism.'"[21] Although Victoria College was a Methodist foundation, Thompson had no religious interests and certainly cared nothing for the Protestant versus Catholic quarrels that often convulsed Toronto. The city was still recovering from the calamitous fire of 1904 that had burned fourteen acres downtown. Public entertainment was strictly limited. The first movie theatre, for example, opened in 1906. When Thompson and his fiancée were courting in 1913, they went walking and botanizing in some open woods called Deer Park,[22] then a relatively wild area north of Yonge Street and St Clair Avenue.

Thompson had very little money when he arrived in Toronto. All he possessed was $300 from his summer work, a small amount from playing baseball, plus limited savings. In addition to his tuition, room, and board, he also needed to assist his mother financially from his modest finances. Neither the University of Toronto nor Queen's, which had also admitted him, offered any entrance scholarship funds; a fact that would have made the choice between education and employment more difficult to make. As he later recalled, "A paying job was very attractive. Mr Jones' arguments were reinforced by visits from representatives of two universities, Queen's and Victoria College, who urged the advantages of their institutions. No doubt they had heard about me from Jones. They did not offer me any financial inducements such as scholarships but only vague statements about the possibility of earning while studying. If there was a province-wide competition I knew nothing about it."[23]

Throughout elementary and high school, Thompson had not been intellectually challenged by any other student. Hence, upon his arrival at Victoria College at the University of Toronto, he had no clear estimation of his abilities when he was placed among an entire cohort of students, many of whom had come from established, often prestigious urban private schools. Moreover, he describes himself as "shy, lacking in self-confidence and socially inept" when comparing himself with some of his "sophisticated" classmates who were there on scholarships he hadn't even known were available. His lodgings, however, provided a refreshing informal education. Since neither Victoria College nor the university had a men's residence in Thompson's time, he lived in a rooming house near the university with ten to fifteen other students, and shared a bedroom with another student. He enjoyed their "bull sessions," recalling fondly that much of his personal university education, and that of the other students, was obtained from such sessions and at the dinner table.[24]

Thompson only realized that he could compete with the best students academically when he received his final examination results during his first year. By second year, his confidence rose even higher as his professors openly recognized his abilities. He began receiving numerous awards: the Edward Blake Scholarship in Biology, Mineralogy and Geology in 1908; the Daniel Wilson Scholarship in Biology in 1909; and later, the Silver Medal in Biology by the Senate of Victoria College.[25] Moreover, professors were welcoming him to their classes.

Given the remoteness and occasional harshness of almost all of his rural teachers, Thompson was surprised and pleased to discover that the relations between faculty and students were cordial and friendly.

The reasons for much of the mutual goodwill were, as Thompson emphasized, the result of the constructive recommendations of the 1906 Royal Commission on the University of Toronto. Even earlier, in 1905, Sir James Whitney's Conservative government had begun to relieve the financial plight of the University of Toronto with the University Act, which allocated half a million dollars for buildings and an annual grant of $30,000.[26] In 1906, the university's constitution was transformed after proposals made by the royal commission were enacted. Academic matters were allocated to faculty councils, instead of the senate, which had been presided over by the vice-chancellor and reflected the jealousies and anxieties of the federated colleges rather than the university as a whole. The president now sat on all the councils and could play a major role in academic issues. A largely non-political board of governors, instead of the provincial government, would now oversee the management of finances. These changes presented the university with the opportunity for growth.

They were largely the result of initiatives undertaken by Whitney, who was elected in 1905 with a Conservative majority after nine successive Liberal provincial governments since Confederation. Liberal premiers from Oliver Mowat, in office from 1872 to 1895, and his successors had starved the university. These politicians shared the prejudices of their voters, the advocates of the various church schools and the many farmers and small businessmen, who viewed the university as a bastion for privileged, spoiled elites undeserving of significant government funding.[27] Whitney and his Conservatives represented a coalition of the old Anglican establishment and those who wanted a big central university in Toronto. Well might the university, therefore, view Whitney as the "greatest friend the institution ever had."[28]

In 1906, Toronto was the largest university in Canada, with 3,545 students. By comparison, McGill, the other major university in Canada, had nearly 2,500, whereas Queen's had an enrolment of approximately 1,500. Moreover, early in 1907, the liberal-minded clergyman, Robert Falconer, was appointed president, a position he held until 1932. Thompson respected and admired Falconer's ability, honesty, and achievements as president which, it can be inferred, helped shape his own concept of how senior university administrators ought to carry out their functions and obligations.

Historians and biographers of Falconer validate Thompson's high opinion. Falconer succeeded in his major challenge to avoid the muddles and political manipulation in appointments and programs that had besmirched the years from 1892 to 1906 when James Loudon was the president. Falconer also had the good fortune to be appointed president immediately after the enactment of the 1906 Royal Commission Report, the "Goldwin Smith Report" as Thompson mistakenly called it.[29] Falconer realized that this legislation provided a fine opportunity to reorganize the entire institution by dramatically improving the academic state of the university. The increased presidential authority and a sound financial base allowed him and his colleagues to develop new and modern departments and programs while recruiting energetic promising faculty to rise to the challenges of the new century. Falconer was able to implement such changes, for example, by working with a board of governors that replaced government appointees and by taking advantage of the distribution of functions whereby the university took over the responsibility for the sciences, rather than leaving them under the segmented jurisdiction of the chronically underfunded denominational colleges. It is not surprising, therefore, that Thompson should assess the royal commission report as "one of the ablest pronouncements on university education which has ever been written for the general reader."[30]

For the rest of his life Thompson believed that the work of the "Goldwin Smith" Commission for Toronto was one of the best things that had ever happened to Canadian universities, since many of its recommendations were adopted elsewhere across the country. Its influence on Thompson was still evident many years later, when, in marginal criticisms of a University of Saskatchewan Faculty Association brief that argued for greater faculty participation in university governance, Thompson scribbled "if you want to go back to pre-1906 Toronto conditions, God help us."[31]

In Toronto, Thompson developed good personal and scientific relationships, particularly with his main professor, R.B. Thomson. In fact, it was in the course of some otherwise routine laboratory work during his second year that a combination of insight, initiative, and Thomson's encouragement led Thompson to make the decision to pursue an academic career.

It was a simple enough exercise: R.B. Thomson wanted his class to be able to identify cells in wood through a microscope. Thompson, finding the dry pine too unyielding for the thin slices necessary, thought a young pine seedling would work and, initially, it did:

> But then an unexpected problem arose. The wood of the seedlings lacked entirely a certain characteristic type of cell. The mass of pine wood consists of long fibers which are oriented vertically in order to transport water from the roots up to the leaves. But it also has a few short fibers which are oriented horizontally along the radii of the stem. They are naturally called ray fibers. All our textbooks stated that they are characteristic features of pine wood. But, although I searched diligently through many good sections, I could find no trace of ray fibers in the wood of seedlings.
>
> Then I conceived what seemed to be an elegant explanation of their absence. A seedling is an embryo which has started to grow. Could its lack of ray fibers be one of those embryonic characters which, like gill-slits in the embryos of man and other mammals, repeat an ancestral condition? The occurrence of such embryonic survivals of ancestral conditions is one of the best kinds of evidence in support of the theory of organic evolution and was used as such in every textbook of biology. As applied to the particular case in question the inference would be that modern pines are descended from trees which never had ray fibers at any stage of individual development.[32]

His professor listened, and to his credit, gave Thompson two weeks to establish his facts and prove his theory. In the meantime, he excused Thompson from other laboratory work.

The result, as Thompson noted, "did not shake the scientific world" but it was "a neat piece of original work" and, even more important, his professor felt he had made a real contribution. Thompson discovered that in the genus *Abies*, or firs, ray tracheids are vestigial or only occur because of some trauma to the wood. Thompson was again excused from all lab work to write his results in a paper, which his professor sent to *The Botanical Gazette*.[33] They were both thrilled, Thompson recalled, when it was accepted for publication.

At the end of 1910, with Thomson's recommendation, Thompson was awarded a British 1851 Exhibition Scholarship, worth £120 a year for two years. It could be used either in Britain or wherever there were recognized university graduate departments. From 1891 on, Canada was awarded two Exhibition scholarships a year for research exclusively in scientific disciplines. The University of Toronto and McGill shared one scholarship, each awarding it in alternate years. The other scholarship was shared in alternate years between Queen's and Dalhousie.[34] Between 1891 and 1914, Thompson was the only biologist at the University of Toronto awarded such a scholarship, since all the other recipients were either in chemistry or physics. The stipend was extraordinarily generous at a time when the pound was worth roughly $4.80. It was well above the annual wages of even the most skilled workmen. The award not only demonstrated Thompson's academic distinction at the University of Toronto; it also prompted him to make a major independent academic decision.

Thompson's professors urged him to take up the scholarship at Oxford or Cambridge. Those were the English universities where Canadians with colonial mindsets traditionally directed their students, both in 1910 and for many decades afterwards. But neither English university possessed a graduate program. It was not until 1914 that Oxford finally introduced a research degree, the first in Britain, modelled on the German and American PhD but still lacking the fields preparatory to a thesis. Thompson never considered graduate work in Canada. As late as 1934, Dean Brett of the University of Toronto was convinced that few faculty members in the country "had become in any significant sense graduate-minded." The University of Toronto only established a School of Graduate Studies in 1922, after World War I had demonstrated just how limited Canadian scientific research was. The federal government had spent less than $300,000 on scientific research up to 1915. To meet this deficiency, in 1916 the federal government established the organization that was later renamed the National Research Council (NRC). Pressed by NRC chairman A.B. McCallum, President Falconer established the University of Toronto's graduate school, as did McGill. Hence, on the surface, Toronto and McGill appeared to be able to offer Canadian graduates an alternative to travelling to the United States or Britain for additional study. But these developments were still in their infancy, and in any event too late for Thompson. Even as late as 1945, historian Bartlet Brebner lamented "Canada does not possess a single fully-rounded graduate school."[35]

From a research point of view, Thompson declined to take up his scholarship in Britain, even if that meant going against the advice of his mentors. He understood that the English universities "made little and unsatisfactory provision for graduate study and earning graduate degrees ... Any need for graduate work was only evidence of deficiency in undergraduate work."[36] In contrast, Harvard had awarded its initial doctorate in 1873 after creating a graduate program in 1872 and in 1890 establishing its Graduate School of Arts and Sciences. Thompson also thought, justifiably, that "no other American and certainly no British institution could equal [Harvard]." Thompson recalled that he was charged by some of his professors (but not by Thomson) with "making a serious mistake ... and it was even implied that I was not being properly patriotic."[37] Thompson, however, had very sensible reasons for wishing to go to Harvard. He intended to specialize in the origin of flowering plants by researching the order *Gnetales*, a field of intense interest among botanists at that time and to the present day. And in Professor E.C. Jeffrey, Harvard possessed one of the world's experts in this subject.[38]

If Thompson arrived at Toronto at an opportune time, the same can be said of his debut at Harvard in 1910. President Charles William Eliot (1834–1926) had just retired in 1909 after forty years spent transforming Harvard from a small college into a great university. Under Eliot's leadership, a graduate department was established in 1872, and made stronger in 1890 when courses were designed for the specific interests of graduate student researchers. To supervise these graduate students, distinguished scholars were recruited by offering higher salaries, sabbaticals were awarded to those faculty seriously involved in research, and a pension plan was initiated to keep first-class faculty at Harvard. Eliot was also instrumental in fostering the development of Radcliffe College, which was soon to become a pioneering women's college.

Thompson described the gifted faculty constellation in the sciences at the time of his arrival. He was especially impressed by the capacities of the leading geneticists, even though he had entered Harvard intending to do a PhD on the evolution of plant structures. He had been attracted by the presence of the leading North American research scientist in evolutionary botany, Edward Charles Jeffrey. Unfortunately, as Thompson was soon to discover, Jeffrey was a most difficult person. Indeed, Thompson blamed him as the primary cause of the Harvard biologists "indulging in so many disputes, quarrels, and feuds" that often led to frequent suffering among the graduate students.[39]

Thompson's research at Harvard, the study of "a peculiar order," the *Gnetales*, included only three, but very diverse, genera: *Ephedra*, *Welwitschia*, and *Gnetum*. The first was native to the southwestern United States but the last two "were on the other side of the earth" – South-West Africa and Java. As Thompson noted, a complete discussion of the affinities of the group would be deferred until other members of the group could be studied. *Gnetum*, the most advanced member, would have been thoroughly investigated but for the great difficulty in securing material.

Having completed his study of *Ephedra* during his first year, Thompson applied, at Jeffrey's urging, for Harvard's Sheldon Travelling Fellowship, endowed by Amey Richmond Sheldon in 1909 in honour of her husband, Frederick Sheldon. The endowment was $346,458.70.[40] Scholars could also apply for additional sources of funding, provided the dean approved.

Thompson visited the graduate school to submit his application. The dean, respected medieval historian Charles Homer Haskins, asked to see Thompson and, after enquiring about his doctoral research project, suggested that he apply for more money than he had originally requested so that he could visit not only German South-West Africa but also Java in the Dutch East Indies, thereby studying all three genera. Thompson's financial situation was further improved when he agreed to do some extra research for Professor Farlow, one of a number of independently wealthy academics at Harvard. Farlow told Thompson that he could pick up the extra amount needed from the bursar. When Thompson went to the bursar, he discovered that Farlow, after telling Thompson that the department would provide the extra finances, had deposited the funds out of his own pocket. Farlow's fund was added to Thompson's already generous fellowship. All told, Thompson had received "$2,000, the largest amount ever awarded for a single year."[41]

While undertaking work with Jeffrey on the order *Gnetales*, Thompson also did some class work with William E. Castle on animal genetics and with Edward M. East on plant genetics. The influential plant geneticist was so impressed by Thompson's work that he urged him to investigate the possibility of parthenogenesis in hawthorns.

Thompson now found himself in a severe personality conflict with his supervisor, Jeffrey. Jeffrey flew into a rage and became "as sore as a boil"[42] when he learned that Thompson, however innocently, had done some work with East. Jeffrey's jealous paranoia made him suspect that East was attempting to lure his student away from him. After Jeffrey threatened to deny his PhD examination, to prevent his thesis from being published, and to have his travelling fellowship withdrawn, Thompson had no option but to sever his ties with Castle and East and the study of genetics.

As Thompson noted ruefully, Jeffrey tended to instigate quarrels with nearly all his graduate students. It is not surprising that he was referred to as "the stormy petrel of botany." One of the most egregious instances of his miserable behaviour was directed at G. Ledyard Stebbins, who later became a great evolutionary botanist at the University of California (Davis). Stebbins had begun graduate work in 1928 and soon found the geneticist Karl Sax much more interesting to collaborate with than Jeffrey. Since he hated Sax "with a vengeance," Jeffrey threatened to prevent Stebbins from defending his thesis. Fortunately, a senior mediator stepped in and ordered the defence to go forward. Thompson's contretemps with Jeffrey never went quite that far, simply because Thompson – who had everything to lose – acceded to Jeffrey's demands; but it did mean that he had to give up any further work with East on genetics. He still had a scientifically important doctoral project in evolutionary botany, although he "regretted" his choice "many times in later years." In any event, after he agreed to continue working on evolutionary botany, Thompson had his supervisor, and other members of the botany department's, full support to continue his PhD research: "my path was made smooth, the way to the doctorate secured without trouble, and the traveling fellowship won."

The *Gnetales*, now classified as the *Gnetophyta*, is a small group of seed plants comprising three genera: the primitive *Ephedra*, the more advanced *Gnetum*, and the very bizarre *Welwitschia*. Each consists of a single family and a single genus. *Ephedra*, a profusely branched shrub with reduced leaves, comprises about thirty-five species and grows in cool arid regions of the eastern and western hemispheres. In the Americas, it is restricted to western North America and parts of Mexico and South America. *Gnetum* lives in tropical rainforests in parts of Asia, northern South America, and certain Pacific islands. Most of the species are lianas (tropical climbing plants that climb high into the crowns of trees). *Welwitschia*, a single species, or *W. mirabilis*, is so named so because it is like no other plant on earth. It consists of a short woody unbranched stem and a crown that bears only two permanent huge strap-shaped leaves – unique in the plant kingdom. The leaf of one giant specimen was measured at 6.2 metres long and 1.8 metres wide and it has been estimated that some specimens were 1,500 to 2,000 years old. Discovered in 1860 by Dr Frederic Welwitsch, in whose honour the plant was named, *Welwitschia* grows in the Namib Desert, Namibia. It is no wonder that Thompson was intrigued.

His project had significance. As Thompson noted in his first article based on this world-wide research trip,

> The *Gnetales* have been called the lure and despair of the morphologist. They are alluring because they promise to give a solution to the morphologist's great problem, the origin of the angiosperms [the flowering plants]. They are despair in that, in spite of many efforts, no one has been able either to establish convincingly or to disprove their angiosperms connection.[43]

The debate among evolutionary botanists remains the same today as it was in Thompson's time. Does *Gnetales* occupy an intermediate position between angiosperms (bearing seeds enclosed in a vessel) and gymnosperms (seeds unprotected by an ovary)? Does *Gnetales* instead represent an evolutionary line that developed parallel to the angiosperm from a common ancestral group? Or is the relationship between angiosperms and *Gnetales* coincidental and the result of parallel evolution? Are there any points of resemblance that were not part of any relationship but independently acquired? Thompson's research trip was an attempt to discover an answer to these complex questions that vex plant taxonomists to this day.

In his study of *Gnetum*, published in 1916, Thompson concentrated on reproduction, including the morphology of the "flowers," and endosperm and embryo development, comparing these characteristics with those in the angiosperms. He came to the conclusion that the genus *Gnetum* should probably be classed with the angiosperms, saying that almost every structure shows some condition that is almost completely angiospermic. He continued that this did not mean that any modern member of the *Gnetales* represented the type from which the angiosperms were derived but that the ancestors of angiosperms were not far removed from the genus *Gnetum*.

Thompson followed his analysis of *Gnetum* with a paper, "The Independent Evolution of Vessels in the Gnetales and Angiosperms," published in the *Botanical Gazette* in 1918, by which time he was at the University of Saskatchewan. This paper is still cited today.[44] In it, he observed that the vessels in the *Gnetales*, i.e., *Ephedra* and *Gnetum*, evolved by haphazardly arranged circular bordered pits of the conifer type enlarging and fusing, whereas the vessels in the angiosperms evolved from cells with many long narrow scalariform (ladder-like) perforations. "There can be no genetic connection between the vessels of the two groups." He added, "to what extent this applies to other points of resemblance between the Gnetales and angiosperms is reserved for future discussion," confirming that "the dilemma of the origin of the angiosperms is still with us, as it has been since Darwin's time."

Thompson's travels in 1912 and 1913 through parts of southern Africa and Java, along with a brief visit to Ceylon, occupied almost all of his fellowship-sponsored research time. He arrived at the port of Swakopmund on 15 September 1912 and remained in German South-West Africa until he departed for Cape Town on 1 November. The plant was in a desert where no rain had fallen for ten to twelve years. After a horseback ride of some forty to fifty miles down the west coast, then inland past the capital, Windhoek, Thompson was pleased to find the *Welwitschia*. It has been described as "the world's most bizarre plant, found only on the Namib Desert, the world's oldest desert," where annual rainfall averaged about one inch a year, when it rained at all. Thompson described the *Welwitschia* as resembling a "huge turnip...five to six feet in diameter" with two leaves that stretch "for twenty feet," perhaps "more than one hundred years old."[45]

In his descriptions of this time, Thompson only occasionally alludes to the growing Anglo-German tensions in South-West Africa. He does not mention, and perhaps knew nothing about, the 1904 German campaign against the Herero people in which some 65,000 out of 80,000 were killed in what has recently been described as the first genocide of the twentieth century.[46] After all, the distances in this huge colony were very great. German South-West Africa is half the size of Alaska. There were fewer than 200,000 people in the German protectorate in 1908, of whom scarcely

7,000 were Europeans. Moreover, since the *Welwitschia* grew close to the Atlantic Ocean littoral of the country, Thompson had no need to travel deeply into the protectorate, since most of the massacre had taken place near Waterberg, which is well north and east of where Thompson carried out his work. In any case, until very recently such massacres were viewed in the West merely as "pacifications." Even African historians did not grasp the scale of the massacre until many years later. What Thompson did remember was the guide with him complaining that "he didn't mind the fleas in his sleeping bag except for their trampling all over him."[47]

Thompson now sailed for Cape Town. There, for the next fortnight, he worked under the generous tutelage of Professor H.H.W. Pearson of the University of Cape Town who had also worked on *Welwitschia.* Thompson and Pearson had a number of scholarly discussions about Thompson's research work and about education in South Africa. Their meetings led Thompson to comment briefly on the state of tangled Anglo–Boer relations after the end of the South African War in May 1902. From 1899 to 1902, British forces had waged war against the Boers to conquer their states, the Transvaal and the Orange Free State, primarily to control the extraordinarily rich gold mines on the Witwatersrand ridge, near Johannesburg in the Transvaal, and to maintain control over the important port at Cape Town and its hinterland. Provoked by British attempts to pressure the Transvaal to grant civil liberties to non-Boers, by October 1899, Afrikaners, led by President Paul Kruger, believed that they had no alternative but to invade the British South African colonies of Cape Colony and Natal and win by a pre-emptive strike. Their attempt failed as Britain poured tens of thousands of troops into the conflict, far outnumbering the Boers. Thompson had the good fortune to engage in two fairly extended encounters with Jan Christian Smuts, whom he met first on Table Mountain when the Boer general and skilled botanist "came along with his vasculum" collecting grasses. Smuts had been one of the most skillful of the Afrikaner commanders against the British.

Thompson described his two meetings with Smuts at some length.

> The episode which stands out most vividly in my memory of Cape Town was an encounter with General Jan Smuts who was then Minister of Finance in General Botha's government and who subsequently became Prime Minister. One day when I was

> on Table Mountain which formed a magnificent background for the city, examining the numerous beautiful species of shrubby geraniums (some similar to the house plants at home), I met a stoutish man with a sandy pointed beard, wearing old clothes and carrying a botanist's vasculum. Since I was carrying a similar vasculum, and since botanists were rare, we made ourselves known to each other. Subsequently Smuts became famous as a leading statesman of the century, as a brilliant military commander during the First World War, and as Churchill's highly regarded adviser during the Second World War. But few people are aware that he was already an authority on the plants of South Africa particularly the grasses on which he wrote extensively. Later he also wrote extensively on the general philosophy of biology. Smuts was viewed by theorists of biologist as an authority in that field. That is why he was elected president of the British Association for the Advancement of Science in 1924.[48]

Thompson next embarked on an around-Africa liner at Port Elizabeth in Cape Colony, sailing up the east coast, with stops at Durban in Natal and Beira in Portuguese East Africa, now Mozambique. From Beira, he travelled on a freighter across the Indian Ocean to Colombo in Ceylon, arriving the day before Christmas 1912. From Colombo, he went by rail through beautiful mountain scenery to the big botanical garden at Peridenya, the highlight of his journey in Ceylon (now Sri Lanka). The garden was well administered by the British scientific staff under the direction of John Christopher Willis. It was there that Thompson first became acquainted with tropical vegetation. He was given all possible assistance by the staff and lived in a small guest house provided by the garden together with servants. The staff tried to make the garden as useful as possible for the native growers of plants important to the tropical economy. Thompson learned much about the cultivation of fruits such as mangoes and pawpaws as well as of tea and rice.

After a fortnight in Ceylon, Thompson visited the prize location on his research trip, the island of Java with the Gardens of Buitenzorg, about forty miles inland from Jakarta. He was to spend almost six months researching in Java, almost totally in the Garden and nearby verdant areas. Java had a rich range of flora and fauna, probably the result of the splitting of two continents in the Malay Archipelago over millions of years ago. Because of that, each continent carried with it indigenous organisms: plants and animals related to Asian species west of the boundary that separates the two zoogeographical regions, and plants and animals related to Australian species east of it.

This geological division and consequent plant and animal separation were noted as early as 1521. The development of the hypothesis, however, is primarily associated with the naturalist, and contemporary of Charles Darwin, Alfred Russel Wallace.[49] In his extensive explorations of the narrow but deep passage between the islands of Bali and Lombok between 1854 and 1862, he described the flora and fauna on one side as significantly different from those on the other, which resembled Australia. The boundary has been named the "Wallace Line."

Thus Thompson had six months to explore the wide variety of plants in the Gardens of Buitenzorg and at the nearby agricultural station, in the company of eight to ten visiting foreign scientists. He worked in its laboratories and with a full-time assistant. The garden, as he stated, "was unrivalled anywhere." Here, and in the surrounding forest, Thompson found many specimens of the genus *Gnetum*, the most advanced member of the *Gnetales*.[50]

These discoveries in Java were to lead to numerous scientific papers, including a fifty-page article in the *American Journal of Botany* "on the reproduction and evolution of the flowering plants as a whole."[51] Thompson also took time to study the culture around him, commenting upon the pacific natures of the inhabitants of the Dutch East Indies. At the conclusion of his graduate student travels, he made some interesting observations about his experiences with a young Buddhist priest in Tokyo. Thompson's few days in Tokyo were spent

> chiefly with Fuji, the most prominent Japanese botanist of the time. Through his influence a day was spent in a Buddhist temple in the company of a young priest who was a highly educated man with a regular four-year course at Tokyo University followed by a three-year course in theology. He not only showed me all parts of the temple, but explained the activities which were carried on in it. From time to time he left me to meet groups of 10 to 25 Japanese people and to speak to them for a few minutes. I understood that these were religious exercises and that part of what he said in a sing-song voice and with little apparent interest was a prayer.[52]

Thompson was only a young graduate student, but he carried with him letters of introduction from – interestingly enough – those professors Jeffrey had so railed against, East and Castle. At almost every stage of his world trip, Thompson arranged to meet with the local leading botanists. In addition to Fuji, these included Hugo de Vries in Amsterdam, Henry Harold Pearson of the University of Cape Town, John Christopher Willis, director of the Peradeniya Gardens in Ceylon, and Melchior Treub in Java. As an undergraduate honours student in biology, Thompson noted, he hadn't read "a single reference to Mendel in a regular class. I learned about him through outside reading. The first textbook to accept the chromosome theory of heredity was published in 1919, six years after I came [to Harvard]."[53] Particularly memorable, then, was his meeting with the Dutch scientist, Hugo de Vries, one of the three men who virtually "simultaneously re-discovered [Gregor] Mendel's laws"[54] after they had remained unappreciated for thirty-five years – perhaps the most romantic episode in the history of biology – but de Vries was famous for his own original contribution, the concept of mutations. He spent the whole day with Thompson, who said he could not have been kinder.

Thompson's pleasure and the intellectual stimulation that came from his meeting with de Vries also reflected his relief after his earlier unhappy encounter with the geneticist Carl Correns, another of the three re-discoverers of Mendel. Thompson went to see him in Berlin, but the German scientist gave him a "rude 'brush-off,'" by asking a young man, who, as far as Thompson knew, could have been "a junior assistant or some kind of janitor," to give Thompson a "few minutes" attention.[55]

Thompson's experience with de Vries reflected what the Nobel laureate Eric Kandel characterized as the generally "open, critical, yet fully democratic and egalitarian atmosphere of university research ... [in] American graduate education." By contrast, Correns demonstrated the atmosphere at a German research university, where "the great scientific leader ordered the hierarchy of his subordinates."[56]

From his undergraduate days through to his year-long research trip, Thompson had certainly acquired broad, first-hand experience of professor–student relations and how easily these might affect the academic career decisions of students – positively, as with Thomson and de Vries, inspiring intellectual curiosity; negatively, when ego appeared to create unnecessary barriers, as with Jeffrey and Correns. And before the start of his trip he was on the receiving end of another positive action when University of Toronto professor J.H. Faull advised him that there was a vacancy at the University of Saskatchewan biology department.

Thompson wrote to the president, Walter Murray, on 15 August 1912 from the ship *S.S. St Louis*, thus somewhat complicating negotiations with the university.[57] "As I had no time to make enquiries," he wrote, "I do not know whether or not I am doing the proper thing in writing to you as I intend to, but it seems to be the only course left, for I am just beginning a year's tour of the world and should like to have my name come under your consideration."[58] Thompson listed both the names of suitable referees and the various contact points on his itinerary where letters would reach him. By 13 March 1913, Murray was prepared to recommend Thompson's name to the board of governors, but the president was concerned specifically about Thompson's lack of teaching experience; thus, the initial offer was for one year with the possibility of the position becoming permanent after that time. As Thompson reminisced, he had "never taught before, never delivered a lecture and only one or two at seminars as a graduate student" when he was offered the appointment.[59] Where Murray was concerned primarily about teaching ability, Thompson had other questions: "I should have wished to learn something more of the conditions particularly in regard to the facilities in time and equipment for the research work to which I am devoted, especially since on the present tour, I have collected a great deal of very rare and valuable material. But as that work will be of value to the University as well as to myself, no doubt satisfactory arrangements will be made, if they do not already obtain." The minutes of the board of governors for their meeting on 8 April 1913 note that the "executive be authorized to appoint ...Thompson, Professor of Biology for one year at a salary of $2,500 and $1,500 for equipment. In the event Thompson's services should prove satisfactory to the President, then the Chair of Biology appointment at the end of one year would become permanent." Thompson formally accepted on 23 April 1913. Years later, his memory failed on some details but his appointment clearly reflected the norm in academic hiring at the university at the time: it was wholly the prerogative of the president.

> There were no appointment committees, no systematic search for candidates, and no invitations to candidates to come and see the place and be seen. I was offered the job without anyone here ever having seen me, without being asked whether I was interested, without even knowing that there was a job available, and of course without supplying the usual curriculum vitae, references, etc. Dr Murray's letter reached me in Java where I was working at the botanical garden on a travelling fellowship. Since he offered me $2500 a year I hastened to accept because that seemed to be a lot of money in those days. I didn't even know where the University of Saskatchewan was. Dr Murray's letter was no help because it was written in long hand on hotel paper when he was travelling, presumably after finding something about me. So help me, I addressed my reply to Regina, which was probably the only place in Saskatchewan I remembered about except Fish Creek and Batoche.[60]

However difficult Thompson's relations with Jeffrey, his doctoral supervisor was professional in the letters that he wrote to Murray. Jeffrey described Thompson as "a most exceptional man," conversant not only with biology but also "unusually well-equipped in the cognate sciences." Thompson's "amiability made him a favourite with all here." Jeffrey also ranked Thompson well above another possible candidate whom he considered "not nearly as able." R.B. Thomson, his main professor at Toronto, described his "teaching ability" [as] "of the highest type," because Thompson had assisted him in a summer course and taken over a class, in a "most efficient and reliable" manner when the professor was ill.[61]

In September 1913, Thompson arrived in Saskatoon to begin his new job. He was given a "cubby-hole" that served as his office, "assigned a desk and a microscope,"[62] and provided with another room that served as a laboratory, lecture room, preparation room, storage room, research room, and students' lunch room. Such limited quarters, Thompson claimed, resulted from Dr Murray's "very low opinion of biology." Both rooms were located at the northeast corner of the second floor in the recently built College Building, then one of the few buildings on the new campus.

Perhaps, Thompson speculated, Murray's low estimation of biology was "the result of an unfortunate experience in school." He further suggested that the president rated biology "far below chemistry and physics" which was, "in part," the reason that the "Biology Department wasn't started until three years after the Chemistry and Physics Departments," and why Murray was content to appoint an inexperienced and untried youngster to start it."[63] This seems unlikely at best, since Murray would have understood the close link between biology and the College of Agriculture, unique in the country for its integral location on the University of Saskatchewan campus.

At the time of his appointment, Thompson appears to have been unaware of the bitter discord that had occurred over where to situate the university. Prince Albert, Moose Jaw, Qu'Appelle, and Battleford had all submitted proposals to host it; but Regina and Saskatoon were the final contenders. The nine members of the board of governors were almost equally divided. The advocates of a Regina site pointed to the fact that the legislature was located in that city, whereas the premier, Walter Scott, favoured Saskatoon "in order to maintain his policy of decentralization."[64] President Murray believed that Regina was the "only possible choice," because the surrounding area had fertile soil; was then the largest city, yielding the most high school students in the province; and perhaps most important, would provide nearness and access to the seat of government. On 7 April 1909, however, the final vote was five to four in favour of Saskatoon.[65] This decision almost led Murray to resign. Nonetheless, in time he became reconciled to the decision and even came to believe that Saskatoon's greater distance from the seat of government offered added protection to the university from government interference.

Murray was adamant that there should be only one state-sponsored university and Thompson shared Murray's position. Many influential Regina citizens, however, were furious about the decision to locate the institution in Saskatoon, a discontent that would smoulder for decades.[66]

When Thompson arrived at the university in 1913, construction of the initial buildings had been completed: the College building, the Engineering building, the Livestock Pavilion, Main Barn, a residence, Saskatchewan Hall, and the power house. Homes for the dean of Agriculture and the professor of Field Husbandry had also been built, as had Emmanuel, an affiliated Anglican college.[67]

Initially, Thompson was the "whole Biology Department" and "taught all the agricultural students for some years."[68] He was convinced that accepting the position at Saskatchewan was "the best thing that could have happened [because he] was able to build up a department in accordance with my own ideas and was therefore happy in it." He was delighted that Saskatchewan was "the only university of any size in Canada which has the perfectly sound arrangement of all biological disciplines in one department."[69] Throughout his career, Thompson implacably opposed the "separation of biology departments" since such a divisive policy was "bound to prevent or hamper the best developments both in research and teaching, even if empire-building is not involved – and it often is involved."[70] What is obvious is that right from the beginning of his life and career in Saskatoon, he settled in quickly and his pleasure at living and working in the university, the city, and the province developed rapidly and with an increasing devotion to western Canada.

During the early summer of 1914, Thompson defended his doctoral thesis at Harvard. He then returned to Toronto to get married. He had met Marjorie "Bobbie" Gordon during the summer of 1912 when she was a graduate student and he was the instructor in her botany lab at the University of Toronto. She was born in Wingham, Ontario on 12 April 1889, the youngest of seven children of Donald McKay Gordon and his wife Margaret, née Palmer. Her father was a dry goods merchant and mayor of Wingham in 1893.[71] The Gordon family was staunchly Presbyterian. By the time Marjorie was of university age, the family had moved to Toronto. Because of this move and since she was the youngest of seven children, she alone of her siblings had the opportunity to attend university. The Gordon family followed an old custom of calling the youngest daughter "Babe," the mispronunciation by a young niece resulting in the nickname "Bobbie." Bobbie became the family name for Marjorie, and was later used by her friends at school and university. Still later, her son-in-law and daughter-in-law also used it.

Thompson and Marjorie Gordon had become engaged before he embarked on his Sheldon travelling fellowship. While he was away, she taught at Whitby Ladies College in Whitby, Ontario. They were married in Toronto in early August 1914 just as World War I began and spent their honeymoon on Manitoulin Island. The island was an appropriate choice for two botanists. It was a botanists' paradise, since the flora and fauna on the north side differed significantly from the flora and fauna on the south side. Thompson then brought his wife out to Saskatoon in 1914, where they rented a house at 1005

McPherson Avenue near Westminster Church before moving the next year to 539 24th Street, beside Knox Church.

The year before W.P. Thompson arrived in Saskatoon, the city, the province, in fact the entire country had fallen into an economic depression that had begun late in 1911 with the collapse both of international credit and world grain prices. The excessive optimism of the economic "boom" of 1907–08 had led civic leaders to massively overestimate the potential of their cities and the province in general. "Saskatchewan cities had enjoyed their 'one great spree.'"[72] The future would be more sober."[73] By 1912, Saskatoon's population was an estimated 28,000.[74] From 1909 to 1913, Saskatoon entrepreneurs had led the way in pioneering considerable building, while at the same time, along with other enlightened citizens, being instrumental in promoting significant cultural developments. The city contained seven public schools, eight cinemas, two live theatres, a musicians club, and a public library. From 1901 to 1912, the population had "skyrocketed" and "thanks to the strenuous efforts of the civic and business elite, all three major railways ran through the city – hence the nickname "Hub City."[75] According to history professor Arthur Silver Morton, the three railways running through Saskatoon provided easy access for students throughout the province and was one of the main reasons why the university was located there. However, conditions in many parts of the city were still primitive. The city still poured raw sewage into the river and on the Nutana side of the river there was a semi-permanent "tent city" for the numerous labourers.[76]

Saskatchewan was the first Canadian university to integrate agriculture with other colleges "at the forefront of the university's activity."[77] President Murray stated in 1909 that the College of Agriculture "must be regarded as the sheet anchor of the University," for it would be the way to "demonstrate its usefulness to the province."[78] That decision in turn led the province to transfer its extension branch to the university, in contrast to other provinces where agricultural extension operated within each Department of Agriculture.

In his own research and that of many of his graduate students, Thompson was to benefit from the incorporation of agriculture into the centre of the university's pursuits. Reflecting in 1970, he declared that, ever since the coming of John Bracken in 1909 as professor of field husbandry, "almost every member of the faculty of agriculture has been active in research. In fact no faculty in the university has been more active and few have equalled it." The historic significance of linking the basic sciences to the agricultural curriculum was justified by the early array of distinguished graduates who advanced agricultural research throughout North America, notably Kenneth Neatby, Cyril Goulden, Robert Glen, and J.B. Harrington in Canada and J.A. Jenkins,[79] D.R. Cameron,[80] and Merton Love[81] in the United States.

The relative informality of hiring practices, not to mention something of both Walter Murray and Thompson's characters, were apparent when, as Thompson later recalled, "One day in 1914 Dr Murray asked me if I had enough work around the Department to keep an untrained man busy for a short time. He had discovered through Knox Church this Scotch family with four children who had recently come over, had spent all their savings, could get no work, and were nearly starving."[82]

As it happened, Thompson needed to hire a technician who could make microscope slides, look after the museum and herbarium, and in later years assist the new faculty, mainly the fresh water biologist, Dr Donald Rawson, and the entomologist, Dr Leslie Saunders.[83] Thus "the much beloved Mr Grant, technician in Biology" was hired in 1914.

Peter Grant was a pint-sized man originally from the Shetland Islands who became such a fixture in the department that Murray arranged for him to have his portrait painted by the artist Augustus Kenderdine.[84] On winter mornings, Mr Grant would ride over the university bridge to the university in Dr Thompson's second-hand automobile.[85] As Thompson noted, although Grant "as what we would now call a technician, he was a very important man in the department and greatly respected ... he stayed with us not for a short time but for many years until his death. He was a well-educated, intelligent man and experienced, and was capable of much better things. But he loved his work, was fascinated by anything original that was being done, and was a great help to everyone. Scarcely a Sunday and few nights passed that he was not back at work."[86]

Thompson's respect for this technician, and for two who came later, Norman Ferrier and Ken Chaney, reflected the high degree of collegiality that prevailed in the department. When the biology department hosted parties, faculty and their wives, students, and the technical staff and their spouses would attend. This sense of community extended to the entire, then small, university where most professors, and certainly President Murray, knew students by name. It was all the more surprising, then, when this sense of collegiality was suddenly shattered.

In March 1919, Mr S.E. Greenway, the director of Extension at the University of Saskatchewan, travelled to Regina to see Premier William Martin. Failing to find him, Greenway then sought out and found the provincial treasurer, Charles Dunning. They met at Greenway's request and in the absence of Premier Martin. Greenway accused President Murray of falsifying a report about university finances, complained of widespread discontent within the faculty over Murray's conduct of university affairs, and alleged that the president faced considerable disloyalty. Greenway's charge of fiscal misconduct was by no means new, for he had been complaining about this issue around the halls of the university since 1913. But he had never before raised the issue formally and certainly not with provincial authorities.

This extraordinary meeting, conducted without Murray's or the board's knowledge, was to lead to a period of turbulence within the university, with serious divisions arising in both the student body and the city of Saskatoon, and unfavourable publicity within Canada as well as in two New York newspapers. The crisis did not end until April 1920, after Greenway and three senior faculty professors had been summarily fired by the Board of Governors on the president's recommendation, a number of contentious meetings had been held, and Murray had suffered a serious nervous breakdown.[87] By the end, however, the president had also been vindicated by the provincial government, the Board of Governors, and a large majority of the faculty. The four men were dismissed at a time when there was no policy of academic tenure anywhere in Canada.

It has been argued that few Canadian universities have ever been more racked by dissension than Saskatchewan in 1919.[88] Despite all the documents and later scholarly writings on the rebellion of 1919, aspects of this case are still debated. At the time, Thompson was unqualified in his support for Murray, and as late as 1964 described the crisis as so desperately serious that it "nearly wrecked the university."[89] Despite both the university and the Court of King's Bench finding the dismissals of the four faculty members "not merely justified but necessary for the good of the university," Thompson noted the affair had "always been treated as if it was a disgrace to the university – a skeleton in the closet."

> Something like a conspiracy of silence has been maintained in regard to it. It had not been referred to in the press and rarely even in conversation among those associated with the university ... It is time that the silence is broken and that a full and accurate account of the affair is written while some of us who lived through it and were in touch with developments are still on the scene. It was an important episode in the history of the University of Saskatchewan; public confidence in the institution was shaken, and many years passed before it gained the confidence, respect, and pride of the public which it later came to enjoy ... Misconceptions which still persist in respect to it should be corrected and justice should be done to the memories of some of those involved in it.[90]

Although there were several possible causes for disaffection on the part of the four men, Thompson believed that the personal ambition of at least two of the four was the driving force, coupled with their conviction that Murray was "autocratic, dishonest, devious and incompetent."[91]

Wartime and postwar inflation contributed to budgetary problems for the university, resulting in low faculty salaries that had not risen in the face of wartime price increases. Such conditions were not, however, peculiar to the University of Saskatchewan.[92] Ultimately, one could argue, "the basic issue was the power of the president."[93] But again, the University of Saskatchewan was not unique in that respect; and numerous other Canadian university presidents were confronted by just as searing and protracted conflicts with their faculty. Perhaps the personalities of the four who revolted at Saskatchewan were made of sterner stuff or they possessed anti-authoritarian personalities to an inordinate degree compared with disgruntled faculty in other Canadian universities. One could also look at the context of labour unrest throughout the country, epitomized by the 1919 Winnipeg General Strike and numerous attendant sympathy strikes, which so frightened "constituted authority" that a "hierarchical society was legitimized" and "obedience stressed." Thompson's interpretation was that "jealousy and thwarted ambition were at the roots of the discontent."[94]

The four disaffected faculty were Samuel E. Greenway and three others, who, in varying degrees, supported him: R.D. MacLaurin, head of chemistry; J.L. Hogg, head of physics, and Ira MacKay, who taught law and philosophy.[95] Since three were heads of departments and MacKay a senior professor, their complaints and alienation from Murray were bound to have serious repercussions, both within the university and among the general public. Hogg was especially angry over the low salaries paid to the faculty while MacLaurin's chief grievance was the conviction that he was not given sufficient research funds. MacKay apparently believed Greenway's charges of financial mismanagement and may also have been disappointed at Murray's decision not to select him as dean of law, an appointment that instead went to Arthur Moxon. Hogg and MacLaurin, particularly of the four, accused Murray of behaving autocratically. Even though faculty discontent over low salaries had been partially alleviated early in 1919 and the provincial government had allocated $25,000 for research, serious discontent still simmered.

At his meeting with Dunning, Greenway accused the president of two financial transgressions. He claimed that Murray had falsified a report regarding university expenses and had appropriated funds designated for extension work for other purposes. Greenway also charged that faculty lacked confidence in the president. Dunning was understandably shocked by the allegations and made haste to meet with Murray and Rutherford, the dean of agriculture, to investigate the charges. Murray was appalled by the charges and angered that Greenway had not brought these issues to him personally before going to the provincial government.

Murray called a university council meeting for 7 April, where he told the faculty about Greenway's charges and asked them to vote on one charge that his accuser had made: that the faculty no longer felt loyalty to the president. After a two-day period of reflection, the Council reconvened and supported Murray overwhelmingly, 27–0, with four members abstaining: J.M. Adams, a professor of physics soon to resign for a position in the United States, MacLaurin, Hogg, and MacKay.[96] At this stage, the Board of Governors took charge, demanding a letter indicating areas of dissatisfaction, if any, with the university's administration, from each member of the university staff. Anyone with issues to report was also invited to speak to the board at its next meeting, on 2 May. All but Greenway attested to their loyalty in their written replies; Hogg, MacLaurin, and MacKay did not immediately respond.

The board summoned the four abstainers to appear before it. MacLaurin and MacKay refused, Greenway attended and offered his resignation, while Hogg only came under threat of dismissal. The first people in the province knew about the allegations was when the "Big Four," as they became popularly known, publicized their case with newspaper announcements on 28 July 1919.[97] The main argument from the four faculty members was that Murray was not only autocratic, but incompetent and unwise in many of his academic decisions. As described by Thompson, the four comprised "a prestigious quartet" in a still-small university in which "the total faculty was thirty-one." The board, with Murray's agreement, dismissed all four on 11 August.[98] Nowhere in Canada to that time had any university ever acted in such a sudden and sweeping manner against such well-established faculty members, all of whom had been with the university for a decade and had risen to become part of the cohort of the ten highest-salaried professors.

Agitation on their behalf continued as the press clamoured for an explanation. On 29 August, W.R. Motherwell intervened in a public letter, insisting that an impartial open inquiry was essential to explain "what unpardonable sin" the four had committed.[99] Since he had been the provincial minister of Agriculture from 1905 to 1917, Motherwell had enormous influence in the province.

Motherwell's demand led to an all-day convocation meeting on 20 November in which three motions were passed, not one of which endorsed holding an enquiry. At one of the protest meetings, according to Thompson, one student, John Diefenbaker, "spoke eloquently and violently" on behalf of the dismissed men. Thompson admitted that he had "never liked John since that time," believing that the entire cause of the trouble was "the ambition and manoeuvring of one of the four [Hogg] to supplant Dr Murray as president." Other students, as well as many in the public sphere, viewed these convocation events as unsatisfactory, and longer hearings were held in March and April 1920 under the aegis of an adjudicator, the lieutenant governor. He transferred his authority to the Court of King's Bench, which then selected three judges from among its members and convened a hearing. The judges accepted the board's decision, stating that it was "regular, proper and in the best interests of the university." Since the four faculty members were not protected by tenure and served at the "pleasure of the board," they lost their jobs and Murray's position as president was reconfirmed by the faculty, the provincial government, and the majority of people in the province.

Politicians in Saskatchewan, accustomed to the "harsher ways" of the business world, had no patience with the four discontented faculty members after Murray was cleared of any fiscal wrongdoing. Dunning, reflecting upon his revulsion at the publicity, compared the four malcontents to the strikers in Winnipeg, and dismissed all four as "the Bolsheviki."[100] "The whole business lasted for more than a year, adding to an atmosphere already made cheerless by the grim news of war casualties and the effects of the influenza epidemic, which shut down the university classes for most of the first term."[101]

Why had the Board of Governors acted in such a peremptory manner? Why, also, had the board initially failed to publicly present any reasons for its action? These questions perplexed and, in many instances, outraged local citizens, many students, local newspapers, and others across the country. Thompson attributed much of the public agitation to a number of conditions. First, two of the four were "eloquent and popular speakers who were well known throughout the province." Second, Thompson faulted the board for not immediately providing "adequate reason for its action" and for failing to inform three of the discontented that the charge of financial impropriety against Murray was a typographical mistake dating from 1913. Moreover, the mistake had in fact been made by Greenway's office in a report he had submitted to Murray,[102] and Greenway had acknowledged this in his 2 May meeting with the board. Third, Thompson blamed the incident on the unsettled public atmosphere, owing to persistent "rumours of trouble at the university" [and] "various criticisms of the administration," much of which he believed had been initiated by Hogg. Thompson viewed Greenway as simply "muddle-headed." Thompson also thought that even the president deserved some blame, however little, because he was so hesitant to "hurt anyone's feelings" by saying "no." By failing to be decisive, Murray frequently left colleagues believing that an issue remained open.[103] But Thompson saw the main cause resting in the ambitions of Hogg and MacLaurin, in particular, to destroy the president and, in Hogg's case, perhaps to supplant Murray.[104]

How can this episode be evaluated? Certainly, under the University Act, the Board of Governors had the power to dismiss faculty, providing that it acted upon the recommendation of the president.[105] Murray had the authority to appoint and fire faculty in that age before tenure and the creation of faculty unions. He alone decided on promotions and research grants. Yet Murray's powers were in no way atypical throughout North American universities at the time, because presidents had extraordinary powers in what was still an age of deference to authority. Thompson, while fully and effectively supporting Murray, concluded that Murray had "learned his lesson," for he thereafter acted "with more force and determination," and devoted lengthy appraisals to all new appointees.[106]

Everything Thompson said about the 1919 predicament was from an administrative point of view. In his academic memoir, he does not refer to any external issue of the time: the Great War, the impact of the Spanish Influenza pandemic, or the unprecedented labour unrest in Canada at the time. Thompson had been courted by the dissidents in the 1919 affair, but had been totally unimpressed by their arguments. Instead, he and Arthur Moxon, then the dean of the College of Law, had, from the first, led the support and defence of the president. Years later, well into his retirement, Thompson spoke at a reunion of the class of 1923, reflecting: "upon the very sad incident in which four members of the faculty were fired ... after all these years it should be safe to mention it. I assure you there has been nothing like it since, although I remember when some of us would like to *have done* something similar."[107]

Was this a reference to wanting to replace J.S. Thomson, the university's second president or Thompson's own unspoken occasional desire, when president, to be able to fire recalcitrant professors? He did not expound on the point.

Thompson never reversed his views on the decision that led to the four faculty members being dismissed. A similar event would have been impossible, or at least very unlikely, in his time as president. It's difficult to imagine professors being dismissed in the 1950s at the University of Saskatchewan for "disloyalty" to Thompson in the sense of talking, however harshly, about his administrative policies and his character generally throughout the university and in the city. In 1965, a professor at Queen's expressed concern, indeed disbelief, over "whether loyalty to an institution should be a requisite for tenure at all; certainly to require loyalty to its officers is completely unjustified."[108]

Never once did Thompson analyze the allegation made by Hogg and MacLaurin that Murray was autocratic. Indeed, Thompson seemed never to have experienced any autocratic behaviour from Murray. When the president considered separating zoology and botany into two separate departments, it was Thompson who prevented this from occurring by threatening to resign. When Thompson needed Murray to call an emergency national meeting in Winnipeg over the wheat rust crisis, the president complied with the request. Moreover, Thompson received many benefits from Murray, such as extra research funds after 1917 when members of the Rust Conference summarily dismissed the geneticist's suggestion that wheat strains be crossed as a possible way to combat rust.

Nevertheless, Marion Evans Younger, the assistant registrar from 1929 to 1941, claimed that Murray "made all the decisions." A secretary who spent her entire career at the university and whose father worked closely with the president at Knox Church, she stated categorically that "Dr Murray was a dictator ... all decisions had to be referred to him." Others accused him of collecting gossip.[109] Thompson, by contrast, accused Murray only of being too kind and perhaps too sensitive. Whatever other interpretations of this event may be made, Thompson firmly supported Murray at the time, and never changed his view.

With the conclusion of the "Rebellion Crisis," Thompson could now return his formidable energies to his genetics research and to his thoughtful undergraduate teaching and graduate supervision.

2

Research: Genetics

I

Right after his appointment at Saskatchewan, Thompson completed the publications resulting from his research on *Gnetales* before embarking on his new interest in genetics. The study of the evolutionary relatedness of *Gnetales* to flowering plants remains one of the most contentious issues in botany.[1] Thompson had collected significant botanical material on his 1912–1913 worldwide explorations. Between 1910 and 1923, he published seventeen highly regarded papers on these aspects of evolutionary botany.[2] In addition, the first MA graduate he supervised had "a specially warm place in my memories." That was Hulda Haining, "who worked out and published the embryogeny of *Gnetum* in 1920" and took a position teaching in an American college.[3]

Thompson recalled in a retirement talk in 1959 that his shift to genetics arose because of the intellectual stimulation he had experienced during his brief and interrupted time at Harvard when he first did preliminary work in the subject. Also, the study of evolutionary botany no longer held his deepest intellectual interest. After his unhappy encounters with Jeffrey, Thompson was "fed up with morphologists snarling at one another."[4] He therefore "found it easy to decide" that wheat genetics would be his research focus.

He thereby responded to the dominant need of Saskatchewan and to the interest that Edward Murray East had engendered at Harvard and E.C. Jeffrey had arrested. His interest had also been fortified by a guest lecture given in 1912 at Harvard by E.B. Wilson on the X chromosome. Soon after Thompson took up his position at Saskatchewan, East sent him some papers on recent developments in genetics.[5] So did William Ernest Castle, the professor under whose supervision Thompson had begun to work on specific problems before Jeffrey interfered.[6] Thompson's decision to shift his research focus to the genetics of wheat chromosomes rather than continue to work on the evolution of plants turned out to be of immense importance to Saskatchewan, the Canadian West, and the country as a whole.

The study of genetics was still in its infancy in 1913: although there had been just over two generations of discoveries since Mendel published his results in 1866. The rediscovery of Mendel's work in 1900 made genetic research only slightly more than a decade old. In breeding experiments during 1856–66, Gregor Mendel first traced inheritance patterns of certain traits in pea plants and showed that they adhered to simple statistical rules. But Mendel was concerned with traits of whole organisms and did not inquire into how characteristics were sorted and combined on a cellular level, which is where reproduction occurs. Hugo de Vries confirmed the German monk's hypothesis that the inheritance of specific traits in organisms came in particles, by 1909 to be designated as genes.

The next significant breakthrough came in 1902, from two scientists working independently, who were examining cell division, Theodor Boveri, a German, and Walter Sutton, an American. Sutton provided evidence that when sperm and egg cells are being formed, the number of chromosomes is split in half and the original number is restored at fertilization, a process called meiosis. This insight provided the basis for the chromosome theory of inheritance: that chromosomes carry the cell's units of inheritance and thus are the basis for all genetic inheritance. But Sutton and the other scientists in the field had no idea where the genes of an organism were located. Although it seemed likely that genes were part of the chromosome, proof was lacking. In 1905, the pioneering geneticist E.B. Wilson at Columbia University discovered the chromosomal XY sex-determination system in molluscs, flatworms, and annelids – that males have XY and females XX chromosomes. In the same year, the emerging scientific ideas were given a name when the English biologist William Bateson first suggested using the term "genetics" to describe the study of heredity and biological inheritance. He then employed the term at an international conference in London in 1906. It soon gained widespread acceptance among scientists.

In 1910, Thomas Hunt Morgan, the Columbia University scientist, argued that genes are located on chromosomes. He had discovered that the white-eye mutation in fruit flies was on the X chromosome and that the pattern of sex chromosome distribution also agreed with Mendel's work. Morgan concluded, therefore, that a specific gene was "tied" to a specific chromosome. Morgan worked with fruit flies, *Drosophila*, because of their short life cycle, ease of culturing, and high fecundity. Large numbers could be reproduced inexpensively in an era before significant government financial assistance to science. In 1911, Morgan's student, Alfred Sturtevant, by experimentation established genetic linkage, leading to the "like beads on a string" theory.

These seminal findings were summarized in 1915 by Morgan and three of his graduate students in *The Mechanism of Mendelian Heredity*, which "set forth the physical basis for the new science of heredity," thereby, according to Nobel laureate Eric Kandel, placing genetics as a science on an equal basis with physics and chemistry.[7] Despite the clarity of the expositions by Morgan and his students, who demonstrated evidence for the chromosomal theory of heredity, some leading scientists remained unconvinced. For example, it was not until William Bateson spent some time in Morgan's "fly room" at Columbia in the early 1920s that the Englishman finally accepted the theory of chromosomal inheritance.

Thompson met Morgan and his distinguished graduate students when he visited the Woods Hole Marine Biological Laboratory in Massachusetts. Thompson spent a week there in the summer of 1915 on a recruiting mission for a biologist for the University of Saskatchewan.[8] That meeting was momentous for Thompson because he soon began to devote his scientific career to the study of chromosomes. He visited Morgan again on his sabbatical to Berkeley in 1929, when he travelled to the California Institute of Technology, where Morgan had moved from Columbia University. Nearly twenty years later, in his 1948 presidential address to the Royal Society of Canada, Thompson imagined a conversation between Darwin and Mendel in which Morgan appears: "Sooner or later in those imaginings the recently arrived shade of their greatest successor, Morgan, always breaks into the conversation ... Morgan's equally great contribution was to elucidate the mechanism of that transmission (of mutations), and the way in which genetic differences are produced and determined."[9]

Thompson's shift to research in wheat breeding genetics, and then, influenced by Morgan, shifting to chromosome work after 1917, and exclusively on chromosomes from 1924 onwards as a cytogeneticist, did not mean that his earlier work on angiosperms had been wasted. There was no inconsistency between working on evolutionary botany and the genetics of wheat chromosomes. From his research in his first field Thompson had understood life cycles and how fertilization occurred. Both fields required many similar lab techniques in preparing slides and searching for appropriate specimens in the field. In Saskatchewan, however, Thompson began to devote himself to aspects of the genetics of wheat, and from 1916 until 1939, he became a prolific researcher in the problems of genetics by focusing on wheat chromosomes. His decision to embark on wheat research reflected the reality of the provincial economy, and, indeed, the economy of the West as a whole. By 1910, Saskatchewan had become the breadbasket of Canada, producing 224,312,000 bushels, 57 per cent of Canada's total crop.[10] As economist Vernon Fowke noted, between 1913 and 1919, "the area devoted to wheat increased by 80 per cent, an amount equal to the total increase of the preceding twenty years."[11]

Initially, Thompson worked on the inheritance of early ripening with a view to obtaining varieties in which that trait could be combined with other agronomically useful characteristics. This inquiry was critical in a province devoted to producing wheat, but where the growing period was brief. Thompson recalled how immediately after his arrival in Saskatchewan he began to collect and grow as many varieties of wheat as possible so that as early as 1914 scores of different species and varieties were growing in his plots.[12] By crossing different varieties, he succeeded in obtaining good strains that possessed most of the characteristics of commercial varieties but ripened two weeks earlier.

At the outbreak of war in August 1914, the federal government encouraged farmers to grow even more wheat to assist the war effort "by feeding Allied troops."[13] Since Saskatchewan grew "almost two-thirds of the entire prairie wheat acreage and produced at least 60 per cent of the wheat grown in western Canada," the wartime economy tied the province even more tightly to a single staple crop. In 1915, there was a "fabulously bountiful crop" of 224.3 million bushels. Coincidentally, the same year Thompson was recognized as the first Canadian scientist to attempt wheat breeding for rust resistance.[14] In 1916, Thompson's earliest initiatives at this kind of breeding became enormously significant, after the most serious rust epidemic in Saskatchewan's history reduced the crop to 147.6 million bushels, a loss of almost $150 million dollars.[15] Thompson described this calamity as "one of the most important events in the history of prairie agriculture."[16] The crisis reinforced Thompson's intention to carry out research into the inheritance of rust resistance in wheat. Moreover, he knew of the groundbreaking work of Rowland Biffen (1874–1949) at Cambridge who in 1905 had discovered that resistance to rust was inherited.[17] Biffen, one of Bateson's most distinguished students, succeeded in breeding a wheat that was resistant to yellow rust, a fungal disease that devastated wheat crops. Thompson was impressed by Biffen's work and cited him in a paper in 1916.[18]

The severity of the 1916 rust problem persuaded Thompson and his colleague, John Bracken, to press President Murray for an emergency conference with the federal Department of Agriculture and the appropriate scientists. Thompson noted that A.H. Reginald Buller[19] of the University of Manitoba had independently requested that the Department of Agriculture call upon the eminent Minnesota wheat pathologist, Dr Elvin C. Stakman, to explore the rust problem – the epidemic had also destroyed some 200 million bushels in the northern and midwestern states.

When Thompson urged Dr Murray to press for a national conference on the rust crisis, the president demonstrated both his tenacity and influence in national affairs by pressuring the federal and provincial agricultural agencies to respond. The blight was, after all, "the worst epidemic of rust this country has ever had." Thompson praised Dr Murray's role in this calamity on many occasions but never more fully than in a speech in 1957. Only by intense lobbying, Thompson emphasized, was Murray able to succeed in convincing government agricultural leaders to convene a conference in Winnipeg in August 1917. He succeeded in bringing about this gathering by "hammering away and pulling many strings in high quarters ... [and pressuring] all the dominion and provincial men concerned ... That conference laid the plans which grew until the problem was solved ... When the original conference remained unimpressed by my proposal that we try to develop rust-resistant varieties ... [Murray] kept the idea alive and he found money, quite outside regular university funds, to support my work."[20]

At the conference, Thompson argued that efforts should be undertaken to produce varieties of wheat by genetic methods that would be able to resist rust. He spoke from experience, however limited. Reacting to the 1916 rust calamity early in 1917, Thompson had already tested two "agronomically valueless species that were almost completely free of rust."[21] One was a dicoccum wheat and the other a variety of durum, an offshoot of dicoccum. The durums were not resistant and neither produced the desired character of bread wheat, but Thompson believed that this was the way to proceed to produce rust resistant varieties. The only formal response Thompson received from this suggestion was from the Dominion Cerealist, Charles Saunders, who had no systematic training in genetics. He dismissed Thompson's proposal as useless because he believed nothing could be gained by crossing a bread wheat with durum or dicoccum. Although Thompson never wrote in detail about the actual discussions at the Winnipeg gathering, he did mention that when he suggested "trying to meet the problem by genetic methods, they weren't very interested: Charlie Saunders said he had tried [with Marquis and others] and had [a] bad time – [producing] weak, sterile plants [so Saunders] preferred early varieties or pathological methods."[22] Thompson's effort to convince the conference members to try crossbreeding was not well received. The conference members thought "so little ... of the proposal that it was not even mentioned in the minutes."[23] The view of those present at the conference, with one exception, was: "You try it; we don't think it's worth bothering about."[24] Nevertheless, the conference members decided that research was to be focused "at the University of Saskatchewan under the guidance of W.P. Thompson."[25] Moreover, the recently formed National Research Council was sufficiently impressed by Thompson to award him a grant of $2,000 early in 1918 to study the genetics of wheat, and later, in 1918–19, grants worth $4,500 "to develop an early ripening rust-resistant wheat, with the promise of future financial assistance if necessary."[26]

One botanist at the conference, however, who worked with the federal government, had understood the importance of Thompson's proposal. His name was W.P. Fraser, a scientist who was shy and modest almost to the point of being inarticulate. Thompson came to regard this profoundly decent man as "the father of plant pathology in Canada."[27]

While at the Winnipeg Conference late in August 1917, Fraser told Thompson about the scientific breakthrough made by his student,

Margaret Newton, at Macdonald College, McGill University. While Fraser was attending the Winnipeg Rust Conference, Newton discovered that the rust fungus had more than one strain. Her discovery came about after a visit from Charles Saunders. Saunders was most famous for developing Marquis wheat, the first modern spring wheat bred in North America. Saunders presented Newton with some Marquis seeds with seedlings. Newton tested the seeds by infecting them with spores of the stem rust *Puccinia graminis*. To her surprise, she discovered that not all of the stem rust spores created the same degree of infection. After Fraser returned to Montreal, he and Newton developed the hypothesis that the stem rust fungus was genetically variable and was composed of more than one strain. When Fraser informed Thompson of Newton's breakthroughs, Thompson negotiated with the federal Department of Agriculture to allow Professor Fraser, assisted by Dr Newton and others, to come to Saskatoon and set up a laboratory in one of the greenhouses to work on the rust problem.

Such faculty appointments would never have come to pass without President Murray's firm endorsement, who consistently supported Thompson's requests. The Board of Governors' minutes record the money paid to Newton and Fraser, and their positions and ranks. Fraser first came to the university in March 1919, but only to teach two hours a week and conduct a lab. He was allotted an office and greenhouse facilities. The minutes for 8 May 1920 record the travelling expenses authorized for Thompson for his visits to St Paul, Minnesota to consult with Professor Stakman and his trip to Ottawa to meet with Dr Saunders. Thompson used these trips to actively recruit Newton. As a result, she agreed to a program whereby she would spend six months at Saskatchewan and six months working on her PhD at Minnesota under Stakman.[28] For some years, Thompson noted, the biology department at Saskatchewan was the only Canadian university working on these wheat genetic problems.

Following the 1917 Winnipeg Rust Conference, Thompson was still encountering serious difficulties with wheat sterility in hybrids in his research on crossbreeding wheat species. His experiments did not produce types of rust resistant bread wheats. According to Gordon Kimber, the first real breakthrough in the genetics of wheat occurred with the work of the Japanese scientist Tetsu Sakamura in 1918, who determined that the three groups of wheat – Einkorn, emmer or dicoccum, and bread wheats – had chromosome complements of

2n=14, 28, and 42.[29] Sakamura's argument was validated the next year by Hitoshi Kihara, another Japanese wheat geneticist. Until then, "no really fundamental advances had been made,"[30] but after grasping that bread wheat and the two species he had used, durum and dicoccum, contained different numbers of chromosomes from those of the Vulgare types, Thompson began to concentrate almost totally on chromosome behaviour in wheat varieties.[31]

By the time of the second rust epidemic in 1923 and a subsequent second rust conference in Winnipeg in 1924, most Canadian wheat rust scientists accepted Thompson's idea of solving the rust dilemma by breeding resistant varieties.[32] Moreover, since a number of talented geneticists had been trained since 1917, the labour could be constructively distributed. Thompson saw his role in this research group as investigating wheat chromosomes in relation to inheritance, breeding, and sterility in crosses that involved species with different chromosome numbers. As Thompson later recalled, the other members of the research team agreed that "in collaboration with my students, I should investigate the whole chromosome situation and behaviour in wheat in relation to its genetics. It was easy to see that many important problems awaited investigation in that field."[33]

Thompson "therefore stopped all my work directly with rust, leaving that to the new researchers, and devoted all my efforts to the investigation of the chromosomes of wheat and its allies." He quickly found that the "investigation soon involved problems of such general and fundamental importance and interest that they became an end in themselves, quite apart from rust."[34] Thompson specialized in a branch of genetics called cytogenetics, the study of all aspects of chromosome behaviour. Thompson was, therefore, neither a plant breeder nor a plant pathologist. Since these fields overlapped a good deal, every year thereafter all the scientists involved in this rust program, including Thompson, met in conference to report on their progress to assess how each of the scientists' results had an impact on the contributions of others[35] and to modify, where necessary, research plans in the light of new knowledge.[36]

Thompson and his research group's investigations included detailed analysis involving chromosome numbers in wheat hybrids he created. For example, in 1926 he crossed the *Triticum vulgare* variety of wheat, the only wheat that had the sufficient number of chromosomes (21) to cross with rye, and then backcrossed (cross with one of its parents) the result. He was successful at a time when many other leading scientists experienced significant difficulties in making such crosses. The resultant successful hybrid possessed great toughness and durability. However, like the similar attempts of other leading cytogeneticists, Thompson's hybrid was almost completely sterile.[37]

Apparently, over "the course of evolution, the wheat and rye chromosomes have become so differentiated that they no longer pair properly."[38] This sterility was only overcome after the discovery of colchicine in 1937 as an agent for doubling the number of chromosomes after the initial cross. Using colchicine, by the early 1950s scientists had created a new cereal crop, *Triticale*, which has developed both as a food and as a major forage crop. This was accomplished by crossing a *Triticum* wheat such as Thompson had tried earlier with rye, or *Secale*, as *Triticum* was technically known.

Also in the mid-1920s, Thompson worked with many graduate students who later became distinguished cytogeneticists. One of the most able was Lillian Hollingshead with whom he published a paper on the progeny of crosses between chromosomes with five times (5n) the number of chromosomes, called pentaploid crosses (plants with five multiples of the haploid number (1n)). Such crosses produced useful hybrid combinations for studying evolutionary diversification.[39] As recently as 2011, this article was still being praised and cited by cytogeneticists as an early attempt to determine the chromosome content of the progeny produced. These scientists noted that while Thompson and Hollingshead could estimate the numbers of paired and unpaired chromosomes, they could not determine the identity of the chromosomes nor easily detect the chromosomal rearrangements because they lacked present-day molecular markers, that is, any site on the genome that shows the position of a particular gene. Thompson and other geneticists lacked the technology needed to succeed in these investigations.[40]

In 1941 and 1942, Thompson attempted to recreate ancient bread wheat in his lab by injecting one wheat species with colchicine. Unfortunately, only a few wheat species were available for testing and he was not able to produce a modern bread wheat from these experiments. Nevertheless, these examples of his chromosome research demonstrate the degree to which he was on the "cutting edge" in his field. Only a few years later, in 1947, modern bread wheat was created artificially by a Japanese scientist.

Thompson and his students published extensive studies on the behaviour of chromosomes in two interspecific hybrids These interspecific hybrids demonstrated the role of chromosomal activity on sterility and on the segregation of characteristics as well as the viability of male gametes (pollen cells) and female gametes (egg cells) with abnormal chromosome numbers. Thompson also did significant chromosomal research on endosperm (the tissue that surrounds the developing embryo of a seed and provides food for its growth) in wheat.[41]

The amount of work he accomplished was extraordinary.[42] No wonder he stated that "work took up all my time and efforts for more than twenty years following 1924."[43] Thompson described his work as laborious, exacting, and complicated. For example, he, not a laboratory assistant, sectioned pollen cells embedded in paraffin at around 30 to 40 microns (a thousandth of a millimeter) with a microtome (an instrument for cutting extremely thin sections of material for examination under a microscope) and then stained the chromosomes so they could be seen under a microscope. Material needed to be prepared in this way to identify the chromosomes from the parental wheat strains and then to assess which chromosomes were present in sterile plants in the first and later generations of a cross. These studies painstakingly traced the path of the chromosomes from the original parents.

The attempt to determine how chromosomes behaved after various crosses was a major endeavour. The amount of time needed to do these studies is difficult to imagine because such work is just not done anymore.[44] Today, chromosomes are marked by molecular techniques that make it easier to see and identify them. Thompson was one of the pioneers studying chromosome behaviour and meiosis. He was also a team leader who encouraged his co-workers in the best way possible, demonstrating a fair-minded professional reluctance to take credit for their research activities. Thompson was convinced that the comprehensive collaborative program he was instrumental in initiating was the ideal way to pursue research, combining plant pathologists, geneticists, biochemists, agronomists, and other scientists.

Margaret Newton worked successfully with Thompson until early 1925, when she moved to Winnipeg to pursue her research at the Dominion Rust Research Laboratory at the University of Manitoba. W.R. Motherwell, by 1922 the federal Minister of Agriculture, offered

Newton the position of head of research, where her mandate would be to conduct research on the biological specificity of sundry varieties of the wheat stem rust, *Puccinia graminis*. Before her departure from Saskatchewan, Newton had been promoted from instructor to assistant professor. In his annual departmental report for 1922–23, Thompson noted that Newton and he were close collaborators, working on a considerable number of hybrids that were resistant to rust strains.[45] Even so, Thompson encouraged Newton to take the new position. Much later, he complimented her by saying she had assumed a post "for which she was better fitted than any other Canadian and in which she did very notable work."[46] Newton in turn praised Thompson as "largely responsible for the idea of a Rust Research Laboratory at Winnipeg and did so much to encourage and stimulate the work of that institution."[47] For many years, University of Saskatchewan scientists, many of them former students of Thompson, dominated the research at the Rust Lab in Winnipeg where they often worked in tandem with University of Saskatchewan scientists. Margaret Newton hired another of Thompson's MSc graduates, Thorvaldur Johnson, and they worked together in Winnipeg on the physiology of rust. Other former students of Thompson who worked for some time at the Rust Lab were Cyril Goulden, who concentrated on breeding research, and Kenneth Neatby, whose research focused on forecasting rust infection. In Saskatoon at the university, four scientists were involved with the research at the Winnipeg Rust Lab: Thompson, W.P. Fraser, J.B. Harrington, and R.K. Larmour of chemistry.

By the late 1940s, of the hundreds of millions of bushels of wheat grown in western Canada, two-thirds came from the rust-resistant variety Thatcher wheat developed at the University of Minnesota, while the remaining third came from varieties that originated in Canada through the collaborative work of the scientists in the "rust program."[48] Marquis wheat, which was excellent for bread making, was extensively grown until 1939, when it proved highly susceptible to new strains of rust. By 1953, Selkirk wheat bred as a rust-resistant strain had yielded 20.6 bushels per acre, whereas Marquis had been reduced to 2.6 bushels by rust. In 1954, Thompson praised his former student, Cyril Goulden, an early statistician of wheat studies and the Dominion Cerealist at the time, who had "just released a new wheat variety, Selkirk, which met the threat of the deadly new rust strain 15B of *Puccinia graminis*, which broke out in 1950.

Thompson was involved early in the development of Thatcher wheat. In 1916, he had proposed crossing Marquis wheat with lower quality emmer wheats, because he knew that Marquis had become highly susceptible to rust. "Using this idea, plant scientists produced a string of rust resistant wheats including Reward, Renown and, in the United States, Thatcher."[49] In Professor T.C. Vanterpool's retirement address, the plant pathologist whom Thompson had hired in the late 1920s, "newcomers to the university" were bluntly reminded about the significance of the research that had taken place in wheat genetics: "if it were not for the plant breeders and plant pathologists, the three prairie provinces would be almost as thinly populated as the northern tundras are today."[50]

In an address to the Royal Society of Canada in June 1949 on the occasion of his award of the Flavelle Medal, Thompson summarized the then-current state of the rust problem: "The rust problem is now solved. It may not stay solved because strains of rust which can attack the present varieties are known and may spread. But we may rely on those who defeated the enemy before to defeat it again. As a matter of insurance they are already taking measures to produce varieties resistant to the newer strains of rust. The struggle may have to be carried on for a long time."[51]

II

Thompson's finely organized approach to teaching genetics was evident in late 1927 when he established a Genetics Club or, as he said to Murray, "really [a] Journal Club." The existence of such a quasi-professional organization, where research papers were regularly presented, no doubt helps explain the later academic success of many of the student participants. Thompson insisted that the graduate students gain no credit for attendance, since participation was voluntary, even though it was "essential that all members of the staff who are interested should attend" but it "could not be conducted as a class."[52] The program that he sent President Murray for the years 1928 to 1931 listed the dates and topics for presentation by the members. Participants were required to prepare an abstract of their work and distribute it at least a week ahead of the presentation. The presentation was not to go beyond three-quarters of an hour so as to leave ample time for discussion. As well as graduate student participants, Professors Kirk and Harrington, as well as Thompson all gave papers.[53]

Thompson's organization of the research in genetics and in the department as a whole demonstrates just how hard he and his colleagues and graduate students worked. In his November 1927 departmental report, Thompson wrote: "It is impossible for the men to estimate with any degree of accuracy the time spent in research. All the full-time members of the department and one of the part-time men spend all their spare time at research, and this includes many evenings. I should very roughly estimate my own time at about 15 hours per week, apart from that spent on the literature bearing on the research. In addition most of the members spend nearly all the summer vacation chiefly on research."[54]

Thompson's main research was conducted despite the lack of a doctoral program at the university. President Murray stated in 1922 that "the University has no intention of preparing candidates for the Doctor's degree ... It would be folly ... to add another feeble graduate school to those that encumber the land."[55] Thompson supervised his MA students exclusively through the biology department or the College of Agriculture. A College of Graduate Studies was not created until 1946, on the recommendation of the survey committee Thompson chaired.[56] In 1948, the university authorized the enrolment of PhD candidates, and in 1952 two physics students earned the first doctorates. Later on, Thompson was to claim that although the College of Graduate Studies had "to wait for many years ... there has been no more important or far-reaching development in the history of the university, particularly when the associated research is considered."[57] Thorbergur Thorvaldson, famous for his discovery of sulphate-resistant cement, was named the first dean. Still, the University of Saskatchewan was only the fourth institution in Canada to form a school of graduate studies, following the early examples of the University of Toronto and McGill, which both instituted graduate schools in 1922, and Laval, which created its graduate school in 1939.[58]

Thompson admired Thorvaldson enormously, and not only for his path-breaking research. They had been contemporaries at Harvard, with Thompson arriving one year earlier. At the retirement dinner for Thorvaldson in the spring of 1949, Thompson reflected upon the long association the two men had shared.

> His name and mine began together in the dim past at the foot of the calendar and floated together to the top of the list as our

> seniors retired or left ... It was more than thirty-five years ago that we were contemporaries at Harvard. My earliest recollection of him is connected with a dinner at the Harvard Canadian Club ... The occasion was, I think, his winning a much-prized fellowship for study in Europe ... I preceded Dr Thorvaldson to Saskatchewan by one year. During that year I was naturally delighted when Dr Murray mentioned that he was thinking of appointing Dr Thorvaldson to our Chemistry Department. Perhaps the best thing I ever did for the University was to help to convince Dr Murray that he should appoint him.[59]

The appointment of Thorvaldson, a major researcher, gave significant distinction to the new College of Graduate Studies. Carlyle King described him "as a scientist of international distinction" who "more than anyone else ... was responsible for the development of advanced studies in the University of Saskatchewan."[60] The new college also demonstrated that by the end of World War II, resistance to PhD work had been overcome, particularly since graduate studies had demonstrated their importance to the recent war effort. The doctoral studies instituted in 1948 were almost exclusively in the sciences. The emphasis on scientific research had been demonstrated in 1947 with the establishment of the Saskatchewan Research Council. The first attempt to found such a council in 1930 had failed. By 1947, however, the Saskatchewan government was eager to create such an organization, mainly to advance the province's development in the physical and life sciences. The grants-in-aid that the council offered enabled university researchers to carry on their work far more effectively, while rendering important services to the province.

Despite lacking a doctoral program until 1948, the University of Saskatchewan produced numerous MSc graduates, many in biology and agriculture, under Thompson's supervision. Throughout the 1920s and 1930s, Thompson built up a cohort of students who earned masters' degrees in genetics under his guidance. Everyone he took under his supervision had successful academic and scientific careers. Many were women: notable among them were "the very brilliant Lillian Hollingshead," his first student in genetics,[61] who graduated in 1923 and became a specialist in cytology and genetics at Berkeley; Myrtle C. Melburn;[62] and Hulda I. Haining. Thompson's secretary remarked that his reputation as a scientist was so high that "he never had any difficulty placing his graduate students in any of the major universities that offered graduate degrees in genetics."[63] A later dean of agriculture at the University of Manitoba, Dr Len Shebeski, went to Saskatoon after his post-graduate studies at the University of Minnesota deliberately to study with Thompson.[64] Speaking in 1955 about two of his graduates, Thompson remarked: "Without the rust resistant varieties [of wheat] produced earlier by universities and departments [of Agriculture], it is likely that the three big crops of the last three years would have been greatly reduced or destroyed. I wish I possessed the money that by a conservative method my modest services in training [J.B.] Harrington and [C.H.] Goulden have meant to Western Canada."[65]

Thompson kept in touch with many of his former graduate and undergraduate students. In 1956, he replied to his former student, the diplomat Gordon Robertson, deputy minister of northern affairs and national resources and later secretary to the cabinet and clerk of the privy council, that he had "gone a long way since you were in Biology II. One of the greatest rewards of an old teacher is to see his former students making their way in the world." In the same letter, Thompson recommended his former student Kenneth Neatby for the position of director of forestry. Thompson described him as a "very brilliant person and an able administrator" but likely not available; much later, Thompson again praised Neatby as "one of the most brilliant men in Canadian agriculture."[66] Thompson next suggested his former student, Dr Robert Glen, who was "the right-hand man of Dr Ken Neatby."[67]

Thompson's focus was not only on students working at a graduate level. Although he disparaged his early endeavours as a teacher, clearly Thompson was successful in encouraging academic interchanges with undergraduate students. One former student vividly recalled the biology class that he took from Dr Thompson in 1928 during his first year of university, along with 150 other students in the chemistry building theatre. Thompson's lectures were "very precise," making it easy for students to take notes from the lectures.[68] More than one student recalled the precision of the man himself, who would enter the theatre right on time, couldn't let any humour in talks but we'd go straight through [and] when the bell rang he'd stop. And start right in on the same spot [the next lecture]."[69] Later, as president, Thompson once apologized for speaking at length by explaining that since he had "lectured three times a day for 50 minutes each time, for thirty years," he found "it difficult to talk less than fifty minutes."[70]

As with any good teacher, word spread among students. One recalled, "there was a huge registration for biology 11 [genetics]; it was not easy to get accepted. This was because W.P. Thompson gave the course and he was such a wonderful lecturer, and made it so interesting, that lots of Arts students wanted to take the course as an option."[71] In the 1920s, Thompson was reckoned by 27 per cent of the students as their favourite teacher.[72]

In June 1929, Thompson embarked on his first sabbatical year in Berkeley, California, to expand his understanding of fresh developments in genetics. Before leaving, the Thompson family took the train to Toronto. This was Marjorie Thompson's first trip to the city since her marriage and, hence, the first time in many years she was able to visit some of her Ontario relatives. In Toronto, Thompson purchased a new automobile and drove the family across the continent to Berkeley. For his purpose, "that institution was almost ideal." As he told President Murray in his report on the year, he was "engaged continuously in research at the Division of Genetics" from mid-September 1929 to the end of July 1930. During the course of the year he published two papers, had two in press and another "nearly ready." He also visited sixteen universities and associated with a constellation of world-class geneticists, both permanent members of the Berkeley staff and distinguished visitors.[73] He was clearly recognized as a major researcher in wheat genetics.

There were good reasons for Thompson to go to Berkeley, where E.B. Babcock had established the first department of genetics in North America in 1912. Thompson had struck up rewarding friendships with Babcock and R.E. Clausen, both outstanding scientists in his field. Babcock secured Thompson's appointment as an honorary member of the faculty and he was "treated as a regular member of the genetics department."[74] In 1929, Thompson visited what was to become the Davis campus of the University of California. He also spent a week at the California Institute of Technology in Pasadena where he met with Thomas Hunt Morgan, who had moved there from Columbia in 1928, and Morgan's brilliant former graduate students, Sturtevant and Bridges. At Stanford, Thompson had a number of conversations with John Dewey, the controversial but influential American philosopher and educator. Thompson was also approached about joining the Carnegie lab at Stanford. Of all the major job appointments Thompson was invited to pursue – later at

Minnesota and at Toronto – his only regrets came from his decision not to follow up the California soundings.

Thompson was proud of a number of his former students who had earned PhDs at Berkeley, notably James Angus Jenkins and Donald Ross Cameron. Lillian Hollingshead was then well on the way to completing her doctorate there, with Babcock and Clausen.[75] There was a moving personal dimension to the relations between Thompson and these three former students. Writing to Dr Murray, Thompson remarked that he had "played the fond (academic) parent in watching two of my boys, Jenkins and Cameron, each take charge of a seminar meeting. They made a good showing ... everyone I meet speaks in the most glowing terms of Miss Hollingshead. She made a great impression here."

Jenkins gave Thompson, Murray, and Babcock considerable concern, when he developed tuberculosis. Thompson immediately told Murray that "everyone here is very much cut up about it."[76] Murray responded the day that he received Thompson's letter. Babcock asked Thompson to write to Murray inquiring if the young student's parents could help in meeting Jenkins's potential expenses. Jenkins had just had his future assured at Berkeley: Prof. Babcock had offered him a permanent position Eventually, Jenkins recovered completely and went on to have a distinguished career at Berkeley.[77]

This episode involved a university president, a distinguished geneticist from Saskatchewan, and the chairman of the genetics department at Berkeley. It demonstrates not only the collegial dimension evident at some university levels nearly seventy years ago; it also illustrates a high level of faculty consideration for students scarcely evident in today's mega-universities. How much time could senior university academics devote to a single case like this today?

Thompson had a fulfilling research career during the 1920s and even during the Depression and drought of the 1930s. Thompson notes that between 1925 and 1945 he, sometimes with his graduate students, published thirty-four papers on chromosomes in major scientific journals.[78] This figure does not include the seventeen papers published on the evolution of *Gnetales* before Thompson turned to genetics. A few of Thompson's scientific papers are still cited today.[79]

In a speech to the biology department in 1968, Thompson spoke of the difficulty of assigning exact credit to himself or to the other main geneticists working in his field. A few other wheat geneticists, especially in America and Japan, were active in the same field and that "neither in the statement of the general nature of the work nor in the explanation of the results which follow, has it been possible to state the precise contributions of each of us."[80] Thompson was modest, though perhaps realistic, about his own abilities, refusing to place himself in the "first rank of academic researchers." He amplified this assessment. "The first rank should be reserved for those who make the big advances – the breakthroughs – which others rush in to exploit by following their consequences. The chief factor in making big advances is originality of mind, and I was not endowed with a sufficient amount of that attribute to make breakthroughs. Therefore my work was largely of the follow-up type."[81] Later, a noted specialist in creating rust resistance in wheat judged that

> At the time Thompson's research ... was among the best in the field. Its significance was recognized by Dr Thompson's election as a fellow of a number of scientific societies including the American Genetics Society, the Japanese Genetics Society, the American Association for the Advancement of Science, the Agricultural Institute of Canada and the Royal Society of Canada in 1921, of which he was President in 1948. It is a credit to the calibre of the research undertaken by Professor Thompson, his associates and his students that their work has been cited in these current world-wide research journals.[82]

III

There was also a more philosophical side to the work in genetics in which Thompson and his international colleagues were involved. Almost from the outset of his career, Thompson often discussed evolution in some of his talks and lectures. Only occasionally did Thompson's ideas on evolution and a suspicion that he was therefore antagonistic to Christianity lead to concern among some churchgoers in the province. Dr Murray carefully endorsed Thompson's lectures on evolution, allaying the apprehensions of a Presbyterian minister by describing Thompson's lectures "as most wholesome ... and never provocative ... to Christianity."[83]

The rediscovery of Mendel led Thompson to make an important generalization. When he arrived at the University of Toronto only six years after Mendel's theory had re-emerged, Thompson soon realized that most of his biology professors were seriously out of date and knew nothing of Mendel's ideas and the paradigm shift that his ideas had brought about. Thompson also reflected that nearly all the older men at the university were committed too deeply to their own fields and therefore were, consciously or subconsciously, resistant to new ideas and fresh projects. Thompson concluded early that an important characteristic of a successful researcher was to know when to drop a problem and take up a new one instead of following the old one down increasingly irrelevant bypaths.[84]

Thompson's first major speech at the University of Saskatchewan was given to the Assiniboia Club in January 1916, a voluntary organization composed of professors and students, who had adopted the name of the organization from an historic one of the old North-West Territories. A fortnight later, a constitution was proposed. Professor Arthur Morton of the history department drew up their mission statement: to study "the present economic, social and educational positions of foreign settlements in our province." "Foreign" referred to immigrants who were not English-speaking. The club's aim was primarily to promote tolerance among the diverse nationalities in the province in a time of war fever, to "learn more and more" about those "who have cast their lot with us" so as "to find the path of justice towards them and do something to win them in turn to those ways which will lead, in spite of much necessary diversity, to the common love of freedom and good citizenship which alone can make our democracy great."[85]

However, the organization also discussed papers on diverse issues designed to stimulate discussion. Thompson was thus given his first opportunity to speak publicly about evolution. His talk on "The Origin of Life" consisted of a rejection of all explanations of creation based on supernatural beliefs while using his considerable knowledge of modern chemistry, physics, and biology to argue in favour of evolution. For Thompson, "the real mystery of the universe is not the mystery of life but the existence of matter and energy and the natural laws which bring about evolution." This conclusion, far from making Thompson pessimistic, prompted his conclusion that "of all the beautiful ideas of creation which have been held by different peoples, none is so impressive as this which is being revealed by modern science."[86]

Thompson also spoke and wrote about evolution in the context of his own thoughts about eugenics. Theories of eugenics had become fashionable in numerous scientific and popular circles in the late Victorian period and remained in vogue with some scientists and laymen into the 1930s. In 1883, Francis Galton, a cousin of Charles Darwin, coined the term "eugenics" to encourage preferential breeding, that is, marriages between individuals who possessed similar traits such as high intelligence while discouraging marriages between couples with low intelligence. He was convinced that mental qualities were determined more by nature than by nurture. Social surveys in Britain from the 1880s on had demonstrated the ghastly wretchedness of many in the urban working class. Many of these investigators became convinced that these conditions resulted from genetic degeneracy. Acting on such views, some opinion leaders promoted fears of national degeneracy. Eugenicist ideas spread through Canada and the United States, particularly in the depression-ridden 1930s, when many economically secure elites came to believe that it was not the economic system that caused such human distress but, instead, moral and genetic failings. In addition, the arrival of millions of often uneducated immigrants led many of British stock to fear that intermarriage would lead to a "mongrel race." In the United States, every member of the first editorial board of the journal *Genetics*, including William E. Castle, and Edward M. East, though not Thomas Hunt Morgan, endorsed the eugenics movement.[87] Eugenics was rendered largely unacceptable socially and scientifically with the coming of World War II, which provided jobs for many hitherto unemployed, who then often developed successful careers and productive lives. Eugenics was also discredited by the realization in the 1930s that the traits eugenicists valued were multifactorial and that therefore any selective program, if feasible, would take many generations to accomplish. Especially damning to the theories, however, was Germany's introduction of eugenicist policies through sterilization (and worse) of the poor and the mentally handicapped, and the increasing revelations of Hitler's racist policies.

These ideas were first popularized at the first International Eugenics Congress in London in 1912. As a young man, fired by the possibilities of the new science of genetics, Thompson briefly supported the study of eugenics and discussed aspects of eugenics in four scientific papers meant for an informed but not scientifically trained audience. In 1916, Thompson gave a talk titled *Heredity and Education* at the Eighth Annual Convention of the Saskatchewan Educational Association in Prince Albert.[88] He argued that the rediscovery in 1900 of Gregor Mendel's laws of heredity had modified "our ideas of evolution, our philosophy, and our ethics" while revolutionizing "our practices in plant and animal breeding." The delay in recognizing Mendel's contributions Thompson attributed to the distractions created by "fighting" between theologians and biologists over Darwin's theory of evolution. From Mendel, he suggested, biologists now knew that acquired characteristics were definitely non-inheritable and, importantly, just how characteristics were inherited. This understanding was critical for the selective breeding of animals.

He went on to reflect on the vexing issue of eugenics, noting that the "human species is the only one in which natural selection is inoperative; man is the only being who protects and cares for his weak and incompetent brothers and allows them to reproduce." Thompson recognized that environment could play a significant role in human development; that heredity and environment need not be antagonistic but co-operative; and that they "pull together" when society attempts to rectify class distinctions "so as to give everyone a chance to get into the class to which he belongs through heredity." But he believed that eugenicist policies were essential if the human race was to be improved. Thus, Thompson lamented the declining birth rate among many of the most intellectually and creatively productive individuals and classes. For example, he stressed the sustained mental and moral qualities of such families as the Darwins, the Lowells in America, and the Oslers of Ontario. By contrast, Thompson argued, criminality and morality might well be inherited, for, he stated, heredity "prevails enormously over environment."[89]

Therefore, he stated, teachers of biology needed to familiarize themselves with the new ideas on the impact of heredity, for "none has more important points of human contact with human life." Hence, "the proper methods of improving the human race are the methods of eugenics – the prevention of the reproduction of the unfit."[90]

Thompson gave this speech when he was still a relatively young man and when his ideas on eugenics were rudimentary, even simplistic. Yet, he was in the company of major thinkers such as Julian Huxley, and the later politician T.C. Douglas, both of whom were attracted, briefly in the latter's case, by what they saw as the optimistic possibilities of eugenics. In 1916, it seemed possible that, led by scientists, especially geneticists, humanity could be guided to a better, more intelligent and more humane world by applying eugenicist policies.

By the time Thompson came to write publicly once more about eugenics, he had developed a more complex and mature understanding of genetics and rejected the simplistic view of eugenics that had characterized his 1916 speeches. For example, in 1930, Thompson, along with a number of other Canadian scientists, refused to support the creation of the Eugenics Society of Canada that had been formed on 6 November 1930.[91]

Thompson addressed eugenics issues in two other papers, "The Biological Conception of Progress," and "The Biological Effects of Race Mixture," the former written in the early 1920s and the latter written in the late 1930s or early 1940s.[92] In the paper on "Progress," Thompson reflected upon the ideas of the English cleric William Ralph Inge (1860–1954), the dean of St Paul's Cathedral, a Neoplatonist scholar and, during the interwar period especially, a popular British journalist. Thompson took as his text Inge's 1920 Oxford Romanes Lecture, a prestigious public talk presented annually at the request of the vice-chancellor of the university. Inge's talk was titled "The Idea of Progress."[93] The dean was haunted by neo-Malthusian ideas of world over-population and advocated selective breeding as a means of checking what he believed was a disastrous path for the human race. He also despised democracy and socialism, believing they led inexorably to chaotic rule by slum-ridden masses. Social reforms for the working classes, Inge believed, merely encouraged the poor and mentally deficient to produce more children.

In his paper, Thompson began by remarking that "we have ... come to think of progress as the normal course of events in human affairs and in living nature in general." This "modern attitude" toward progress, he suggested, was largely due to recent scientific advances. By contrast, he noted, Dean Inge, "in an essay that has not detracted from his reputation for gloominess ... contends that there is no justification for this faith." Without initially contesting or agreeing with the cleric, Thompson set his task as one of examining the "general biological conception of progress." In biology, Thompson stated, "we have agreed to define progress as change in direction of increasing complexity of structure and function," and suggested that the "complexity which accompanies specialization is the only workable test of progress in biology." But increasing specialization may lead to a lack of adaptability.

So Thompson saw "no law of nature which ensures progress." Indeed, "retrogression has been very common in the history of life." In terms of the human species, he suggested, there has been "no physical progress at all since Cro-Magnon man," nor any evidence of mental progress over the centuries, for "knowledge is not intellect." Thompson agreed with Inge in believing that there had not been any moral improvement in man's nature. In fact, from his own experiences, Thompson asserted that "the natives of the interior of Java are more moral then the average Canadian." Additionally, he stated, since man had eliminated natural selection, the human species would probably not improve physically or mentally. This state of affairs was not likely to change, particularly as eugenics was "little more than a philosophy." And Thompson saw it as "inconceivable that the eugenicist will ever be given power." Still, Thompson had hopes for the future of mankind, by social reforms that "man has only begun to travel." His conclusion, completely at odds with that of Inge, was the basis of his belief in social democracy. "Though physical and mental progress may be at an end, social progress is rapid. In this path there is specialization and cooperation of whole human individuals."

Thompson had rejected his earlier endorsement of eugenics as far too simplistic and as opening the door to fanatical racists. In his second paper, on race mixture, he began his analysis of popular hostility to "race mixing," starting with the English novelist Israel Zangwill's description of North America as "a melting pot" – a concept that Thompson saw as completely invalid scientifically. Following Mendel, Thompson argued that the mingling of races will not "blend into an intermediate condition; they will not cancel each other or be diluted." Instead, those genetic traits once characteristic of particular peoples "will be shifted back and forth, combined, dissociated, and recombined in every possible way."[94] Therefore, "the frequently expressed belief in a general degeneration of a mixed people is quite unjustified." "Differences do not necessarily mean inequalities."[95] Indeed, Thompson dismissed the "superstition of Nordic superiority," an idea that had guided American immigration policy in the 1920s. Thompson argued that no "one race has a monopoly of any attribute." [96] His opinions continued to mature, so that by 1945 he stated categorically: "*There is no biological argument against race crossing* for Peoples of highest achievements have been racially mixed."[97] Thompson concluded this paper with the injunction that, "We educators have a great responsibility and duty in combating race prejudice." When Thompson wrote this 1945 paper, the full horrors of Nazi racial policy were just being revealed.

In 1959, Thompson was invited to present a lecture at the Royal Society Symposium on Evolution to celebrate the hundredth anniversary of the publication of Darwin's *Origin of Species*. In 1960, this essay was published in *Evolution: Its Science and Doctrine*. Thompson's fourth essay, and chapter, was "The Cause and Mode of Evolution." His main theme was his praise of the ideas of Charles Darwin. Thompson remarked that fifty years earlier he had attended a lecture at the University of Toronto in which the speaker had presented very few findings since Darwin's *Origin of Species* of 1859, either in fact or in theory. Since most of genetics had developed after 1909, there had been very few breakthroughs on the mechanics of genetic development. Although it was true that Mendel had been rediscovered in 1900, few biologists grasped the "great significance of these principles in relation to evolution." Even the idea of the inheritance of acquired characteristics had persisted for many years after 1900 and had recently been resurrected in the Soviet Union by Trofim Lysenko. But now the fundamental problem for geneticists in the mechanics of evolution was how and why mutations occur. Finally, by 1930, scientists agreed that the great majority of hereditary mutations are "small and barely detectable" and that Mendelian heredity is universal. A new species would arise when an original population had split and diverged genetically over time so that the two populations were no longer capable of interbreeding. But the developments of genetics since Darwin in 1859 validated Thompson's views that evolution was an opportunistic phenomenon. These four essays are some of the ways Thompson sought to convey his scientific work, especially in genetics, to the general public and, in the last instance, to fellow scientists.[98] More important perhaps, they provide some glimpse into the evolution of his thinking. There is no evidence that Thompson's earlier acceptance of some eugenicist arguments ever adversely affected his personal research, his mainstream evolutionary views, or his liberal social outlook.

Thompson and the university as a whole prospered during the 1920s. The "dirty thirties," however, led to serious, indeed desperate problems. University faculty and staff were confronted with the fact that their salaries had to be cut dramatically and building projects postponed. Between 1930 and 1934, the provincial grant to the university was cut by forty per cent. Thompson's professional career, however, continued to go from success to success, despite the human tragedies of the period, the cuts in university funding, and the diminution of scientific grants. He was able to appoint three talented scientists to the biology department during the 1920s and secure the services of two more in the depths of the Depression. In 1924, he hired Les Saunders, an entomologist, parasitologist, and invertebrate biologist who was also a fine painter and a distinguished photographer. In 1928, Thompson was able to hire T.C. Vanterpool, a specialist in plant diseases. The next year, Donald S. Rawson, who was to become an internationally known fresh-water biologist, joined the department. Then in 1934, the department secured Thomas Arnason as a plant geneticist; and that same year, entomologist J.G. Rempel was seconded to teach at Regina College. These five departmental faculty members were to be the last full-time, permanent scientists in biology at the University of Saskatchewan until 1950. The ongoing Depression and then the exigencies of World War II curtailed any further departmental expansion.

Thompson believed that during the Depression years "Saskatchewan was more severely affected than any other part of the country."[99] Since education was a provincial responsibility, the near collapse of revenues for the government in Regina left the university in particular, impoverished. The annual university grant from the province fell from $676,727 in 1930–31 to $398,000 during the years 1930–34, while the average per capita annual income in Saskatchewan fell by 72 per cent.[100] During the academic year 1933–1934, the straitened economic conditions of the university were marginally alleviated by a grant of $50,000 from the Carnegie Corporation. It was this gift that allowed the university to take over the bankrupt Regina College and assume all its liabilities. Much as the United Church was reluctant to part with the junior college, the church authorities agreed to the transfer, believing it to be "in the best interests of higher education."[101] In 1937, the worst of the drought years, Saskatchewan's wheat yield, which normally averaged 15 bushels per acre, dropped to an average of 2.6 bushels per acre. Compounding this problem, the drought spread northward to the parklands, while in the south of the province an infestation of army worms and a growing equine encephalomyelitis epidemic developed that not only killed over 15,000 horses during 1937 and 1938, but also affected human beings. The University of Saskatchewan also suffered because the "Great Depression ... hit Saskatoon the hardest of any English-Canadian city."[102]

The economic plight of agriculture in western Canada was all too often ill-understood in eastern Canada, notably in Quebec. For example, in 1938, the future prime minister, Louis St Laurent, then acting as legal counsel for the Rowell-Sirois Royal Commission on Dominion–Provincial Relations, had a heated verbal exchange with T.C. Davis, Saskatchewan's attorney general. When Davis stated that no more money could be raised by taxes, St Laurent responded by expostulating "Have you ever thought of soaking the farmers?" According to his biographer, St Laurent, even at this late stage of the Depression, still envisaged the "western agriculturalists driving Cadillacs" and spending "their winters in California." This extraordinarily ignorant remark, when reported in the press, occasioned an outburst of prairie rage and contempt.[103]

Thompson was convinced that, owing to President Murray's wise leadership and organization, the University of Saskatchewan emerged "in better condition that might have been expected under the circumstances."[104] Murray was particularly pleased to record that "members of staff were unanimous in preferring a general reduction of salaries to dismissal of a certain number," for the brunt of wholesale dismissals "would have fallen upon the junior members of staff."[105] Moreover, during Murray's presidency, no permanent faculty members were dismissed. Despite Murray's fine work, the fiscal crisis brought on by the Depression severely curtailed the development of the university building plans, especially a library and an arts building. The economic crisis also demoralized many faculty members. Dr Murray not only reduced the salaries by at least as much as twenty-four per cent for married faculty, but he also required unmarried men to take a year's leave of absence with only three months' pay. Some bachelor faculty members, such as Dr Les Saunders in Biology, were able to take this loss as an opportunity to travel and take other, often short-term, appointments.

Also affected were research funds, as Thompson noted in one of his annual reports.

> The research work of members of the department has been seriously affected by lack of funds particularly for assistance. The effect will probably not be to cause the discontinuance of the work of any member of the staff but seriously to change its

> nature. Large and important projects can scarcely be undertaken without prospects of the necessary assistance to yield returns. The tendency will therefore be to attack smaller problems, or phases of problems which can be carried out by one man or promise results within a reasonable time to the work of one man. Most of the best work of this department involves programs which must continue for long periods. Such work is specially affected by lack of assistance, and most of the problems in those fields not so affected are relatively minor.[106]

"No era promised fewer rewards for hard work than did the depression-ridden years."[107] Some of the university's best students had no alternative but to give up all thoughts of an academic career. Such was the case of the distinguished physicist and outstanding athlete, Orvald Gratias. As a Rhodes Scholar, Gratias had completed a doctorate at Oxford in nuclear physics, with Bertrand Russell as his external examiner. The effect of the Depression both on the university and the city meant that he had no chance for employment at either. Therefore, he had no alternative other than to enter the business world in Eastern Canada, where, according to his son, "he was never happy" for "he wanted to be in the lab."[108]

"Because their families were too poor to pay, one-third of the seventeen hundred students at the University of Saskatchewan had their tuition fees deferred in 1934–35."[109] The economic straits of so many citizens of Saskatchewan meant that the university charged the lowest fees in Canada.[110] In 1934, promissory notes were received from six hundred students unable to pay their fees, representing one-third of the total student body.[111] Faculty who were able to keep their positions also experienced severe fiscal constraints. In his retirement speech, T.C. Vanterpool recalled graphically just how the Depression forced the biology department to confront extreme economies: "I came across a memorandum on onionskin paper from Dr W.P. Thompson, then head of the department. It was dated 1934 and read: 'Our library appropriation for books is $32.00. This should allow Saunders and Vanterpool to get two books each, and Arnason, Rawson and myself one each. Next year Saunders and Vanterpool will get one each and the other three staff members two each.'"[112]

Despite such meagre financial support, the University of Saskatchewan, according to Harris, made more advances during the decade than the other Western universities, with the exception of Alberta, because of the "excellence of the leadership provided by ... W.G. Murray."[113] Harris makes this assessment on the basis of Thompson's claim in his history of the University of Saskatchewan that "the skilful adjustments and reactions which the university administration made...brought the institution through its adversities in better condition than might have been expected ... and even enabled it to make some modest advances." One of the far from modest was the collaboration of Dr Spinks with President Murray in bringing the world-famous molecular physicist, Gerhard Herzberg, to the University of Saskatchewan in 1935. Murray's bold decision came after both the University of Toronto and the National Research Council had rejected his requests that one or the other institution take the scientist to save him from the Nazis. Murray was also the imaginative creator in 1935 of the Emma Lake Art School, which continues to flourish and diversify to this day.

Thompson later painted an account of the university during the Depression that was extravagantly pessimistic, somewhat inaccurate, and at odds with his above verdict when he addressed the Association of Universities of the British Commonwealth in Saskatoon in the autumn of 1958: "We will celebrate our fiftieth anniversary next year. Considering that for 20 of those 50 years there was no progress whatever – the years of the two wars and the decade of economic depression in the thirties – we feel that we have not done badly."[114]

Because of his stature as a scientist, Thompson attended quite a few international scientific meetings in an era when financial considerations prevented many other scientists and scholars from travelling extensively. Moreover, most of Thompson's and other researchers' academic journeys often required lengthy and slow travel, whether by railway, bus, automobile, or ocean liner. The era of frequent air travel was really just dawning as Thompson was retiring. One of his most stimulating trips was to the Seventh International Genetics Congress held in Edinburgh from 23 to 31 August 1939. Thompson was able to attend because the board, advised by President Murray, authorized payment of Thompson's rail and boat fare from Saskatoon to London and Edinburgh return and gave him an advance of $350.[115] He thanked the president, noting that he was "now working hard trying to prepare a worthy contribution."[116]

Thompson later wrote and talked about the history of this gathering, brought together on what turned out to be the eve of World War II. Originally, the congress was scheduled to be convened in Moscow in 1937 after the leaders of the Soviet Union authorized the distinguished Russian geneticist Nikolai Ivanovich Vavilov to issue an invitation at the 1932 Congress at Cornell University in Ithaca, New York. This invitation coincided with the rise in Russia of Lysenko, the infamous advocate of Lamarckian ideas about the possibility of plants and animals inheriting acquired characteristics. Lysenko denied the theory of chromosomal inheritance and the existence of genes, thereby completely rejecting the ideas of Vavilov and other Russian geneticists. Among many other fallacious claims, Lysenko declared that by treating seeds with various temperature regimens, yields could be significantly enhanced. His views suited the Stalinist hierarchy, because of the problems confronting Russian agriculture. Lysenko became so powerful that Vavilov was forced to resign as president of the Lenin Academy of Agricultural Sciences and ultimately was sent to prison in 1940, where he died of starvation in 1943. In protest at the Stalinist cancellation of the proposed 1937 Moscow Congress and the Soviet persecution of Vavilov, the Congress was moved to Edinburgh in 1939, where it was attended by some 400 geneticists.

On the way to the congress, the delegates stopped briefly to visit University College London as well as Kew Gardens, the Courtauld Institute of Art, and Cambridge. Because this was his first trip to London, Thompson enjoyed the cultural sites immensely. He was especially pleased to wander among the Charing Cross second-hand "wonderful bookstores." Along the way, he purchased a complete set of Shakespeare in one volume for two shillings. The habit of book collecting, evident from his high school days in Hagersville, obviously remained one of his dominant interests. "St James Park ... with magnificent flowers is a wonderful place,"[117] he wrote his daughter, and found the Mall "a wonderful boulevard."[118] He noted to her that "they are taking the possibility of war very seriously" for there was a long "blackout" all over southeast England, including London. Airplanes flying all night made it impossible to sleep, while underground shelters and barrage balloons were present throughout the centre of the city. Thompson's observations concerning preparations for war were probably not relayed to his wife, for in Saskatoon she was consumed by anxiety for his safety.[119]

Thompson and the other geneticists were driven by bus from London to Edinburgh. On their way, the bus passed through Shrewsbury. This was a very roundabout route, and implies that the English organizing committee deliberately intended the geneticists to go through this small market town very near the Welsh border so they would pass through Darwin's birthplace. On the other hand, perhaps this route reflected the fear of imminent war, that the British government did not want the Great Northern Road from London to Edinburgh cluttered with non-military vehicles. In any case, as the bus trundled through Shrewsbury, Thompson casually remarked that this was where Charles Darwin had been born and spent his early years as a schoolboy. The others in the bus scoffed at Thompson, indeed "rubbed it in" for what they saw as an incorrect – and silly – comment. Thompson felt embarrassed. Then, as the bus was leaving the city, the wife of the American geneticist, Albert F. Blakeslee, spotted the imposing statue of Darwin. The bus stopped and all the passengers got out and examined the statue in the park. Immediately, as Thompson recalled to his family humorously, he felt his self-respect had been restored. But he did express surprise that famed geneticists would be so ignorant about Darwin's life.

Soon after the scientists arrived, the Congress began to disintegrate, although Thompson remembered all his life just how fine Julian Huxley's "performance had been in summarizing the important ideas presented at the Congress."[120] German and Dutch delegates left early because of the imminence of war. On the last projected day, 31 August, the Congress concluded. Many members had difficulties reaching their homelands. Indeed, three American geneticists who sailed on the passenger liner *Athenia* were drowned on 3 September, the day Britain declared war on Germany when a German submarine torpedoed the ship in the first sinking of the war. The U-boat captain had contravened the Hague Convention and the subsequent Prize regulations by attacking an unarmed passenger ship. Thompson has left no record of when he returned to Canada, although he had no alternative but to go back to Canada by ship. On 29 September 1939, *The Sheaf* printed a picture of Thompson, with a short note that he "had returned home safely … from the Conference in Edinburgh."[121]

Providentially for Thompson, and for Saskatchewan as a whole, the economy of the province began to improve in 1939, not least

3

The Administrator

The decade of the Depression also saw the start of Thompson's career in senior administration. In 1934, while remaining head of the biology department, Thompson accepted the appointment as dean of Junior Colleges, a position created to assist Arts and Science dean George Ling. Ling was not only overworked, he was also burdened by attending to his ailing diabetic son. Apparently Ling had told Murray "he wouldn't have anyone but Thompson messing around in his records." Thompson's appointment was considered "a temporary arrangement to help Dean Ling through a difficult period," and Thompson, who admired the mathematician greatly, "would have done anything to help Ling." Nonetheless, Thompson envisioned the administrative duties lasting a month or two. "But once in administrative work," he wrote later, "it seemed impossible to get out."[1]

Both Walter Murray and George Ling, both of whom he met in his first years at the University of Saskatchewan, had a profound impact on Thompson, both personally and professionally. Years later, in a public forum, Thompson stated unequivocally, "You could give me no task into which I could put my heart more than into paying tribute to Doctor Murray. He was like a father to me."[2] Murray had been appointed president in 1908 and remained in that position until he retired in 1937 at age seventy-one. Ling, a mathematician, was one of the original four appointments made in 1909 by Murray. He was dean of Arts and Science from 1912 to 1939, when he retired. He died shortly thereafter, in 1942. Speaking in December 1949, then-President Thompson was unstinting in his praise of these two men. "Any fitness, which I possess for this post, is due to those two great figures in the history of the university, Dean George Ling and President Walter Murray. They were the two closest friends I ever had and they gave me not only their direct help but – more important – the example of their character and actions. It must be a unique experience for a man to succeed to the positions, one after another, of his two closest friends."[3]

Ling held Thompson in equally high regard. Writing to Murray concerning a possible successor to the summer school directorship, Ling said that Thompson would probably not take the position because of his summer research, although "W.P.T. is good enough to deserve first chance at anything."[4] Unfortunately, in their later years Murray and Ling became estranged. When Murray retired as president on 31 August 1937, Ling was the logical choice to replace him. The board of governors, however, believed that Ling was too old and too preoccupied looking after his only son. Instead, the board conducted an extensive search for Murray's replacement, with a special committee considering a wide list of possible successors, before settling on James Sutherland Thomson. Thomson had grown up in Scotland, taken degrees at the University of Glasgow in philosophy and theology, served in World War I, and had taught at Pine Hill in Halifax since 1930. In this last capacity, he could be said to have followed Walter Murray, but he had no administrative experience and was "not known for his tact and empathy."[5]

Ling was convinced that Murray had conspired against his succession, which was not, in fact, the case, and for the rest of his life, he refused to speak to Murray, despite the best efforts of their mutual friends to bring them together. Thompson recalls how, "in the middle of one of my efforts, Ling interrupted me quietly: 'W.P., you can go to hell, and don't raise the subject again.'"[6]

Dean Ling is now almost forgotten in the history of the university. Thompson regretted that in his lifetime Ling never received even in his lifetime the credit and recognition which he well deserved. In Thompson's considered judgment, "no one in the history of the University ever had a greater influence for good."[7] Thompson remembered the constructive influence that Ling had on countless numbers of students, his insistence on maintaining high standards in teaching, in setting and grading examinations, in student conduct, and in sound university regulations. Ling was also "an ideal committee man, always willing to do the drudgery as well as the thinking" while avoiding "the slightest trace of domination."

Thompson was by no means a novice at administration when he took on the position of dean of Junior Colleges, since he had begun his career by establishing and developing the biology department. As soon as Thompson became involved in administration beyond the departmental level, however, he became more aware of the issues in the entire College of Arts and Science and in the university as a whole, issues he had not had to concern himself with previously. One such problem was the university's policy of admitting students with only Grade 11. Thompson was appalled at the high percentage of Saskatchewan undergraduate students who were failing, and failing badly. So he undertook a mathematical survey of grades over many years and discovered that practically no student with an average of less than 65 per cent in Grade 12 "ever succeeded in university." Thompson urged Murray to raise the university entrance requirements to an average of at least 60 per cent at the student's graduation from high school. Murray demurred at first, fearing that such a change would antagonize the Department of Education. After a good deal of reflection, however, the president concluded that Thompson was correct, because by failing so many students the university was "stigmatizing" students as "failures" and damaging their morale when they could well be successful in other pursuits. This change in policy had the almost immediate effect of dramatically decreasing the percentage of failures.[8] Saskatchewan was only the second university in Canada to adopt the rule that no students would be admitted without a Grade 12 standing of 60 per cent.[9] The importance of higher entry standards was confirmed as Thompson later extended his analysis to examine the correlation between IQ tests and university success. Every student took an IQ test, which was fashionable in all Canadian universities at the time. Thompson again was concerned about those students who, while scoring well on IQ tests, nonetheless, earned poor grades. As he discovered, "One can predict from the average student's Grade 12 marks his degree of success in first-year university almost but not quite as accurately as one can predict from his first year university mark his degree of success in later years. The Grade 12 marks have considerably better predictive value than have intelligence tests."[10]

Thompson also introduced tutorial classes in each subject at the beginning of the academic year as well as a week of orientation classes on study methods and on how students could best use the library. Thompson's purposefulness was also evident in his provisions to gain some uniformity in grading, his requirement that deans give initial talks to students entering their faculties, and that guidance officers and senior students hold discussions on social activities.[11]

In 1939, following Ling's retirement, Thompson was named dean of Arts and Science. A few days later, a revealing, if somewhat flattering, portrait of Thompson was published in *The Sheaf*, the student newspaper. Under the title "Swivel Chair and Pipe Still Favourites of New Dean of Arts," with the subheading "Left Research in Africa to Come Here," the article describes Thompson's confidence, interests, and workload:

> Tilting back in a newly acquired swivel chair and still backward to talk about himself, W.P. Thompson, new Dean of the College of Arts and Science, was little perturbed about his promotion when interviewed Tuesday. A person in ignorance of Dean Thompson's ability and his academic standing would little realize that this man, tilting in his chair, and nonchalantly drawing on his mellow pipe, has headed our Biology department ever since he came to this University in 1913, has been Dean of the Junior College since 1934, took a year's travelling fellowship in German South West Africa (now a British mandate), and Java, and contributes regularly to scientific journals, not to speak of the journal on which he serves on the editorial board. But most important of all, a layman sizing Dean Thompson up would never guess that this man with the dreamy eyes and the ready grin, is the foremost plant geneticist in North America.

The reporter also noted that despite being "haunted" by publishers to write books on genetics, Thompson dropped the idea after drafting "three or four chapters," finding writing less interesting than research, "and devoted more time to his work on the behaviour of the chromosome." The piece ended by noting

> The Dean will carry the load of his biology department, of the work of the Junior Dean, and of the Dean ... His last words were that he would like expectant graduates to file their application for graduation right away so that he can check their record and make sure that they have all the requisites for graduation. The Dean intends to patch up the college careers of any delinquents

so that the possibility of graduating will be improved. He fears that some have taken wrong classes or have failed to take their physical instruction.[12]

Indeed, Thompson's door was always open for students. After all the exam results were in, Thompson would examine every one, paying particular attention to the grades of students who had earlier demonstrated evidence of ability but had recently failed to do well. In those cases, he would ask the particular professor to speak with the student and Thompson would then often call the student in for a chat to discern what problems might be holding back successful exam results. All of these meetings involved significant amounts of time, effort, and patience. Just as Thompson's scientific research was characterized by minute and exhaustive attention to detail, from which emerged general interpretations, so also his work with students demonstrated both attention to detail and a capacity to implement policies based on academic principles. He was concerned that students fulfill their potential, especially since many came from farms and other economic areas badly damaged by the depression of the 1930s.

On a family level, Thompson's elevation had a significant impact on his wife, leading her to become more involved in university social affairs. *The Sheaf* records numerous references to Marjorie Thompson's roles as patron at such events as "Big Sister – Little Sister" teas, and the "Sadie Hawkins Flare to Pente Kai Deka Dance." Many of her social duties were reserved for the College of Arts and Science, but they also included university-wide events. She successfully carried out these obligations with ease and apparent pleasure.

Thompson's new position also involved him more in undergraduate activities. He spoke at numerous student departmental gatherings and alumni functions. He took an active interest in the Biology Club, formed in October 1939, and spoke to the members of the organization on 9 February 1940. He chose as his topic a theme relevant to students in biology who would soon be seeking employment: "Openings in Field Biology." He combined narrative with films, for he thought that the films would be especially helpful to students as they developed their future career plans. He emphasized "foods and nutrition," "heart and circulation," "fruits and spraying," as well as "trout and shark fishing."[13]

During 1940, Thompson devoted much time and energy to curriculum reform by initiating new courses of study. He argued that in spite of the Depression, "the College of Arts and Science made more progress in curriculum and maintaining a high standard of work during that decade than during any period of similar length before or after ... which may deserve the term revolution."[14] Thompson's reputation as an administrator must be based partly on his dominant role in this restructuring, because his refashioning gave coherence and a balance among disciplines. With faculty approval in 1940, he established four different types of curricula: Types A (languages and literature), B (social sciences), C (sciences), and D (theology).[15] He was also chairman of the Joint Committee of the Board of Governors, Senate, and the Council on Art, Drama, and Music that had recommended the establishment of the Type E Arts curriculum in fine arts in November 1946.[16] With some modifications, this structure has remained in place to the present day.

The general philosophy behind this work was to ensure that "the student shall learn something about each main field of human knowledge and a great deal about some one field," and was furthered when Thompson gained faculty approval in 1940 to establish introductory courses concentrating on a wider curriculum, rather than the disorganized and unfocused courses previously offered. For students in the arts who had no education "about the essential principles or generalizations of either the physical or biological sciences," Biological Sciences A and Physical Sciences A were created; similarly, students in the sciences would be obliged to take two courses, one in humanities and another in social sciences. One such survey course would concentrate on "principles and generalizations of economics and political science," whereas another would "concentrate on philosophy and history." In this way, Thompson attempted "to deal with a body of knowledge that was generally regarded as important for a liberal education." *The Sheaf* noted that because of the new Arts curriculum, the freshmen of 1941 would be the first to have the advantage of the wider courses.[17]

Moreover, Thompson insisted that these first year survey courses be taught by the best teachers. He thus chose the professors, who would initiate the courses and remain as the teachers. President J.S. Thomson enthusiastically supported the new curriculum, so fulsomely, in fact, that Dean Thompson asked him to present a course that would "introduce students to philosophical thought by giving a course on the history of ideas." Thus, for the remainder of his time at the university, Thomson "took part in its teaching."[18]

A leading historian of universities in Canada, Robin Harris, concluded that "the general education courses introduced at Saskatchewan in 1941–42 must also be regarded as unusually successful since, in conjunction with a course in English literature and composition, they remained for over twenty years the core of the arts and science program."[19]

Thompson had also hoped to start a course on comparative literature but it failed to come to fruition after Harry Steinhauer, a scholar in German literature, distinguished for his writing on the 1912 Nobel Prize recipient Gerhart Hauptmann, and the one faculty member Thompson believed to have both the "learning and courage" to teach such an interdisciplinary course, left the university. Thompson mentioned his dismay at the loss of Steinhauer at an address to the Alumni Association, lamenting that his loss was "very great," for Steinhauer was in the "very top of flight of literary scholars in this country ... in spite of great difficulties he has continued to publish his scholarly work regularly." In April 1943, he told his daughter about the impending loss to the university: "[Harry] Steinhauer is leaving to take the headship at Manitoba. I did my damndest to keep him, raising his salary $600.00 and offering him a separate department (of comparative literature). But he doesn't like the conditions of work and J.S. [Thomson] has used him rottenly. He is about the only real scholar we have on the literary side."[20] Some of W.P. Thompson's persistent irritation with J.S. Thomson arose not only because he believed that the president was incompetent and hierarchical, but also because he had treated Steinhauer badly.[21]

As the dean, Thompson also supported initiatives in creating new departments, including Slavic Studies in 1944, Drama in 1944, and Psychology in 1947. There were many reasons to establish a department of Slavic Studies: Saskatchewan had unusually large Ukrainian and Russian populations. The decisive role of the Soviet Union in World War II and Russian literature were also powerful intellectual stimulants. Finally, Dr George W. Simpson, head of the history department,[22] was a pioneer during the 1930s in introducing Ukrainian studies in his history courses. He initiated Slavic studies at the university and was the first Canadian historian to learn Ukrainian with the intent of reading original sources in Ukrainian history.[23] He also edited the first history of Ukraine published in Canada.

The Drama department was originally funded in 1943 by a grant from the Rockefeller Foundation and the first class was given at Regina College. Difficulties in Regina led to the enterprise being transferred to the Saskatoon campus, where, in 1945, under the direction of Emrys Jones, it became the first such department in Canada and the first in the British Commonwealth.[24]

Thompson was also the architect of the four-year honours program. He was emphatic in his insistence that the "time is simply too short to do honours work in 3 years, for any university does its best work and produces its greatest effects through its honours men. And we must give them the best we have."[25] As the beneficiary of a four-year undergraduate degree at Toronto, he was convinced that the three-year degree policy failed to provide sufficient intellectual depth, especially for the ablest students and those among them who aspired to go on to graduate school. Thompson received strong support on this issue from chemistry professor Thorbergur Thorvaldson. With his support, Thompson's plan carried the day, despite widespread faculty protests that the cost of an extra year would severely burden students financially, especially since this proposal came at the end of the Depression. Thompson managed to alleviate this cost somewhat by persuading the board to assign a number of bursaries to deserving fourth year students.[26]

Thompson's rapidly growing interest in university governance was stimulated by these years as dean. One of his first actions was to hire a capable secretary. Avis Kirkpatrick had recently completed an excellent undergraduate degree in which she had demonstrated exceptional organizing skills, mathematical knowledge, and a capacity to work with statistics in two classes she took from Thompson. She also had an engaging personality. Thompson hired her in July 1939 and soon gave her increasing responsibilities. This talented woman wrote an account of her time as Dr Thompson's secretary that illuminates important aspects not only of him as dean but about the culture of the university throughout World War II. Soon after her graduation in 1938, she was called in to see President J.S. Thomson, who scrutinized her academic record closely. Then, she noted with relief,

> Dr W.P. Thompson walked in. He was my professor in the two biology classes I had taken – he was ... the most articulate, the most organized, the best professor I had the whole time I was there ... [He] had just been named the new Dean of the College

> of Arts and Science – and had accepted the position of Dean provided he had someone capable enough to assist him with all the administration since he wanted to do some research ... Dr Thompson and I would work out my duties and that my pay was to be *$100 a month!!!* (A fortune)!!! ... Dean Thompson soon knew that I was as interested in organization as he was, and changes were made in the College that hadn't been dreamed of before. We set up a new system of keeping students' records, and they were meticulously kept up to date; new statistics were done each year for the College (also my responsibility) ... More and more Dr Thompson relied on my dealings with students and assisting them in selecting courses.[27]

In December 1940, Avis married a master's student in biology named Harry Williamson who left soon after for Britain as a soldier. Avis was fired when news of her marriage came to the attention of the senior administration, for "the President and the Board of Governors" told her "no married women were allowed on staff," now that she had "a husband to support and look after me. (Try that today!!)," Avis stated to her niece. Dean Thompson was furious at losing Avis and waged a campaign for nearly two years against the decision of the board of governors. Finally, in August of 1942, when Avis was in Eastern Canada, Thompson phoned her saying "We've done it! How fast can you get home?" Avis was "the first married woman ever to be hired to the staff of the university. A milestone, I guess ... for women's rights." She remained as Thompson's secretary until her husband returned from the war in November 1945 and they moved to Ottawa.[28]

Avis Williamson provides revealing information on how Thompson functioned as the dean. Her memories are particularly pertinent and important, since she is the last living person to regularly sit in on his decanal meetings and can describe his skills as an administrator, skills that from 1949 to 1959 were to distinguish him as president. One of her first tasks was to consolidate all student and other college records in the adjoining offices that she and Dr Thompson occupied, thereby allowing them to avoid running back and forth between the registrar's office and their own. Thompson took pains in "keeping his Faculty well informed,"[29] preparing agendas well in advance of meetings and circulating them in advance whenever possible. Avis, as recording secretary, was always present and Thompson always began meetings by first thanking her. He would then begin by setting out his own view of the issues to be considered, and then encourage others to speak without fear of ridicule or retribution. An open-minded leader, he never attempted or, apparently, desired to thrust his own views upon others. Avis emphasized just how gentle his nature was and what a gentleman he was at all times. Calm and stable by temperament, these characteristics, coupled with Thompson's maturity, were essential elements in his success as a policy-maker and opinion leader. On occasions when his gout caused him significant distress, particularly after tense periods such as registration, Avis would gather up all the necessary documents and go to the Thompson house where Marjorie Thompson would provide them with tea as they worked.

As dean, Thompson was responsible for the junior colleges. Although by 1929 there were seven junior colleges affiliated with the university, four became the largest and most firmly established – Campion College (Catholic), Luther College (Lutheran), and Regina College (originally Methodist, then United Church) in Regina; and St Peter's College (Catholic) in Muenster.[30] Regina College, with the largest enrolment and near the legislative buildings, was by far the most important, its establishment predating World War I.

The powers and functions of these junior colleges had been defined by the University of Saskatchewan Senate in 1924. Although the rationale given publicly was that they would "enable students to take university work inexpensively near their homes" while assisting "struggling church colleges," the real reason was to stop requests for the right to give full degree courses and grant degrees.[31] As many of the smaller junior colleges failed, Thompson's conclusion was that "the history of the Junior Colleges in Saskatchewan [gave] no support for the establishment of such institutions elsewhere in the province."[32]

In November 1942, Thompson was appointed acting president at a salary of $7,500 per annum when J.S. Thomson took a leave of absence to become director of the CBC. He did not, apparently, expect to return.[33] The news of Thompson's appointment and George W. Simpson's as acting dean was in *The Sheaf* on 23 October 1942. Thompson was the logical temporary replacement, although he later humorously recalled that "logic" did not appear to play a role in his selection. Thompson spoke of the dinner at the faculty club where the chairman of the board announced the appointment:

"The only good thing, which the chairman knew of or could think of to say about me, was that he and I lived in the same section of the city and had the same milkman and bread man and postman, and that they had informed him that I was really quite a nice fellow. It scarcely seemed sufficient reason for making a man acting-president."[34]

One of his first major public roles was to give the annual convocation address. In May 1943, Thompson used the occasion to discuss the impact of the war on the university. He noted, for example, that 700 students had enlisted out of the total enrolment of roughly 1,650 regular students and 800 graduates had left their jobs to join the armed forces, while "hundreds of others" had taken scientific and technical positions in war industries. In addition, eighteen faculty members were on active duty in ranks from lieutenant to major general. Other faculty members had taken wartime positions with the National Research Council and the Wartime Prices and Trade Board, and many were engaged, either on or off campus, in wartime scientific work. All physically fit male students not otherwise exempt were expected to train in the Canadian Officers' Training Corps (COTC) or the auxiliary battalion while carrying on their studies, and 400 female students were taking the Women's War Training Program. The need for specific training, together with changes in recruiting policies, meant that for the first time, engineering became the largest college. This was completely different from the situation during World War I, when every faculty member and student in engineering had enlisted, effectively briefly closing the college. This increase in enrolment in scientific courses resulted in only thirteen of the 170 men in first year arts and science taking non-science courses, while sixty percent of the women in their first year in the college were taking science courses. Thompson noted that monies from the provincial department of education, the Dominion Wartime Bureau and large private donations meant that for the "first time in the history of the province a large proportion of young people who wished to come to University and whose academic records showed them to be brilliant students, were able to come because of this financial assistance."[35] Thompson warned that the already overcrowded university would confront a significant challenge after the war when the veterans, both men and women, returned to pursue higher education, for their numbers would be "much larger than after the last war." In fact, the veterans' "bulge" of the immediate postwar period actually began in 1943 with the arrival of "air crew [from the RCAF] and those who had been wounded, sick or disabled." In the space of two years, 1944–45 to 1946–47, enrolment numbers nearly tripled, from 1,530 to 4,195.[36]

Most of the veterans did very well at the university. Thompson's statistical studies and some others, notably those of Professor Herman H. Ferns, adviser in studies to the veterans, demonstrated their academic successes. Thompson later reflected upon these facts: "the superiority of the veterans was a common topic of conversation among the faculty of the time and for many years afterwards."[37] Thompson was warmly remembered by many veterans for his consideration of their needs. In 1959, he received the following letter from a former soldier and undergraduate, Charles Waywell:

> Above all I want to thank you for your kindness that morning in the summer of 1945 when I walked into the College Building for the first time after being overseas for almost four years. When I got back to Canada the words of welcome from my wife had been "It had not mattered to me whether you came back or not." When I arrived at the station no one met me. Not long after that I went up to the University with no clear idea of what I was going to do, and little thought of picking up the loose ends from where I had left off more than five years ago when I joined the army ... when I walked in to the hallway of the College Building I was not expecting you to look up, recognize me immediately, and come over to me with a big smile and an outstretched hand and say "Hello Charlie! I'm so glad to see you back!" The feeling that someone cared what happened to me changed everything ... it was this incident – which you have probably forgotten – which pulled me up from the very depths of despair and cynicism, and helped me on my way. I shall always remember you and be grateful.[38]

Thompson believed that some of the roots of war had come about through the West's lack of attention to character, discipline, and morals, "due in part to the increasing influence of science," and was not due solely to the rise of Nazi Germany.[39] Though science must be objective, "when the methods and attitudes of scientists are carried over into fields where [humanistic] values are important and responsibilities are great the results may be disastrous." Thompson suggested that "humanist scholars, observing the great success of scientists, had tried to become coldly scientific, neutral, objective ... refraining from judgments involving moral choice." That did not imply, he claimed, that morals must be taught as a subject distinct from the curriculum. In fact, exhorting students to be good might have the reverse effect. Thompson argued that humanist teachers "face the most supreme intellectual challenge of our generation, for it is only by the unconscious effort of their character, [and their integrity,] that morals will be learned through individual influence and example."[40]

In November 1943, J.S. Thomson returned to the office of president from the CBC, where his weaknesses as an administrator were accentuated. Both the board and the provincial government were increasingly irritated by his determination to discuss university matters only with the premier, rather than the minister of education.[41] Additionally, as early as 1944 two influential members of the board of governors, Justice Donald MacLean and Arthur Moxon, had concluded that "Thomson's irresponsible [faculty] recommendations" had to be curbed. Apparently, Thomson had sought information about future appointments without consulting any advisory committee and often failed to take into account advice from knowledgeable persons when hiring professional faculty.[42] The result of this pervasive dissatisfaction led Maclean and Moxon to advocate the establishment of the Survey Committee in January 1945. Both men were old friends of Dr Murray, whom they knew to be also upset with Thomson's administration.[43]

Dissatisfaction with Thomson, however, was not the only reason, although it clearly was a dominant cause, for creating the survey committee. Other reasons were the challenges and opportunities that the university confronted as the war was drawing to a close, particularly the subsequent expansion of the student body as hundreds of veterans enrolled.

Another reason was the need to adapt to the demands – and dynamism – of the new CCF government. On 15 June 1944, the CCF, led by T.C. Douglas, won an overwhelming electoral victory, with forty-seven of fifty-three seats, leaving the Liberal Party with six seats and denying the Conservatives and the Social Credit any representation. Saskatchewan at that time bore the heaviest burden of debt in Canada. In addition, because of its dependence on an economic base of agricultural exports, the province was not an attractive manufacturing location and therefore had been "denied" by private investors "any important share in the postwar industrial boom."[44] Despite such daunting obstacles, the first CCF budget allocated 70 per cent of its expenditures to health, welfare, and education.

Premier Douglas and his cabinet had already revealed their aim: to draw upon the scientific resources of the university and the talents and skills of the institution's economists, as well as agricultural and other experts. The election platform of the CCF on the eve of the 1944 election had also demonstrated a major commitment to educational reform. The CCF placed significant emphasis on planning, promising equality of education for all, advocating adequate scientific research and assistance for farmers at all times, larger school units for greater efficiency, and, especially, health reforms. In January 1944, the CCF Education Committee had proposed, if elected, tentative expenditures to establish a medical college and university hospital at the University of Saskatchewan, projects that "had long enjoyed support within ... University circles."[45]

All of these imperatives pressured university leaders to revise the structure and procedures of the institution, and the CCF was determined to bend the University of Saskatchewan to many provincial needs. Soon after the election, Premier Douglas had shown his dissatisfaction with the oligarchic Board of Governors.[46] For their part, many in leadership positions within the university grasped both the new CCF imperatives and the opportunities this new provincial administration opened up for their institution. Members of the Board of Governors understood the CCF aim to proceed rapidly. At a special meeting on 16 September 1944, the board was informed that the government had issued an order-in-council for $25,000, to be used in planning the early stages of both the medical college and the hospital while the board began discussing possible sites for the structures. Dr W. Stewart Lindsay, head of the School of Medical Studies, was authorized to visit various medical colleges and hospitals.[47]

The CCF emphasis on education was significantly different from decades of relative Liberal indifference to education and often outright hostility to university professors. For example, the former Liberal premier in the 1930s, and by 1944 federal minister of Agriculture, James G. Gardiner, had in the 1930s sneered at some academics who advocated "planning" as "silver spoon-fed monstrosities" by "academic nonentities."[48] Similarly, at least one university administrator believed the Conservative government of J.T.M.

Anderson "had no idea of what a university was and what academic freedom meant."[49] In contrast, soon after the CCF electoral victory, Douglas recruited members of the university to advise the government. George Britnell, Vernon Fowke, and F.C. Cronkite began serving on the government's economic advisory committee.[50] As Spafford remarked: "In relative terms ... Douglas did have an ideal of the university ... set priorities, and pressured the university to clean up its finances (not new). It had a larger sense of its role ... but there were limits. Most important, perhaps, Douglas and co. respected the university, saw it as *the* post-secondary educational institution and were concerned to work for its betterment. This is all to their credit (there are easier and cheaper ways to get votes)."[51]

Finally, the CCF was predisposed to collective organization by employees and decreed that all employees under its jurisdiction should have unions. Soon after the 1944 victory, support staff at the university unionized, which probably made the board more sympathetic to faculty participation in determining salary scales, appointments, promotions, and other personnel issues. In any event, the board displayed cordial willingness to work with the faculty relations committee after 1946 and the subsequent Faculty Association. Such new circumstances led the Board of Governors to see the necessity of reviewing the original constitution of the university. As J.S. Thomson noted, many changes were long overdue, because by 1945 many aspects both of the organization and the administration of the University of Saskatchewan had become woefully antiquated by any sensible, fair, and efficient criteria. New clearly defined procedures had to be introduced to deal with the responsibilities of all administrative officers. The "cosy, comfortable" administration of Dr Murray no longer suited the larger community that the university had become.[52]

At its 29 January 1945 meeting, the Board of Governors grasped the nettle, and attempted to confront in a sweeping manner the activist needs of the CCF administration and the challenges and opportunities now facing the soon-to-be postwar Saskatchewan. Justice MacLean moved and Moxon seconded a groundbreaking motion:

> That as there has been no substantial change in the University Act since 1907 and as the University is now entering an important period of expansion and development, it seems desirable

> that the Board of Governors, the Senate and the Council should at this time appoint a committee of review to study and investigate the present constitution and organisation of the University, and in so doing, shall give particular attention to the administrative practices and to the power and duties of the Board of Governors, the Senate, the University council and the chief executive officers of the University. It shall make due enquiry among suitable and experienced persons in this and other Universities and report its recommendations on such matters and any other matters that may seem advisable, to the Chancellor. The committee shall have the power to fill any vacancies. This resolution not to be acted upon until it has been approved by the Senate and the Council.[53]

The adoption of most of the recommendations of the survey committee by the university Board of Governors and their incorporation by the provincial legislature early in 1946 marked the most sweeping amendments to the 1907 University Act ever made. The committee's mandate was wide enough to deal with many aspects of the university, but it focused especially on studying the constitution, organization, and administrative practices of the institution with a view to recommending appropriate changes. The Board of Governors asked W.P. Thompson to chair the committee, with the classicist Dr Francis Leddy as secretary.[54] Two other faculty members, dean of law F.C. Cronkite and Dr Neil Hutcheon, professor of mechanical engineering, and four board representatives were included: Walter Francis, Arthur Moxon, M.E. Hartnett, and G.W. Robertson. To his annoyance, President J.S. Thomson was not invited to be a member. Thompson later recalled the importance of this committee, singling out Dr Leddy for praise. "I was chairman and Dean Leddy secretary. Neither of us wanted the jobs because we knew that we would have to do some unpleasant things; but we were the only men who were willing to stick our necks out. That committee brought about many important changes."[55]

After meeting frequently – eleven times from the end of August to mid-December 1945, usually in all-day sessions – the report was ready and was presented to the board and the president on 14 December 1945.[56] The recommendations were passed by the legislature in March 1946 as the University Act 1946, revising the original 1907 legislation. Though the 1946 Act did not constitute a "root and branch" transformation of the original Act, it embodied major alterations that modernized the University of Saskatchewan, allowing it to function far more effectively in the postwar decades by bringing it in line with other major North American universities. If Thompson's research demonstrated his intellectual inquisitiveness and persistence, his ideas expressed on the survey committee revealed his ability to grasp what changes were needed and his capacity to effect the requisite new directions.

The committee ranged far and wide to gather information from other universities that might be pertinent. Leddy was charged with visiting the University of Alberta where President Robert Newton had carried out extensive changes in the constitution after the report of that university's own survey committee. Dean Cronkite visited the University of Manitoba to assess constitutional changes there. Leddy was also directed to acquire as many statutes as possible of other Canadian universities, to provide context for the committee's work. Documents from many American universities were also gathered for comparative analysis. The statutes of many Canadian universities revealed the "very considerable influence of the report of the Royal Commission which recommended the present Act of the University of Toronto in 1906." This Act "was carefully consulted and copied whenever new university acts were being drafted for all four Western Universities" and had been especially "true of the University of Saskatchewan."[57]

The committee first resolved to lessen the heavy burdens and powers of the president, whose workload had become filled with minor, but very time-consuming, items. President J.S. Thomson himself believed that he was seriously overburdened by routine work and invited the survey committee to devise some method of reducing his workload.[58] To distribute this workload more efficiently, the survey committee advocated increasing the hitherto undefined positions and powers of the deans and department heads. This led to numerous presidential powers being shifted to the deans. To alleviate the president's workload of student issues, the position of adviser on student relations was created, leaving the president to deal only with intractable problems or students who were dissatisfied with the adviser's assistance. To develop policies that could only be resolved with expert assistance, a Planning Committee was created to consider the university's activities in academic, business, and administrative issues, especially those with implications extending "far into the future."[59] The planning committee would advise the board and also obtain the opinions of the academic staff more effectively than before. Although the survey group rejected the proposal to create an executive assistant for the president, the office of business manager, first established in 1920, was given larger responsibilities. The bursar's office was also allocated more staff, space, and equipment, and given the responsibility of adopting a more up-to-date accounting system. The registrar's office was expanded by adding two additional staff with executive experience. The authority of the superintendent of buildings was enhanced. He was no longer required to consult the president or the business manager concerning every maintenance issue. A separate budget was provided to cover such matters and the superintendent was given the power to supervise and direct employees within his jurisdiction.

A major recommendation affecting presidential authority addressed Thompson's belief that the greatest weakness in the university's administrative practices was in the making of appointments and promotions, since he considered these practices to be the most important for the long-term interests of the University. No longer was the president able (or compelled) to decide on all faculty appointments, promotions, and salary scales, although the final prerogative of making recommendations to the board still lay with him. Instead, Thompson advocated the establishment of appointment committees, composed of at least four people, for each appointment to the rank of instructor or higher, the choice of the academic staff at McGill, Toronto, and several large American universities. The president would now be able to make academic hiring recommendations to the Board of Governors only after consulting with advisory committees, made up of the president, the dean, a member of the board, and the department heads. Soon after he became president, Thompson secured two additional changes to this procedure: every advisory committee had to include a faculty member chosen by the executive of the Faculty Association (formed in 1952) and "the responsibility of searching for suitable candidates and gathering information ... was transferred from president to dean" who, in turn, could delegate the duty to the department head.[60] These recommendations were crucial in transforming the university from a paternalistic administration into a modern institution with an emphasis on collegiality.

The survey committee also recommended establishing a Faculty Relations Committee consisting of six members to represent each college, and made up of members from each rank. Minister of Education Woodrow Lloyd suggested that this body could act as a "bargaining agency" for members of the staff in cases of difficulties with the Board of Governors over salaries, terms of employment, or general matters affecting the welfare of the staff. This committee would be obliged to meet at least once a year. Moreover, a salary scale with clear upper and lower limits for the entire staff was created. As Thompson wrote, "up until 1946, salary schedules, when they existed at all, were drawn up by the board and handed down to the faculty."[61] The survey committee remedied this unsystematic, and often unfair, approach. First, it accepted Thompson's recommendation that, the standard annual salary increase for the academic staff be $100, as long as positive reports were given for members by their head of department and dean of their college; Second, junior academic staff, namely instructors, when recognized as "first-rate in every respect" by their heads and deans, should be allotted $200 annually, until reaching "the maximum salary of assistant professors." Third, standard annual increases for non-academic staff should be $60, based on recommendations for good service.

The third major recommendation was controversial. Since CCF cabinet ministers, especially Douglas and Lloyd, intended to play a greater role in university affairs, the deputy ministers of finance and education were added to the permanent membership of the Board of Governors. The survey committee concluded not only that the university would benefit from a closer link with these two government departments, but that membership of the board should be increased from ten to fourteen to allow members to take a more active role in university business, especially by working on sub-committees. The provincial government insisted that the board be restructured to allow for an equal number of members to be selected by the cabinet and by the university senate. The final survey committee report concluded that the "present board is too small to permit the full use of ... [sub] committees, and it is accordingly proposed that the membership be increased."[62] Some university members, both at the time and later, criticized this provision for increased government participation in university affairs. Thompson was well aware of this critique, but believed that increased government involvement in university decision making was no cause for disquiet. Writing in 1969, he argued that he had seen no evidence of political interference arising from the addition of the two deputy ministers.[63] Many years later, Francis Leddy wrote, echoing Thompson's view and challenging the opinion

> that the appointment of the majority of the Board of Governors constitutes, in itself, a dangerous threat to university autonomy. It remains my firm conviction that there is no *necessary* or *fundamental* connection between the proportion of governors appointed by the Provincial Government, and the opportunity of political interference ... I was responsible for suggesting the compromise that ... the division should be evenly balanced. The proposal ... was inspired by the conviction that it was more sensible to have them on the Board, involved in its business, and responsible for its decisions ... In short, it was better to have them onside, rather than off-side, and this certainly proved to be the case in my experience with them.[64]

Advisory councils for the colleges of medicine and education, similar to those already existing for the college of agriculture, were also established. Finally, in light of the growing significance of graduate studies and research work at the university, the survey committee recommended that the graduate school be raised to the status of a college, with its own dean.

Thompson's satisfaction with the procedures and outcome of the survey committee reflect his orderly, disciplined mind; his capacity to articulate overarching themes; and his desire for a fair degree of shared governance in the university. These changes paved the way for the extraordinarily constructive relationship W.P. Thompson was to establish with both Douglas and Lloyd. Because of his education portfolio, Lloyd was the minister who dealt most directly with the university or, as Thompson noted, "the minister ... through whom all communications between University and Government pass."[65] The provincial treasurer, Clarence Fines, was also of critical importance in negotiating and allocating the University's annual budget. Both Lloyd and Fines remained in these cabinet positions throughout Thompson's years as dean and as president. Fines left politics in 1960 and Lloyd became premier when Douglas left provincial politics in 1961 to become the leader of the newly formed federal New Democratic Party.

When J.S. Thomson informed the board of governors in the autumn of 1948 that he intended to move to McGill, Thompson was the undisputed choice as successor. He had been a successful acting president in 1942–43 and a consummately effective dean. In 1947, the Board of Governors had made him their permanent choice to serve as acting president should the need arise. By 1949, he was a proven administrator and a known quantity.

But postwar society was changing rapidly and so were expectations of the role of universities. Thompson was well aware that the increasing prosperity of the province would allow more students to attend university. Despite the departure of most of the veterans by 1949, enrolments continued to grow. As Thompson related in his first presidential report to the senate and Board of Governors in August 1950, the number of both established and new professional colleges in Canada had increased. Among the professional colleges, in 1900 medicine and engineering had existed only at the University of Toronto and law had been developed in only two English-speaking universities. Over the next half-century, newer colleges in such areas as agriculture, education, pharmacy, nursing, journalism, social work, and household science were established in most universities. These newer colleges, as well as engineering colleges, accounted for most of the increase in student numbers. By 1950, critics of the so-called "ivory tower" culture of universities, who had often patronized them or sneered at the institutions as impractical, had shifted to blaming universities for becoming too practical, too much like training schools, in which cultural values were being neglected.[66]

Thompson emphasized the changing nature of the courses on offer, enabling the university to be of even greater service than had been the case when universities "were concerned almost entirely with recondite academic subjects. Their chief aim was to produce an elite group ... But Universities now provide a great variety of professional, semi-professional, and vocational courses," as industrial and commercial conditions became more complex. Thompson here expressed what had become a stronger and stronger argument, developed both by contemporary universities and parents of potential students: "Formerly only the sons of the wealthy and leisure group went to university. The courses were designed for them. Now our students represent a fair cross section of the population. For example right now 20 percent of our university students in Saskatchewan are sons and daughters of the labour group. And if I interpret official statistics correctly that is just about the proportion of labour to the total population in Saskatchewan."[67]

Thompson received many congratulations upon assuming the presidency. Few would have given him as much satisfaction as that from Gerhard Herzberg, a future Nobel Prize winner, then at the National Research Council, and a former University of Saskatchewan colleague. "Ever since the resignation of Dr Thomson was announced, all those interested in the University of Saskatchewan here in Ottawa have been worried about its future but I am sure that everybody feels, like myself, that it will now be in competent hands and that there is nothing to fear."[68] Woodrow Lloyd, the minister of education, had written warmly about Thompson's appointment, offering his personal congratulations and "assuring you and the University of all the support that I can provide."[69] Thompson replied, emphasizing how much Lloyd's letter meant to him, because it showed just how pleased the minister and the other members of the cabinet who "have the most to do with the University" were by the appointment.[70]

Thompson's first presidential actions were to surround himself with a good administrative team. He had made two conditions prior to accepting the position. First, if they were to move into the president's house, his wife would need some assistance. Second, he would need a good executive assistant: Colb McEown, to be precise. McEown had already "made himself quite indispensable and very popular with the staff." Two dominant board members, Arthur Moxon and W.B. Francis, had suggested the appointment, and as Thompson acknowledged, he had "always leaned heavily on those two very able and devoted friends of the university, but they never gave me better advice than on that occasion when they suggested appointing Colb McEown."[71] Throughout Thompson's tenure as president, he and McEown were able to work so well together that at the end of his term, Thompson noted if he "were to give a course now on training prospective university presidents, by far the most important thing which I would have to tell the trainee would be 'Get an assistant like Colb McEown.'"[72] Dr T.H. McLeod, dean of commerce at Saskatchewan from 1952 on, and earlier the CCF deputy treasurer in the late 1940s, commented on how effectively Thompson and McEown worked together: "Whoever managed to have both Dr W.P. Thompson and Colborne McEown in the president's office at the same time was a genius. WP was interested in policy and educational programs, while Colb was a born administrator. They ran the university as an institution should be run, and the university community respected them both."[73]

Thompson appointed a number of other colleagues to senior administrative posts and granted all of them significant autonomy. They included Jack Pringle, the comptroller, who succeeded Dugald Graham in 1956. These men, with their fine administrative capacity, attended to day-to-day university business affairs. Thompson claimed that all that he "knew about business is what I have picked up incidentally from them. It is true that they occasionally do me the honour of consulting me about something after they have decided what their decision should be."[74] However jocular Thompson's words were, he was adamant that "One of the most difficult problems of a president is to restrict his participation in business affairs so that he can be a real educational officer and carry on the duties of such an officer effectively. In practice this means that his only concern with business should be in helping to make the major decisions that directly influence educational activities."[75]

In a major speech delivered to a large alumni gathering, Thompson reflected, as he officially took up his new duties, on the difficulties presidents confront on the business side of a university's affairs, "for the modern university has become big business." He explained how many American universities had, for that reason, modelled themselves after business corporations. This had led, in Thompson's estimation, to a large number of [American] universities "deliberately subordinating the academic side and choosing presidents of the executive type who make no pretence to acquaintance with academic problems." Recent examples were Columbia University's choice of Dwight D. Eisenhower and the University of Pennsylvania's choice of Republican presidential hopeful Harold Stassen as president. This trend disturbed Thompson who argued that there "had to be a solution other than subordinating the academic to the business interests." After all, he claimed, "the business side of the university is solely to provide the necessary conditions for the real university which is the community of students and teachers."[76]

Thompson also ensured that he had the secretary he wanted, bringing Muriel Stein with him from Arts and Science.[77] Thompson felt settled as soon as he was in his new office, where he hung his own pictures and had "my old secretary who is a wonder."[78] He thought so highly of her abilities that when John Spinks was chosen as his successor, he wrote a personal note urging Spinks to retain Stein, since "she is an ideal person for the president's office – in ability, discreetness, handling of people etc."[79] Spinks must have had the same high opinion of Miss Stein, for she became his secretary during some of his presidential years 1965–74.[80] Years later, near the close of a letter to Dr Spinks, Dr Leddy remarked: "I was very sorry to see news of the death of Muriel Stein, someone whose service to the university I much admired."[81]

During his years as president, Thompson relied especially on three board members, Arthur Moxon, Walter Francis, and the chancellor, Hedley Auld. He also counted on several faculty members to chair particular committees, to speak powerfully and effectively in council, and, generally, to provide thoughtful advice. For example, in addition to his virtually daily meetings with Colb McEown, early in his presidency he relied on Francis Leddy and then, increasingly, on George Britnell, Vernon Fowke, and Kenneth Buckley from the Economics and Political Science Department, Balfour Currie from Physics, John Spinks from Chemistry, Dean Tommy McLeod from Commerce, Dean Wendell McLeod from Medicine, and occasionally Carlyle King from English. The president was not one to attempt to get his way by exhortations or dramatic statements. Quite the contrary. Thompson tended to communicate his wishes in subtle ways. Dean Riddell of Regina College read the president's signals in the following way. "When relaxed, his pipe drooped at a comfortable angle." But when he confronted "disagreement or, on rare occasions, mild criticism, his pipe cocked up to the highest point possible."[82]

Although it was not a condition of accepting the presidency, Thompson made another significant decision when he took up his new position. He stepped down as head of the biology department, a position that he had held since coming to the university in 1913. Thompson approached Professor Donald Rawson, a noted limnologist, to succeed as head, but with one proviso: Rawson must maintain the unity of the department. Rawson agreed, remarking that when he observed the "lack of cooperation between biology departments at Winnipeg, Edmonton and Vancouver," he fully realized the importance of a single department.[83] Thompson replied that although a committee would be struck to choose his successor, "it would be influenced largely by what I say." Thompson realized that "Les [Saunders] is the senior man, a grand fellow, and a good teacher. But I think it is essential to have one who is more active in research."[84]

When he was appointed president on 1 January 1949, Thompson was sixty years old. Over his thirty-six years at the university, he had demonstrated many clear, consistent, character attributes. He was calm by nature and not quick to anger. There is no evidence that he ever blamed others for mistakes that he made or that he held grudges. He was a decisive researcher and administrator who consulted carefully with the board and faculty members whose knowledge and judgment he respected most highly. He made clear decisions and did not agonize over his actions. He was good at assembling relevant facts, particularly numerical data, before arriving at his decisions. Though he was a thoughtful, reflective, and well-read man, he was not deeply philosophical by temperament and intellect. His values and instincts were democratic and he was hostile to unearned privilege. He never became a rich man and never seems to have desired to become wealthy; he and his wife never appear to have talked about money nor did he demand personal salary increases. His salary as president began at $9,000 a year. By contrast, when Wendell Macleod, a medical doctor, began in 1951 as dean of medicine, his salary was $12,000.

He was also a very private man. His autobiography, *An Academic's Progress*, is almost completely opaque on aspects of his family, friends, and private life. Both his parents had died by the time he was twenty, and although he briefly roomed with two of his brothers, Samuel and Jim, while attending the University of Toronto, he appears to have had little contact with his siblings and extended family later in his life. An advanced education, especially one marked by taking a PhD, tended to separate these fortunate few from many of the rest of their families because of the profoundly different circumstances. Such divergent lives may have been a reason why Thompson saw so little of his siblings in later life, as could the simple fact of the physical distances between them following Thompson's move west.

Since no letters have survived revealing any contact between Thompson and his siblings we simply do not know of any later relationships. He did name his only son James Scott, presumably after his brother and his brother-in-law. When Thompson does mention a few family members, it is in the form of occasional meetings or correspondence with cousins, in-laws, and nephews and nieces. When he was in Toronto, he saw his cousin Leta Teeter fairly often, and she was instrumental in assisting him in collecting family genealogical data. He also found time to visit his wife's brothers, Scott and Roy Gordon. When in Toronto, Thompson also met with his maternal cousin Jean Newman and her family.[85] Newman was the Toronto city controller for the Liberal Party. A close ally of Mitchell Sharp, an outstanding Liberal cabinet minister in the 1960s and 70s, she ran unsuccessfully against Nathan Phillips for mayor. Thompson may have had as much interest in her political career as any familial ties.

Above all, he cared about his daughter and son and their families. The depth of his affection is amply demonstrated in the scores of lengthy letters that he and Marjorie Thompson wrote to them, beginning in the early 1940s. Certainly he was very much at ease with his granddaughters, who recall that some of their happiest memories are those arising from their all-too-infrequent visits to Saskatoon. They remember Thompson reading to them, walking in the garden of the president's residence together examining various flowers and, above all, listening to them talk about what they were reading and what their educational plans were. His clear affection for them was reciprocated, for his grandchildren all speak of their enduring devotion for their Thompson grandparents.

After the Thompsons moved to the president's house in 1949, both the private and public aspects of their duties increased and, to a certain degree, merged. Large receptions at the president's house were managed by Marjorie Thompson with the aid of a couple of ladies from the University Women's Club. Frances Morrison, the chief librarian at the city's public library from 1961 to 1980, recalled Marjorie asking her if she "could please come and help me in the kitchen," a task Mrs Morrison was only too willing to undertake.[86]

After long Board of Governors meetings, members did not return to the president's house for refreshments before leaving for home in Saskatoon or elsewhere in the province. Instead they often went to the McEown house, for the Thompsons did not serve alcohol. Marjorie Thompson disapproved of drinking, and her husband had almost no interest in alcoholic beverages. Although her position required Marjorie to host numerous teas and other receptions, and the university community provided many congenial acquaintances, deeper friendships were reserved for a limited few: Dean Laycock of Education and Edith MacKenzie from the English department, and especially board members Moxon, Francis, and MacLean, and, in earlier years, Walter Murray and George Ling.

In 1934, Dr David Baltzan and two other Saskatoon doctors founded a weekly Saturday luncheon club that met regularly at the Bessborough Hotel for many years. Attending these gatherings was one of W.P. Thompson's main social activities. The gatherings allowed him to mingle with many men, both "town and gown," for whom he developed a high regard. Typically the tone was extremely congenial; by light conversation and jests they were able to "humanize" the laconic, inordinately serious Ling, for example. The lunches were an excellent venue for making significant contacts with the business and professional elites of the city, and membership also allowed Thompson to be an effective ambassador for the university. He well understood that the depth of local alienation former president Murray had confronted during the 1919 "rebellion" of four university members was partly caused by his lack of contact with civic leaders who had little awareness of university affairs. Other club members have described the meetings. University comptroller Jack Pringle recalled "about twelve prominent people from downtown" who "brought [Thompson] up to date with what was happening downtown and quizzed him about the University."[87] Businessman Herb Pinder noted that "Pat Waldron [publisher of the *Western Producer*] often led us off, speaking on current or sometimes esoteric subjects, and often W.P. Thompson brought up university or education matters but usually in low key and cautiously as I recall."[88]

As some men moved away or died, others were invited to join. Until he retired to British Columbia in 1951, Father Henry Carr was a member of the group. Carr had taught at St Michael's College at the University of Toronto and had founded the Pontifical Institute for Medieval Studies. He was then instrumental in establishing St Thomas More College at the University of Saskatchewan in 1936. Thompson praised him, calling the association of the Catholic college with the University of Saskatchewan "an unqualified success."

Thompson was most comfortable with this kind of small group. He confessed in 1963 in a talk to the biology department that, though he was obliged to speak frequently, "in spite of much subsequent [speaking] experience – too much – I have always disliked public speaking and feared it – which is a great fault in a president."[89]

Although these lunches gave Thompson intellectual stimulation and fellowship outside the university, he knew that he had to ration his energies during his work week, for each day he returned home at lunch for a nap. During these midday rest periods, Marjorie Thompson routinely told anyone who phoned for him that her husband was not at home.[90]

Thompson also found respite from his duties by his sustaining interest in botany. His letters to his daughter Mary Smith in Raleigh, North Carolina, almost always mention, during the appropriate seasons, various flowers, their stages of development, and their diversity. Thompson derived much pleasure from working outside in the flower garden, both at the house on 24th street beside Knox Church and later at the president's residence. In July 1951, he reflected humorously to his daughter:

> The garden is lovely now. I told Siggs (the old man whom the University has working around the place) that I would be at home for a month and wanted to do the things that would keep me out in the sun and give me some exercise, so he could work up at the U. He was quite shocked that I wanted to do them – beneath presidential dignity – and listed a lot of things that only he could do! However, we agreed on a number of things that I could do ... Have been picking a pint of strawberries every day for three weeks, and the raspberries are beginning to turn.[91]

Occasionally, the Thompsons would rent a cottage at Waskesiu, a beautiful area north of Prince Albert, for two weeks,[92] especially after participating in meetings in Eastern Canada or abroad. When visiting their son James in Edmonton, they would take time to visit Jasper and other Alberta parks. Nevertheless, Thompson most often spent his holiday times in Saskatoon, tending the garden.

Thompson was sympathetic to the progressive left, an outlook that may have been shaped in part through meeting James Shaver Woodsworth, socialist, labour activist, and one of Canada's leading advocates and practitioners of the Social Gospel, a widespread Protestant movement that tied Christian ethics to social reform. Thompson referred to Woodsworth as "the saintly founder and leader of the CCF party," noting that "we saw a good deal of Mr Woodsworth before there was any CCF party, because he was a great friend of Dr Murray and frequently visited the campus."[93]

After playing a dominant role in the Winnipeg General Strike of 1919, J.S. Woodsworth was invited to speak at the University of Saskatchewan on 22 March 1920. His talk was announced as "J.S. Woodsworth's Address tells the 'Inside' of Strike,"[94] part of radical labour's call for "One Big Union." A police detective investigated Woodsworth's speech and audience by speaking with Professors Swanson and Elliot of the Economics department and Professor Morton of the History department, who had arranged the talk. The newspaper reported the RCMP's interest in investigating the incident, although the RCMP took no further action.[95]

Thompson similarly admired the ideas and social activism of the poet, legal scholar, and civil libertarian, Frank Scott, of McGill. Scott had assisted Frank Underhill in drafting the 1933 "Regina Manifesto," outlining the political ideas and political aspirations of the CCF Party, of which he was national chairman from 1942 to 1950. From 1944 to 1950, Scott also acted as legal advisor to the provincial CCF government, and frequently travelled to Saskatchewan.[96] Late in his time as president, Thompson wrote Scott asking him if he had any interest in assuming a position in the Faculty of Law at Saskatchewan. Thompson said that he had written this letter of invitation "entirely off my own bat" and had not even "consulted Dean Cronkite."[97] There is no evidence to show whether Scott considered accepting the offer.

Despite his progressive sympathies, Thompson was careful never to jeopardize his position as president by aligning himself with any particular political party. He proclaimed his political neutrality publicly at a dinner hosted by the CCF government early in 1959.

> I have always been careful to have no public politics and to say or do nothing that a member of one party could interpret as favouring another party or prominent member of it. That is the proper attitude not only for a president but also for every member of the staff of a state university. In other words in the best interests of the university no member of a faculty should be active in politics, because at any given time a large proportion of the population will be adherents of a party other than that in which he is active. And since party feeling may be strong, he is likely to arouse antagonisms and therefore to injure the university.[98]

In his private correspondence and in letters to his daughter and her family, however, Thompson made no secret of his CCF sympathies. In a letter to the well-known journalist and University of Saskatchewan alumnus James Burns McGeachy, Thompson thanked him for his kindness in writing warmly about his retirement, saying he remembered McGeachy well. Thompson then mildly chided McGeachy, "Dare I say to an easterner and a member of the staff of the *Financial Post* that much of the great progress of the university in recent years is due to the fact that we have a socialist government in Saskatchewan?"[99]

As for his formal obligations, Thompson was pleased, for example, to have cordial relations with the Catholic Church in the province. Writing to his daughter in 1951, he observed that he had to sit on the platform in the Capital Theatre at a farewell for Catholic Bishop Pocock, who had been made Archbishop of Winnipeg. "For a worldly sinner I stand in remarkably well with the Catholics, which is a good thing for the university."[100] Despite his high regard for a number of Catholic clergymen, Thompson thought many Catholic ideas "beyond the pale." As he remarked to his daughter when he was in Quebec City for the Royal Society meetings in June 1952, the priest at Ste Anne de Beaupré Church expressed "stories and beliefs ... equal [to] anything from darkest Africa."[101]

Thompson, it must be emphasized, had no religious convictions about any form of Christianity or any other religion. He demonstrated his unbelief unreservedly in a letter to the creative flower breeder and philosophically minded thinker, Percy Wright of Sutherland (a small town on the outskirts of Saskatoon). Wright had written to Thompson, who knew him pleasantly as a fine former student, asking for a critique of his essay exploring thoughts on "spirituality":

> I am not competent to judge this [essay], much less criticize it. Before I gave up thinking about such things, I had reached a simple – perhaps naïve – concept, and have seen no reason to change it. It is that mind is simply the functioning of brain. It evolved along with brain and nervous tissue from the general sensitivity of living matter, and you can introduce it at any stage you like, even with the first life. There is no break. To me "spirit" presents no problems. There isn't any, apart from mind. Ideas are reactions – part of the functioning and therefore "physical." They involve energy exchange. How (or if) relativity comes in – no comment.[102]

Religion offered Thompson no consolation in the pains and illnesses of life he endured, both the everyday setbacks and those that were more difficult. By 1949, Thompson had already suffered persistent if periodic bouts of painful gout that would "lay him up" for up to a week at a time, and of sufficient concern that it almost forced him to turn down the presidency.[103]

In August 1952, Thompson remarked to his daughter that he had recovered sufficiently from another bout of gout to reach the chesterfield. "And mother is pretty well tuckered out with running up and down stairs to look after me. This has been the worst yet – all around my ankle and even up my leg, over the whole instep, in the joints on both sides, and even down into two of my toes. Couldn't touch my foot to the ground from Sunday to yesterday [Thursday]. It's a good deal better today and I was able with the help of a cane to get here in the living room."[104]

His condition proved so difficult, he drafted a letter of resignation. "my attacks of gout became so severe and so frequent that they were seriously interfering with my work. But before I submitted [my resignation], Dr Baltzan informed me that he had learned of a new treatment for gout that was very promising. Since he had started to use that treatment [c. 1952] I haven't had a single attack. Again I was fortunate not only in having a good doctor but in that the cure came along at just the right time."[105] Thompson was still a voracious reader. He wrote about reading John Dewey's *Journey to the Far Pacific*, which he "found ... very interesting," since, during his doctoral Harvard research, he "had been to some of the places, particularly Java, Hong Kong and Japan." Thompson found the book "much more penetrating than the usual travel book" and his opinion of Dewey "had gone up." It is worth remembering that Dewey and Thompson had spent some time together during Thompson's sabbatical at Berkeley in 1929. As president, however, he remarked that his "reading underwent a great change. Previously it had been three-quarters scientific; now it is largely educational. And the difference between the two is very striking."[106]

Thompson would normally have been expected to retire at sixty-five. Premier Douglas mentioned to a potential presidential applicant that he might think about applying in 1954, by which time Thompson might have been considering retirement. Therefore, upon Thompson's appointment, the Board of Governors recognized that his "tenure of office will in all probability be a very short one, since he is approaching superannuation age."[107] This possible limitation on Thompson's term as president was changed a few months later. He informed his daughter: "We have made no plans about retirement.

There's no knowing what we may want to do then. The Board of Governors at their last meeting passed a motion exempting the president from the rule requiring retirement at 65. They did it deliberately now so as to have the way clear when the time comes. They made it quite clear that that they wanted me to stay indefinitely. Of course I made no promise and may be glad to quit before that!"[108]

4

The Humanities, the Social Sciences, and the Ascendancy of the Natural Sciences

Thompson hoped to be understood, by at least some of his staff, as honest and fair, for he was well aware of the numerous conflicting interests that he would need to judge and of the subsequent antagonisms that would inevitably accumulate against him. He saw his greatest academic responsibility as "helping to determine who his colleagues will be and their precise positions and duties."

He was particularly concerned about establishing a fair salary schedule where none had existed before. As he noted, up to 1946, salary schedules, in so far as they existed at all, were "drawn up by the Board and handed down to the faculty." From 1946 to 1949, the faculty relations committee met with the board occasionally to discuss salary issues. Yet, as Thompson commented caustically, salary records "left something to be desired." In 1949, with board approval, Thompson built upon the work of the survey committee which had established annual increases and an early form of merit pay, and negotiated a new salary system: both structure (that is, ranks), and rates of pay. Postwar inflation and the effect of the American economy on Canada were having their effect; faculty salaries were to increase significantly during the 1950s. On 20 May 1951, Thompson reflected upon their deliberations in a letter to his daughter. "We are in the midst of trying to decide about a salary raise for the staff. Have had consultations with the cabinet to get more money. The Board of Governors is meeting on Tuesday to make the final decision. It will be about $500 each. Have already given them $100 this year. Your inflation has caught up with us because economically we are only a small tail on a big dog."[1]

The structure was finally settled to Thompson's satisfaction, and that of the recently formed faculty ssociation. In 1953, the president established two levels of full professors, "professors B," with a salary ceiling $500 higher than that of "professors A." "The former rank was reserved for faculty members of special distinction or who had particularly important duties," a rank to which "only a few were admitted."[2] It was also a method to attract outstanding academics from other institutions. In 1954, the $500 ceiling was removed; by 1959–60 the maximum salary for a professor B stood at $11,700, an increase of about $1,500 higher than the previous year. Earlier, in 1946, the rank of associate professor had also been instituted, placing the university in line with accepted practice elsewhere.[3]

During his tenure, Thompson continued to have serious concerns about salaries, not least because he "deplored," like many university presidents, the "effect upon staff morale of any ... salary differential."[4] His concern here arose particularly from a study by the Saskatchewan professor of economics, Vernon Fowke, who presented it to a special universities conference in 1956. The study demonstrated statistically that some university faculty in medicine, science, and engineering were being paid two to three times as much as professors in the humanities at the equivalent rank.[5] This issue of salary disparities was particularly disputatious in the medical faculty. Two senior specialists wrote to Thompson in May 1955 complaining that they were not being paid what they initially had been offered and that "there was no uniformity in the salaries." This complaint led to intensive discussions with the Board of Governors. Thompson remarked that he was tempted to point out "that neither the Dean of Medicine nor the President of the University is now receiving as much as the head of any clinical department. It is probable that we don't deserve any more than we are getting! But it is also probable that most people would think the comparison should be in our favour."[6]

Thompson faced the same salary inequity quandary with the law faculty. In the autumn of 1955, Dean Cronkite sent a memo to the president arguing for substantially higher salaries for members of his faculty. His argument was straightforward, namely that to hire and keep law faculty they had to be paid at roughly the same rate as private lawyers. Full professors needed a ceiling of $12,000 whereas assistant professors should have a base of $7,500. Moreover, he believed that, as dean, he ought to receive an administrative stipend, as he was certain that this was the practice in every other Canadian university.[7] These salary dilemmas graphically reflected the problem: that faculty with relatively lucrative possibilities in the private sector, especially medical doctors and lawyers, had far greater financial bargaining power than most other academics.

In 1957, Thompson wrote a speech that addressed these problems and prepared to present it to the Hamilton Alumni Association. For reasons unknown, he decided not to use it. The concerns expressed in his draft reflected some of the most serious staffing and salary issues confronted by universities in Canada.

> All universities are going to have great difficulty in securing and retaining suitable staff to handle the great increase in the number of students. They are already competing vigorously with each other and with business, industry and the professions for an adequate supply. A serious feature of the situation is that we are recruiting few students for university teaching. Few are taking the honours and graduate courses necessary for university posts. Well-paid jobs for graduates with the first degree are too abundant. And university salaries were too low too long. Although there has recently been a marked improvement, it is doubtful whether it will have much effect, or if it does, whether the effect will be evident in time to meet the situation.

Yet Thompson took some consolation from staff retention rates at Saskatchewan. "Last year only seven members resigned, although I know of at least 30 who received offers of jobs elsewhere mostly at considerable advances in pay. The other 23 rejected the offers. That speaks well for our conditions of work and the morale of our staff."[8]

On the eve of his retirement, Thompson, publicly, seemed reassured about salaries, at least as far as the University of Saskatchewan compared nationally. In the spring of 1959, just before convocation, Thompson rebutted an article in *The Sheaf* that charged the university with failing to pay decent salaries. Thompson stated: "The facts are that at the present moment the minimum salary of a full professor at the University of Saskatchewan is $9,700, and at McGill $8,000; of an associate professor at Saskatchewan $7,700, and at McGill $6,500. Professors may be the unworldly people they are supposed to be, though I have seen little evidence of it. But they are not so unworldly that they will line up for a job paying $1,200 less than they are receiving."[9]

Indeed, by 1959 Thompson could state that salaries at the University of Saskatchewan compared favourably with the top "five or six."[10] His claim was corroborated independently in a 1959 report that found that, "Substantial salary increases during the past few years have placed the university's faculty among the best-paid in Canada," noting that the university's 1960–61 salary schedule would match the University of Toronto scale.[11]

Closely aligned with this work on salaries was Thompson's continuing interest in appointments. Thompson was insistent that the university choose the best faculty possible for every position, because the development of tenured appointments made it difficult to discharge unsatisfactory members. Perhaps even then reflecting on the residual effects of the university's "1919 crisis," he emphasized in his 1955 presidential address to the National Conference of Canadian Universities (NCCU), that the "extreme action of dismissals is almost always inexpedient even when it is possible, because it is likely to injure the institution more than the continued employment of the man."[12] Thompson had been more emphatic about the difficulty of faculty dismissals in a speech to the Phytopathic Society two years earlier, exclaiming that "no university professor is ever fired for anything short of murder."[13] Hyperbole aside, Thompson was "strongly of the opinion that the appointment of faculty members is the most important, interesting, satisfying, and rewarding of the numerous tasks which a university president has to do. The appointment of even one very outstanding man may have a far-reaching effect for good on the long future of his institution. And the appointment of even one 'dud' may have unexpected harmful effects."[14]

However, the element most inextricably linked by Thompson with the issues of hiring and compensation was his continuing emphasis on research, in some respects a measurable output of faculty engagement although by no means the only device for identifying the outstanding faculty member "of special distinction." Thompson's view of the primacy of research was evident early on when, in their correspondence leading to his appointment, Thompson asked about facilities for his research while Walter Murray countered by asking pointedly whether Thompson had any teaching ability. A proven record of research had been his reason for wanting Rawson, rather than Saunders, as head of biology; and why the university could rightly boast "work of fundamental importance"[15] was being done by faculty such as Thorvaldson in chemistry. Thorvaldson's major scientific achievement was to determine that sulphates in ground water were destroying concrete structures.[16] In his annual report for 1952, Thompson could not only take note of Thorvaldson's "remarkable capacity as a scientist," but he could also praise the specific effect of Thorvaldson's contributions: "Many of the problems solved by his wide knowledge and experimental ability have been directly related to economic improvement ... in amounts considerably greater than have been spent on the construction and maintenance of the University during its entire history. He has built up a Department of Chemistry that has carried the fame of the University wherever his students have gone."[17]

However, as dean of Arts and Science during the war years and later as president, Thompson was particularly critical of what he and many others saw as the weaknesses of the Arts section of the college. He was convinced that too many humanists, in particular, did little scholarship of merit. The issue was not with any specific area of research, but with output: Thompson simply believed that there were too few faculty members in Arts who were interested in scholarly inquiry, much less with reputations as established authors. Moreover, the apparent contrast with the output from the science faculty was striking. In his 1949–50 presidential report, Thompson praised the sciences at Saskatchewan for such a high scholarly reputation. He claimed that the departments of physics, chemistry, and biology compared "favourably with those of any institution in Canada," as "measured by the ... number and quality of published works, membership in scientific societies and election to office in such societies, and grants-in-aid for research from bodies like the National Research Council and Defence Research Board."

To some extent, there were external issues at play within this perceived imbalance. The war years, in particular, had helped establish a climate less conducive to the humanities in general. At convocation in 1946, President J.S. Thomson, speaking "with brutal candour," noted that up to that point "most of the University's money had gone into provision for those who work in the pure and applied sciences." Carlyle King later lamented this, noting that while "a choice probably had to be made," it was "understandable, if regrettable, that the educational and political leaders ... should value good poultry more highly than philosophy and should prefer bridges to books."[18] Since

Thompson also believed that faculty members in the arts, unlike scientists and engineers, were unable to contribute substantially to the war effort, he was generally unsympathetic to their needs throughout World War II. In 1942, a number of influential university presidents and government leaders, including Prime Minister King, proposed suspending all courses in arts, education, commerce, and law as long as the conflict lasted, as students in these subjects were not considered essential to the domestic war effort. This issue bedevilled North American universities, with the Americans drafting all students, regardless of their course of study. Canadian universities, directed by government, insisted that students completing courses vital to the war effort, notably those in engineering, medicine, and science, remain in school. Thompson supported the initiative by Principal James of McGill and Principal Wallace of Queen's that students in programs not deemed directly related to the national interest were required to be available for the military. On 23 November 1942, Thompson wrote to the NCCU secretary stating: "We can no longer defend encouraging students who are of military age and physically fit to attend universities to take courses in the Humanities and Social subjects. If the National Selective Service decides that such men should be called up, I think the Universities would make a big mistake to protest and attempt to prevent it."[19] The James-Wallace proposal did not secure passage because members of the Social Science Research Council (SSRC) successfully fought it, in the process helping to create the Humanities Research Council.

Nevertheless, students were radically altering enrolment in some programs. Thompson noted in 1943 in a speech to alumni in Winnipeg how war work was intensifying the drive toward the sciences: " There has been an enormous increase in the number of students taking scientific and technical courses. For example there are 340 students in First Year Engineering. There has been a corresponding decrease in other courses. For example there are only 13 men in non-scientific classes in First Year Arts and Science ... Education has very few, and all women. Law is a way down. Pharmacy has nearly vanished."[20]

The sciences continued their ascendancy postwar. The development of the Cold War, from 1947 on, and especially the Soviet launching of satellites Sputnik I and II in 1957 dictated many of the scientific directions. Sputnik electrified America and the rest of the world, leading to hand-wringing in the West, for the Russian success "seemed to signal defects in scientific and technological education in the West that cried out to be fixed."[21] For example, the Soviet accomplishment prompted President Eisenhower to sponsor the Defense Education Act, which channelled students, and vast sums, toward science. The prestigious scholar of English literature and president of the University of Toronto, Claude Bissell, published an article in *Maclean's* in April 1958 that demonstrated Canadian alarm: "Universities Must Answer Sputnik with Higher Standards."[22] In a speech in 1956, Thompson told members of a co-operative school that within the past half century an enormous change in curricula had taken place in universities. For example, even though the population had grown, the proportion of scientists had "increased 8 times as fast as the population." The proportion of engineers to total population had multiplied six times during those fifty years, whereas the proportion of elementary and secondary school teachers had grown by only "one-half." Nearly every week the newspapers included calls for more engineers, more scientists, and more doctors and nurses, he told them. "And frequently the demand is accompanied by a frightening comparison with Russia's output."[23]

Thompson was convinced that universities must nurture science, both by facilitating faculty research and in the teaching of students. Without provision for the intense development of the sciences, he contended that any contemporary university would be isolated from the modern world and never become first-rate. Allan Blakeney, a CCF cabinet minister throughout almost all of Thompson's presidency, was certain that Thompson was correct in emphasizing "the scientist's approach" to the university and to the province. By 1949, when Thompson became president, Blakeney suggested that the university "needed an emphasis on the world of science and what that world had to offer to the people of Saskatchewan." The university had become "a multiversity as all great universities are" for "we as a society have decided that we want to use universities as scientific, societal service centre[s];" and a "liberal arts college ought to be able to survive in the bosom of a multiversity." While Blakeney believed that there was some truth in the complaints of humanities and social science faculties about the "over-emphasis" on scientists' research, no university "can dispose of funds between scientific and humanities and social sciences totally at its discretion."[24]

Thompson identified a series of other potentially contributing factors for what he saw as an unsatisfactory situation in the humanities and the social sciences: library deficiencies, limited employment opportunities compared with the scientists, greater government interest in the sciences, and poor office conditions for work. The main library at the university was situated in the College Building, which was also the location of many administrative offices, including that of the president. Thompson lamented the lack of a "visible location or home on the campus" for Arts and Science students at an Arts Dinner in 1948. He further deplored the "lack of proper offices such that professors are placed 2, 3, or 4 to a room in what has been intended as bedrooms," while for "class rooms we must use rooms intended for other colleges but which they do not need." Thompson was not blaming the administration, for, he argued, "no one could have fought harder for the Arts Building than the President [Dr J.S. Thomson]. But no one can fight successfully against a climate – an intellectual climate. The simple fact is that the things for which Arts stands for are not highly enough regarded in this time and place."[25]

The first plan to build an arts building had been cancelled when the engineering college burned in 1925 and funds went to replace it. In 1929, the legislature had passed an appropriation of $100,000 to cover the cost of plans and preparations for a combined arts building and library.[26] But by 1930, when the architects had completed the plans and tenders had been received and approved, the Depression had begun and the government learned that the cost was to be $885,832.00 for the same two buildings, which also included biology, household science, accounting, a small women's gym and a museum.[27] With farmers on relief and the depression deepening throughout the province, the government refused to approve the project. Thompson reflected ruefully that this action "had a profound effect on the nature and development of the institution. It severely handicapped the humanities and social sciences and directed development toward the sciences and professional training."[28] Even the 1929 plans, however, had their drawbacks: as Thompson noted, "at that time no one had the presumption to think that arts professors rated individual offices."[29] It wasn't until 1957 that Thompson was able to report to the board concrete progress toward the construction of an Arts building.

All other factors aside, however, Thompson placed the blame for the imbalance directly on the research limitations of the humanities professors. The cause, he said, was "basically a matter of personnel." All too many non-scientific faculty members, he believed, were not as capable of research as many of the University's scientists.[30] Despite some individuals who were doing "outstanding original work ... the general level of scholarly attainment of those [humanities] departments is not equal to that of our scientists." The situation was by no means unique to the University of Saskatchewan. Of Canadian universities as a whole, it could be said that "[faculty] of the forties had qualifications that were relatively low and extremely various. Outside of the sciences, few professors had doctorates, and many had the sort of British MA that is earned not by formal work but by the effluxion of time ... Perhaps they were serious about teaching because they could not hope for recognition as researchers."[31] Thompson, too, frequently emphasized "that in recent years there has been an enormous criticism of Colleges of Arts and Science everywhere. Faults and shortcomings are constantly being pointed out ... A new book on this subject comes out every few months."[32] It was an issue he felt compelled to address. Thompson's concern over the arts pervaded every one of his annual decanal reports during the 1940s. For example, in his report of 1943–44, he wrote ruefully that "the Arts...are at their lowest ebb in many years." In 1948, he again stated that "we must still deplore the eclipse of the humanities." His views were most clearly documented in his decanal report for 1946–47 in an addendum marked "Not to be published." In it, Thompson praised the scientific staff for the number of papers they had published in the past year. In addition, he remarked on the number of scientists who had been elected to national and international scientific societies and noted those who had been elected to an office in those societies. In particular, he was proud of the fact that by 1947 seven members of the scientific staff were Fellows of the Royal Society of Canada, including three who had been elected president of their section and one president of the entire Society. By contrast, only one staff member from the non-scientific societies had been elected as a Fellow – then-president J.S. Thomson.[33]

President Thomson agreed with these criticisms, and thanked Thompson for requesting that the research achievements of scientists in the arts and science faculty not be published in the annual report of the president for fear of demoralizing the non-scientific faculty. For some time, J.S. Thomson had been "concerned about the ill-balanced record of productive work within the faculty comparing the scientific and other departments." He did not believe that "mere lack of library facilities [was] the real reason" for, in his view, the university had never "denied library facilities to anyone who really wished them." Perhaps, Thomson reflected, he should be "more active in giving some leadership to see whether we could not produce at least a symposium of real creative work from the Faculty of Arts."[34]

Thompson had a more immediate and practical solution: early in his presidency he instituted a policy of summer research grants to assist humanists and social scientists in accessing often difficult to reach research sources. One of the reasons why some humanists tended to be discouraged from research, Thompson believed, was the gross financial imbalance between science and humanities, for almost all the money went for research in the natural and applied sciences and scarcely any for research in the humanities and social sciences. He noted that 97.7 per cent of the listed total research expenditure was allocated to science-based research whereas the Humanities Research Council and the Social Science Research Council had "pitifully small amounts to spend and what little they have comes mostly from American foundations."[35]

The Social Science Research Council (SSRC) had been established in the autumn of 1940. For the next seventeen years, until the creation of the Canada Council, the Rockefeller Foundation gave $499,795 to the council, while the Carnegie Foundation provided $61,130 over the decade 1940–50. On the eve of grants from the Canada Council in 1957, the SSRC received $150,000 from the Ford Foundation to tide the social sciences over until the new Canadian grants took effect. The SSRC was also the recipient of some small sums from universities, private organizations, and private individuals. Over the seventeen-year period, about two thirds of the SSRC's monies were spent on funding scholars to help them complete research projects or publish the results. A similar organization was established for the humanities at the end of 1943 and its first plenary session was held in May 1944, again with the main purposes of providing aid to potential scholars while assisting them in publishing their work.[36] By contrast, in 1960 the total amount of federal funds provided for scientific research was over $15 million, with, for example, the Defence Research Board providing $1.7 million and National Health and Welfare allocating $3 million.[37]

However, the postwar Liberal government of Louis St Laurent was preparing to help Canadian universities, influenced by the continuing pressure arising from the wartime advocates of a culture of reconstruction. Votaries of that kind of reconstruction emphasized developing an elitist culture that would instill in Canadians "a capacity for intelligent and cultured living," for example, by following Britain's policies of generous support of music and the arts while promoting education, both at the community and university levels.[38] Only after the establishment of the Royal Commission on National Development in the Arts, Letters and Sciences (the Massey Commission), did Canada create the main, and most visible, agency, the Canada Council, to define and deepen the country's national cultural identity. Hilda Neatby, one of the four members on the Massey Commission, recalled that the Commission was

> engaged in an examination of the "plight of the humanities" in Canada. One problem was the inaccessibility of research materials except in a few large centres. It was with immense pride that I was able to say that at the University of Saskatchewan the recently appointed president had inaugurated a system of grants for those who were free to devote their summers to research. These are commonplace now. I think I am right in saying that no other university in Canada made them at that time.[39]

Neatby was referring to grants given by Thompson with the approval of the board of governors on 23 May 1950 for the academic year 1951–52. The sum of $1,500 was placed in the 1951–52 budget to give grants to faculty members in non-scientific departments to aid them in research.[40] The modern equivalent (in 2011 dollars) would be just over $13,000. Then on 13 February 1951, the board, at Thompson's initiative, "set up a committee of three: himself, Leddy, and board member E.F. Whitmore, to provide grants of $300 each to a number of prominent and promising scholars.[41]

From August 1949 to July 1950, the Massey Commission held hearings in Canada's leading cities. Thompson was present on 8 September 1949 when the commission met in Ottawa with the National Research Council. In response to the invitation to meet with the commission members, Thompson, as president and as a prominent NRC member, requested an appearance at the commission's hearing in Saskatoon. In his letter to the commission's secretary requesting his appointment, Thompson appended ahead of the event two densely written sheets, noting the matters that he wished to "bring to the attention of the Commission."[42]

Thompson's brief to the commission on behalf of the University of Saskatchewan emphasized first that the federal government should help universities out of their financial plight by allocating money for general needs, not scholarships that would force the institutions to undertake additional expenses. Second, he advocated the introduction of "Grants in Aid of Non-Scientific Research" that could be administered by a body similar to the National Research Council like the British University Grants Committee. Such an awarding body would need to be familiar with conditions in each department and the scholarly work of each faculty member. Moreover, Thompson suggested graduate scholarships similar to those in the sciences administered by the NRC needed to be made available to students in the humanities and social sciences. As well, he believed that some provision should be made to provide scholarships and loan funds to undergraduates using the model then in place at the University of Saskatchewan.

Thompson made these same suggestions in person when, as the only university representative, he met with the Massey Commission in Saskatoon on 18 October 1949. Thompson speculated to the commissioners that a single body for the humanities and another for the social sciences would provide the expertise of referees essential to assess the quality both of individual students seeking aid, and for group projects. Thompson also favoured granting scholarships of small amounts to a large number of students and larger grants to "top ranked" students.[43] As for the total numbers of students, Thompson announced flatly that "Canada should be educating several times as many college students as it is doing, if it [is] to be a really advanced nation."[44]

When the final report was written, Thompson's suggestion that the Massey Commission establish a national body akin to the NRC for the humanities and social sciences to devise and administer a system of scholarships was rejected. The commission members reasoned that to erect such a system would "subject them too rigidly to scientific techniques and methods of organization."[45]

The Massey Commission Report of 1951 did, however, contain a separate section titled "The Plight of the Humanities." The commissioners lamented: "Apart from the work of a few brilliant persons, there is a general impression that Canadian scholarly work in the humanities and social sciences is slight in quantity and uneven in quality." By contrast, "in the fields of the natural sciences Canada has been able to make important and worthy contributions."[46] The commission argued that when scientists, notably those in the applied sciences, lacked a basic background in the humanities, too many of them, "especially in certain fields of applied science, are only glorified technicians." Lacking proper immersion in the humanities, a student in the sciences all too often lacked the "mental discipline" and the "intellectual curiosity and interest which enrich his life."[47]

Had this ever been the case, however? Thompson endorsed the views of Harvard President James B. Conant, who argued that in the past, all too often what passed for an "appreciation of the arts and letters" exemplified merely a combination of "antiquarianism" and "old snob appeal" that did a grave disservice to the humanistic tradition.[48] Thompson denied that there had ever been a golden age for the humanities in Canada, or anywhere else in his experience. Reviewing his own education at the University of Toronto, he dismissed as illusory any thought that early in this century students in the natural sciences were treated to any significant immersion in the humanities and social sciences. Until recently, Thompson argued, arts students tended to take humanities courses on the strictly utilitarian grounds that such a path opened the way to the single prospective profession, teaching, whereas science students had access to all sorts of avenues into scientific areas that had only came into existence recently, whether chemical engineering, or widespread developments in medicine or biochemical scientific research, or graduate studies in general.[49]

By no means did Thompson have unalloyed admiration for the pursuits, morals, and characters of many scientists and other educators. On 18 September 1951, he gave a paper to the Canadian Education Association titled "Education and Moral Values"[50] at a convention hosted by the university. Attendance at these annual conventions, usually about 370 persons, was largely made up of ministers, deputy ministers of education, and senior departmental officials from each of the provinces.

In his speech, Thompson remarked that although "Germany was one of the best educated nations, with a system which enjoyed the greatest prestige," her universities were among the "first ... to be taken over by the Nazis and used for their own ends" as their "educational leaders lacked the character to resist." A similar lack of educational ideals was evident in the Soviet Union despite the country's "enormous strides in education." Thompson believed that modern education was weak in moral training and he would not credit earlier education by religious authorities or immersion in classical values as effective "moral training or character building." Thompson also dismissed the idea that the scientist "must be deliberately indifferent to values and social consequences," believing instead that immersion in great literature and history provided crucial moral guides for both teachers and students. Above all, he was convinced that the example of the respected teacher possessed of "outstanding character and integrity" was the finest "really effective means of moral education."

And, despite Thompson's own concerns regarding the "plight of the humanities," they were by no means neglected in his appointments during his presidency. Thompson's success in the 1950s in hiring some notable humanists and social scientists was in large part a result of the increased revenue at the university's disposal. Much of this revenue can be accounted for by better economic times, especially from the mid-fifties on, and, more decisively, by added federal government funding.

Thompson had important contacts with the federal government from 1949 onwards. He was active in the only national organization for the universities of Canada, the National Conference of Canadian Universities (NCCU). Founded in 1911 to create an agenda for an imperial universities conference, the Canadian university presidents (including Walter Murray) who had been leaders of the conference, resolved to meet annually to discuss common educational issues. During the first forty years of its existence its members met almost as "a private men's club" to reflect, often casually, on matters such as strengthening the liberal arts, developing teacher training and graduate work, as well as urging university pension schemes.[51]

During World War II, the NCCU finally developed a reasonably high profile nationally. Early in the war the federal government had decided, "partly as a result of persuasion from university heads," that generous financial support should be offered to veterans who either wished to begin or continue their university studies after demobilization. In response, the NCCU appointed a committee on postwar problems to examine and assess the veterans' program of providing $150 per student per year. The success of this government financial program demonstrated both "the value and the feasibility of federal money being used to support higher education."[52] These activities meant that by "the end of hostilities in the second world war the NCCU had established itself as the recognized spokesman for the Canadian universities."[53] Since education under the British North America Act was allocated to the provinces, the success of the NCCU in persuading Ottawa to intervene in this fashion was a major accomplishment.

But it was not until 1949 that the NCCU began to have a fiscal association with the federal government beyond that of assisting veterans. Coincidentally, Thompson was a member of the NCCU finance committee that had met in March 1949 with Prime Minister St Laurent. This gathering was the first in a series of meetings that soon led to a close working relationship between the Liberal cabinet and the NCCU. Thompson commented on this initial meeting in February 1952:

> of the greatest importance to all Canadian universities, namely the decision of the National Government to extend substantial aid to all Canadian universities. It should go a long way towards putting the universities on a sound financial basis and removing the very real danger of deterioration due to rising costs ... The Government asked a committee of the National Conference of Canadian Universities to advise it regarding which institutions should be eligible ... I happened to be a member of that committee.[54]

Earlier, writing to Woodrow Lloyd on 22 June 1950, Thompson had said that the NCCU would be making an application to Ottawa regarding financial aid to universities. The NCCU requested that the federal government make a per-capita grant of $100 per full-time student in all faculties. Such grants, if approved, would be made to the provincial governments rather than to the universities directly.[55] Lloyd agreed to provide support for the application and agreed with Thompson that "across the board" grants to students were "fairer than the grant for certain types of professional education."[56]

When the NCCU submitted another brief in July 1949, this time to the Massey Commission, Prime Minister Louis St Laurent joined the NCCU participants for lunch. He promised some way for the universities to receive the financial assistance they so badly needed. The NCCU then requested an annual grant of $12,842,000, an amount that at that time was beyond federal consideration. About four months later, St Laurent addressed this request, advising the NCCU to embark on a nationwide publicity campaign to win the approval of the public and the press. This drive was greeted sympathetically across the country. As a result, on 1 June 1951, St Laurent announced in the House of Commons that, in the national interest, the government would allocate $7.1 million to the universities, which worked out to about 50 cents per capita. This federal money was paid to the universities directly. Surprisingly, there was virtually no federal consultation with the provinces. Almost immediately after the prime minister's parliamentary notification, Thompson wrote a memorandum for the Board of Governors to consider that it set out a new teaching staff salary schedule based on the use of the federal grant.[57] Both a small across-the-board salary increase and an across-the-board cost-of-living increase was recommended and carried. Writing to his daughter, Thompson commented that the university now possessed "the first surplus almost within living memory. During Butch's [J.S. Thomson's] regime they accumulated a deficit of $500,000 which the government wiped out ... The Board of Governors were incredulous ... that we had a surplus."[58]

Thompson spoke warmly of the impact of federal financial aid in an address to the alumni in 1952 when informing his audience that he expected the university hospital to be opened late in 1953 and the acute medical centre in the fall of 1954. By the autumn of 1956, Thompson had even more reason to be enthusiastic. As a former president of the NCCU, he had been informed earlier of the federal Liberal government's intent to assist universities financially at a higher rate than originally proposed and to have that revenue distributed by the NCCU. On 10 October 1956, G. Edward Hall, the current president of the NCCU, contacted Thompson to tell him that St Laurent was considering "the possibility of federal monies being paid to the NCCU, and of having the NCCU distribute the money, on the stated pro-rated population formula to the various universities of Canada ... [and] is prepared to recommend ... that the amount be increased from the 50 cent per person basis to $1.00 per person."[59] Thompson replied immediately:

> In my opinion the universities would be silly to do anything but accept the proposal and agree to make it work ... The NCCU would have to be incorporated [which would provide essential liability protection] ... It would be very undesirable for the Government simply to hand the money over to the NCCU and

> leave the distribution to that body. The Government should by legislation lay down the ground rules similar to the present ones – so much per capita of the population; the institutions of each province to receive a total amount in accordance with the population of the province; each institution within a province to receive a proportion of the provincial total in accordance with its enrolment. The NCCU might decide what institutions are to be eligible for assistance, what types of students are to be counted, etc.[60]

Thompson's hopes had been realized and his support validated. On 18 January 1957, the NCCU was legally incorporated as the National Conference of Canadian Universities and Colleges (NCCUC), and was able to administer the federal subsidies. The NCCUC now became a very complex structure, largely because it now included member colleges and some subsidiary organizations. So in 1959, the Canadian Universities Foundation (CUF) was created and incorporated as the executive agency of the larger organization to simplify its administration so it could manage the subsidies. In one of his last talks as president, Thompson reflected that

> Friends of any university and of higher education in general should be very grateful to the federal government and parliament for that decision. They should also be grateful for the promptness with which the decision was announced following the publication of the Massey Report, and particularly for the announced federal policy of exercising no control over the way in which the money is used; in fact the federal government is to require no report or accounting for the way in which it is used. It is gratifying also to have the public announcement of the premier of the province that federal aid will make no difference in the provincial grants to the university.[61]

Thompson was an active advocate federally, writing to his daughter, "Tell [Francis] Leddy [Dean of Arts and Science] that I got in a good plug for the Canada Council in my speech at the and also in private conversation with Mr St Laurent and Mr Howe."[62] Nevertheless, public policy objectives did not always align with Thompson's aims. Other Leddy correspondence shows that Thompson did not endorse the objective of the Canada Council to support only the arts.

When the Canada Council was created in 1957, Leddy stated that Thompson was angry that none of the allocated revenue was designated for the sciences. The president had written to the local MP R.R. Knight, asking for a copy of the bill that established the Canada Council, since he gathered that "the capital grants to universities must be used for non-scientific purposes." If that restriction was accurate, then "the usefulness of the grants in meeting our crisis will be greatly reduced." Thompson proceeded to lament that the "great need is for accommodation for scientists and engineers."[63] Indeed, such was Thompson's disapproval that Leddy believed Thompson also was irritated by Leddy's appointment to the Canada Council.

Nevertheless, the investment in post-secondary education was so significant that Thompson was able to be extraordinarily active in making appointments to all of the university faculties during the decade 1949–59. As he reminded faculty and board members in a speech in September 1960, seven of the (then) eleven deans, four directors and sixty per cent of the professors "were appointed on my recommendation, of course after the necessary committee action." They included not only a significant number of distinguished scientists, but also quite a number of humanist and social science scholars.[64] Among them was Murray Adaskin. In 1931, with financial assistance from the Carnegie Institute, the University of Saskatchewan had been the first university west of Toronto and Montreal to create a Chair of Music; in 1952, Adaskin became the first head of the music department. That year, Thompson remarked: "the question which I have been asked most frequently during the past summer is 'How in the world did you manage to get Murray Adaskin out here?'"[65] The answer was that in the spring of 1951, the dean of arts, Francis Leddy, had invited Adaskin to apply for a position at the University of Saskatchewan, which was planning to set up a new music program. In January 1952, Adaskin came to Saskatoon to meet with the president privately and then with other members of the search committee. An appointment was not expected to be made until May or June. The next morning, however, Adaskin was summoned to Thompson's office and offered the position of full professor, with tenure, at $5,600 a year. Thompson regretted that the university could not offer more, but Adaskin accepted, and in the summer of 1952, he and his wife, the accomplished singer Frances James, arrived in Saskatoon.

Thompson's concern for Adaskin went well beyond merely appointing him. Adaskin recalled meeting the president frequently and randomly during the winter in the faculty parking lot. He remembered Thompson asking him if he had enough time to compose, which was the main reason Adaskin had come to Saskatchewan. When Adaskin replied that all was going well with his work, the president pressed him: "Now Murray, if there is any aspect of the work that turns out to be too much for you, do not hesitate to ask me about it." As Adaskin later commented, "what a wonderfully smart man he was to deal with people in that manner."[66]

Another significant appointment was that of Eli Bornstein in art. Bornstein was professor of the art and art history department from 1954 to 1971, and has often reflected upon Thompson's interest in furthering his work. He stated categorically that Thompson had been more interested in and contributed more to the arts than any subsequent president.[67] Paying tribute to his old colleague and friend Murray Adaskin, Bornstein noted that:

> Murray Adaskin spent the majority of his years as a professional musician and as one of the leading composers of Canada at the University of Saskatchewan, and ... often regarded the sojourn in Saskatoon as the most rewarding. Owing to the support offered by W.P. Thompson, then President ... for making the University of Saskatchewan a primary patron of the arts in the province of Saskatchewan and beyond, Murray Adaskin embarked on the task invested within him of creating a cultural centre of pre-eminence within the province.[68]

Thompson often spoke of the university's good fortune in having two distinguished artists on its staff at the same time.

> a musician whose original compositions are bringing such renown to himself and to the institution and also a man whose paintings and sculpture are doing the same in the field of art. And we may compliment ourselves on the abundant evidence that both these men are happy in their surroundings and opportunities in a prairie university where some people would not expect artists to feel at home ... We have long had good reason to be proud of the achievements of the university in the sciences ... But now we can also be proud of our achievements in the fine arts.[69]

Other notable scholars and teachers hired included Clarence Tracy, William Blisset, and Douglas Cherry in English, Charles Lightbody, James McConica and Roger Graham in history, Moishe Black and Ron Ridgway in French, and Constantine Andrusyshyn in Slavic Studies. In the social sciences, Thompson approved the hiring of Edward Safarian and Kenneth Buckley in economics and Norman Ward in political science, to mention just a few. Moreover, he agreed with the leading members of the political science and economics department, Mabel Timlin and Vernon Fowke, that it was imperative that the university bring George Britnell, a well-known agricultural economist and political scientist back from his wartime work in Ottawa.[70]

Emrys Jones, head of the drama department, stated in his 1951–52 report that his former student, Frances Hyland, had recently "been given a starring role" in London in *A Streetcar Named Desire*. Her achievement, he noted, "has brought as much favourable attention to this university as the achievement of any other graduate for many years."[71] These departmental annual reports are valuable documents, for they also include statements about the various needs of the departments, the fulfillment of many, though not all, of those needs, and diverse expressions of satisfaction and dissatisfaction with the administration, and the president in particular. The head of the English department, Carlyle King, noted in his 1950–51 report that his department was the first in Canada to revise its first-year program by adding an hour of lecture time per week so that two hours a week were devoted to literature and another two hours to English composition, in an attempt to improve students' writing skills. Both Queen's and the University of Toronto prepared to adopt the Saskatchewan program. In his 1952–53 report, King stated that the department "had received sympathetic consideration and generous treatment ... in recent years," having been allocated adequate staff and satisfactory office accommodation and effective teaching arrangements. Like almost all the other department heads, King lamented the heavy load of speeches and other extension work imposed on the staff. The history department, particularly after the publication of Hilda Neatby's *So Little for the Mind* in 1953, was overwhelmed by requests for lectures and addresses. Yet the chair, Dr Simpson, expressed gratitude in his 1953–54 report to the president and the board for "the financial assistance given to our members for the purposes of research." By contrast, the head of the art department, Gordon Snelgrove, lamented the lack of support for the visual arts and contrasted that neglect with what he saw as the heavy emphasis on science. Snelgrove claimed that art students produced creative work in the face of "indifference on the part of the university." In 1956–57, however, one problem was resolved for the art department, namely the need for consolidation, when new integrated quarters were provided on the second floor of the administrative building.[72] This integration may have resulted from the distinction professor Eli Bornstein was bringing to the university from his numerous exhibitions in major American and Canadian cities, as well as the numerous awards that he won. Ironically, financial and spatial considerations prevented the creation of a fine arts building.

In 1957, the president had an opportunity to allocate much larger research grants to faculty in the humanities and social sciences. Writing to his daughter, he told her of a recent financial gift to the university. Because it was so large and unprecedented, he was able to assist those two faculties to a much greater extent than ever before. Thompson remarked that, unlike in America, "The industrialists here haven't yet got beyond making grants for specific researches and for scholarships, except in one case ... The one exception was International Nickel which gave the U. of S. $50,000 without strings. I got our Board to use it for awards of $800 each to faculty members in humanities and social sciences who undertook to spend the summer in approved full-time research. It was a very popular move."[73] Thompson added that he only accepted this grant and similar ones, provided the university controlled their use, for it would be "fatal for them [corporations] to have any say in the spending."

In 1957, a grant of $800 was a substantial sum of money, amounting to $6,588.10 in today's funds in sixty-two allotments. That sum would allow any historian, economist, novelist, or musician to work in reasonable comfort for the summer on his or her research project, whether in Ottawa, at the Library of Congress or, for Murray Adaskin, at Canoe Lake in Algonquin Park. Those who wanted to use research sites in Britain or continental Europe also would be able to spend extended periods of time in archives or libraries overseas.

Thompson distributed the summer grants widely among departments and to a diverse group of faculty members, both those who were already established and others who were just beginning their scholarly careers and demonstrated promise. One major recipient, C.H. Andrusyshyn, author in 1955 of a *Ukrainian-English Dictionary*, the first such work published outside of Russia, thanked the president for two grants as well as other financial assistance in publishing his book.[74]

Ultimately, Thompson's pride in the scientific accomplishments at the university was graphically demonstrated when he was asked in the fall of 1958 to indicate the names and kind of influence of those who had contributed the most to the university. This request came from the chairman of the Committee Studying Higher Education in Canada, appointed by the NCCU, but funded through the Carnegie Foundation. The chairman wanted Thompson to cite in chronological sequence those who influenced the university and what their main contributions were: (1) before 1914, (2) between 1914 and 1939, and (3) since 1939.

The president outlined in a rough time sequence those whom he considered the dominant contributors. Only Walter Murray had a background in the humanities. Thompson placed Murray (1908–37) first, since "he laid the foundations, set the whole tone ... established the philosophy of service ... to the people of the province." Second, he placed Dean W. J. Rutherford (1909–1930) for his "big influence in an agricultural province" and his partial responsibility for "a science curriculum." Third, Dean G.H. Ling (1909–39; a mathematician) was noted as he played "the same role as Murray for the College of Arts and Science." Fourth, Thompson named Dean T. Thorvaldson (1914–49), who was "one of the strongest influences in promoting research and securing its recognition as a normal duty of faculty members." Fifth, Thompson identified Dean C.J. Mackenzie (1912–39), who "created the College of Engineering" and then became president of the National Research Council, and, sixth, he chose Dean Wendell Macleod (1952–61), who was "chiefly responsible for a first-rate Medical School." In last place, Thompson placed himself, for, "There are possibly some people who think that I myself had some influence."[75]

5

Governance and Governments

During his ten-year presidency, Thompson took an active interest and great pride in developing not only a strong research and teaching faculty but also a group characterized by collaboration and dedication to the university and, as much as possible, by commitment to the needs of the province. In these pursuits he was following the ideals of Walter Murray, albeit in profoundly different times. Although he probably did not know every student by name, as Murray had, he certainly knew each faculty member by name and took a personal interest in the professional endeavours of each. And, despite their growing numbers, he was anxious for the faculty to get to know one another.

Thompson's interest in faculty concerns was concretely demonstrated by his interest in and support for the creation of the Faculty Association. In 1952, George Britnell and Vernon Fowke, from the Department of Economics and Political Science, spoke for the faculty relations committee in advocating the establishment of a faculty association. They made their request when the climate of opinion among many Canadian academics was shifting from automatic acquiescence in administrative policies to a critical, indeed proactive role. This assertiveness had been signalled in 1951 by the formation of the Canadian Association of University Teachers (CAUT) to protect and extend the interests of the profession, with a particular goal, in its early years, of increasing faculty salaries.

This national initiative happened just before Thompson agreed to the request to establish a faculty association. "Strongly in favour of" the association, Thompson played a constructive role in convincing the few board members who "dragged their feet," because they believed that the Faculty Relations Committee was sufficient.[1] Thompson described the development of the Faculty Association as of "far-reaching significance" for it would be "independent of the college faculties and the council" and had as its primary function the representation of the faculty "individual and collective, in their relations with the government and administration."[2] Thompson explained its functions publicly in his 1952–53 annual report: The association was "to promote the professional interests of the members, including relations with the administration, salaries, conditions of employment and to co-operate with national and international associations." It would also have an "important voice in all promotions through the presence of a representative on the committee that makes recommendations to the Board." In addition, a member of the Faculty Association would also be a member of the committee on grants for research. In these ways, Thompson believed that the faculty could then "play a real part in important matters of administration."[3]

The cordiality and effectiveness in discharging business that prevailed between the Faculty Association and the Board of Governors is captured well in the report Britnell presented to the association in November 1952.

> I should like to say a word about the atmosphere in which negotiations with the Board representatives have been carried out. The new system of committees from the Board of Governors sitting down around a table and actually negotiating with each other constitutes a radical departure from the paternalistic tradition. Yet from the first meeting last May the representatives of the Board have displayed friendliness and courtesy in discussion, interest and patience in exploring problems, and a spirit of cooperation and fairness in reaching agreement. The President both in these meetings and in innumerable less formal discussions of details has been most cordial, considerate, and helpful. I can hardly conceive of informal, voluntary, collective bargaining being carried on under more favourable auspices.[4]

In a similar vein, Walter Smishek, a board member then with the Saskatchewan Labour Institute, reported to the union members in February 1953 about how constructive this new organization was:

> During the past year our professors formed what is virtually a union and formed it with the blessing of the administration. They didn't really call it a union and it is not certified. But it functions as a union with collective bargaining rights etc. I was one of the representatives of the Board of Governors, who met with representatives of the professors' association on several occasions during the year. We sat around a table and as a group of individuals discussed salaries, pensions, promotions etc in a spirit of the friendliest goodwill. And we reached complete agreement. Also, the chairman of the professors' association has been named by the Board of Governors as a member of the committee that deals with promotions and salary changes.[5]

The Thompson era also witnessed the beginnings of tenure regularization. After 1945, and especially by the time of the increases in enrolment in the 1950s, the president realized that the university would not be able to compete nationally and throughout North America with universities eager to hire increasingly scarce suitable faculty members unless a system of greater security was created. Thompson's awareness of this need was well understood by the leaders of the newly created Faculty Association, especially the chair, George Britnell. Early in 1954, the Board of Governors, at Thompson's urging, passed the following resolution. "That in future all appointments to the rank of Assistant Professor be probationary for a period of two years; such appointments to be made permanent on the recommendation of the President after consultation with the general committee on promotions ... It is agreed that this regulation should not come into force until the Faculty Association has been consulted."[6]

On 3 March, Thompson wrote to Britnell informing him that the Board of Governors had approved the resolutions of the Faculty Association, that the probationary period for instructors would not exceed three years. Under special circumstances, the board could appoint an assistant professor without a probationary period. Moreover, the probationary period would count toward the time required for a sabbatical leave.[7]

Faculty involvement in governance became a realistic, if limited, development at Saskatchewan during Thompson's presidency. Thompson, however, was still primarily influenced by the pioneering University of Toronto Royal Commission recommendations of

1906 for a proper, constructive form of university governance, most of whose features were later applied to other Canadian universities. When implemented at Toronto, and then at the University of Saskatchewan, the commission's recommendations put university governance in the hands of an independent Board of Governors. There was to be no direct control by the provincial government. Moreover, although the Saskatchewan provincial government had a significant influence on university policies, and, after all, provided most university funds, the Board of Governors was now the dominant policy body in all business and financial matters. It was the board that negotiated with the government for the annual budget. By the time Thompson retired, the academic decisions, in practice, were largely under the purview of faculty committees. Speaking at a government dinner in his honour early in 1959, Thompson stated:

> In form he [the President] may have considerable power; in practice, if he is wise he will take very little. The staff must determine all policies collectively. All important administrative decisions should be made ... by the administrative officers collectively acting under the direction of the Board [of Governors]. Donald Creighton, speaking for the faculty, reminded the new president of the University of Toronto that a good university is fundamentally a *constitutional* monarchy. Decisions may be made and actions taken in the name of a monarch but that is only a historical fiction. If he tries to do anything important on his own, he would have his fingers rapped.

Further, he noted: "Another intangible is the general esteem in which the university is held by the people of the province ... I doubt whether any university anywhere does more in service to its constituency quite apart from intramural teaching ... This policy has led the university into kinds of work which many older universities and some of our own staff regard as below the level of legitimate university endeavour. I am not greatly concerned about that criticism ... it is a proper field for the university."[8]

Throughout his career at the university, Thompson had had good relations with the Board of Governors, many of whom he held in the highest esteem for their devotion to the university and their willingness to work long hours on behalf of the institution. He also seems to have had excellent relations with businessmen, both in Saskatoon and throughout the province. Where he separated himself from the business world and from trends in North America was in his firm conviction that businessmen ought not to be chosen as university presidents. Thompson's solution was for universities to do what Saskatchewan had already done with the appointment of Colb McEown: to create an executive, or business, manager. Initially, Thompson noted, some faculty members criticized McEown's appointment because they thought that a former high school teacher ought not to have such an important position. But the criticism soon ceased, Thompson stated decisively, "when they became acquainted with his work."[9]

Thompson had been sympathetic to faculty aspirations for a role in helping to make new appointments, as evidenced by his work on the survey committee, allocating more authority to appointment and promotion advisory committees (although still not binding the president to accept their advice).[10]

In March 1960, after his retirement, Thompson commented at length on a twenty-eight-page document from the University of Saskatchewan Faculty Association advocating significantly increased faculty involvement in university governance.[11] This document reflected to a large extent the sweeping rise in academic self-consciousness and self-confidence throughout Canadian universities.

Both the document and Thompson's commentaries were written within the context of the academic crisis created by "the Crowe case," although Thompson never referred specifically to this conflict about the nature and boundaries of academic freedom. The case arose in March 1958 at United College in Winnipeg, now the University of Winnipeg. The two people at the centre of the crisis were the principal, Wilfred C. Lockhart, and an associate professor of history – and alumnus of the college – Harry S. Crowe. Crowe, along with two other left-of-centre academics, made up the history department. All three were discontented with the administration of the college.

The crisis started when Crowe wrote a letter to a colleague critical of the college. An individual, never identified, took it from the mail room and placed it on Lockhart's desk. The principal was shocked when he read Crowe's disparaging remarks and, with the approval of the Board of Regents of the college, dismissed him. CAUT was asked to investigate the matter and appointed a committee composed of

Vernon Fowke of the University of Saskatchewan and Bora Laskin of the University of Toronto. Their report concluded that the dismissal of Crowe constituted a severe violation of academic freedom, due process, and natural justice. Although Crowe was reinstated, thirteen professors ultimately resigned in protest over his initial dismissal amid storms of debate within Canadian university circles.

This crisis transformed CAUT. Even though, before 1958, it represented nearly eighty per cent of Canadian university teachers, it was primarily concerned with salary issues and other terms of employment, But it was not a union and had no national office, it was in a parlous financial condition, and it was staffed by volunteers. Crowe's dismissal "led to its first ever committee of inquiry and hastened the establishment of a national office. Most important, the case significantly affected the self-image of the professoriate and the idea of academic freedom in Canada."[12]

Thompson's comments demonstrate his detailed knowledge and thorough understanding of the University Act as well as the long and often hesitant process by which faculty gained some degree of influence in university policies. His marginal comments were often acerbic, reflecting what he believed was inaccurate or at least incomplete faculty understanding of the evolution of senior university administrators' ideas and policies about governance as well as the evolving and limited nature of the administrative authority of the Board of Governors. Thompson argued that many of the Faculty Association's generalizations were incorrect and some of the policies their members promoted had already been achieved. When the Faculty Association members praised English universities for what they saw as "democratic self-government," Thompson noted that academic self-government in Oxford and Cambridge had led to such "stagnation and decay" that Parliament had had to intervene to reform the two universities. His marginal annotation to the Faculty Association's claim that "full participation" by faculty in university governance would be "the best guarantee of academic freedom and security of tenure" was caustic. "Have you any fears? I often wished that a faculty member could be dismissed. I could have strengthened the university greatly, if it were possible."[13]

When Thompson assessed the association's outline of the powers of the Board of Governors, he argued: "*A very important provision of the [university] act is omitted.* Under duties of *president* (83 (e) before recommending any appointment he must consult a committee set up under regulations of [the] board. And those regulations ensure faculty control."[14] On the association's listing of the president's powers to promote or remove faculty, Thompson inserted a suggestion in the margin that would enhance faculty authority: "Faculty should recommend that [the] president can't make a recommendation re: promotion or dismissal without consulting a committee as for appointments."[15] He also corrected a statement by the association that the Saskatchewan Board of Governors had similar powers to the boards of the six other provincial universities, noting that Saskatchewan was "very different from Alberta where [the] Board has ultimate power in academic matters." Thompson believed that the association's fears that the board had so much authority that "the danger of a 'managerial revolution'" existed were groundless, arguing that "whenever any question before the board clearly involves academic considerations, the board always tries to get the opinion of faculty ... and if there is a clear expression, [the] board regards it as its duty to implement it if possible." For this reason and others, Thompson was critical of the association's aspiration to change the composition of the board by adding seven faculty members. He outlined at length the grounds for his opposition to the proposal:

> Have had much experience with both faculties and boards and am definitely of the opinion that board members of the present type do a much better job of the type of work that they have to do than an equal number of faculty members would do. In addition there is the likelihood that some [faculty] members would be elected by the vote of the more vociferous and less responsible faculty members. Any government will take seriously the duty of appointing board members and will try to appoint the most suitable.
>
> Government has to provide very large sums of money. Can they do that without naming [the] majority? Would the legislature vote the money to people not responsible to them through Government? ... A board composed of or dominated by faculty members is most unlikely to have that confidence to [the] same degree as [the] present type. It is no good to say that governments show confidence in professors by appointing them consultants or to commissions. They are consulted as experts in their specialized field not as administrators.[16]

This debate took place on the national stage in February 1960 when Percy Smith, of the university's English department, argued in the CAUT *Bulletin* that "all senior administrators, including the president, should be elected for fixed terms," and the same policy ought to apply to at least fifty per cent of the members of Boards of Governors in Canadian universities. The boards would then constitute an executive council of the faculty. Many CAUT members protested that such a proposal did not go far enough and that all, or at least a majority, of board members ought to be elected.[17] Again, these demands can only be understood as stemming from widespread national faculty outrage over the behaviour of the United College administration in the Crowe case.

The December CAUT *Bulletin* contained Thompson's response. He stated that Smith was too preoccupied with the formal, as opposed to the actual, role and powers of Boards of Governors and rejected Smith's statement that budget decisions above the departmental level ought to be made by faculty members. As Thompson saw this issue, "Faculty members do their best to avoid decisions which may injure particular interests or persons ... And for the welfare of the institution such decisions must be made. It is better to leave such decisions to experienced, thick-skinned administrators who expect to have to make them."[18] CAUT rejected, temporarily, Thompson's argument, an argument that, in his old age, reflected his growing conservatism about questions of university governance. But by April 1961, CAUT had come to the conclusion that without more data and a serious investigation there was no way of finding out whether it was Smith or Thompson who "pictured conditions 'not as they are, but as they might be.'"[19]

Thompson's often sceptical comments about the Faculty Association's requests and similar demands from CAUT for significantly increased authority in university governance are not just the reservations of a retired former president who had enjoyed much success under the old regime. Many of his criticisms were wise and constructive. But his views reflected the fact that he personally admired the work, intelligence, and judgment of most of the board members who were active during his time as president – and he remained concerned about the intellectual and material well-being of faculty members. Often he took a personal interest in their lives and work, a point Eli Bornstein has frequently highlighted. Moreover, when the Board of Governors was preparing to choose his successor, he convinced the members to admit one faculty member into their deliberations, providing that member acted as an independent voice and not as a representative responsible to the Faculty Association. This qualification was not acceptable to the association. But at least Thompson had made the attempt.

On the other side of the coin was Thompson's approach to students – and student involvement in university governance. By his own assessment, Thompson's relationship with the student body differed from his predecessors'. Dr Murray, he thought, "constantly had his finger in student affairs," but was so subtle that the students "often did not realize that they were being directed." Dr Leddy corroborated this view of Murray, emphasizing his paternalistic relationship to students. The second president, J.S. Thomson, had behaved differently, calling students in "on the carpet" and giving a bad time to any of those who had offended in some manner. He issued "blunt orders about what could not be done and what was permitted." Thompson, by contrast, believed that "thinking faculty and administration, as well as the public" should rely upon students' "sound judgment, sanity, and good taste ... except possibly [on] a few occasions. And we shouldn't legislate for the many as if they were the few."[20]

One of the clearest expressions of Thompson's convictions about student rights and responsibilities was in a Color Night speech that he gave in 1955:

> Probably I realize and appreciate more than most people the excellence of the student government this year, because, for example, I was under tremendous pressure to suppress *The Sheaf* when it became a disgrace and published stuff which wouldn't be published by the yellowest paper, and wouldn't be read outside a men's smoking room frequented by travelling salesmen. But I was confident that ... the S.R.C. [Student Representative Council] would deal with the matter properly and effectively ... it was far better for all concerned that the student representatives should take that responsibility than that I should do as I was urged to do by many persons ... It all goes to confirm my conviction that the students must have complete self-government, provided they continue to elect able officers who are prepared to take the responsibility which must go with self-government.[21]

Shortly after his retirement, Thompson reflected on students' exemplary conduct in a speech to law students, stating that "no president anywhere has ever had less trouble because of unseemly student conduct than I have had."[22] But this was within the sphere of student self-government, not university governance. As he noted,

> Up to 1959 the students were content with having won full self-government. They did not realize that they had grievances or that they should have representatives on the senate and board of governors. It never occurred to them to demand a voice in the making of general policies, constructing curricula, appointing and promoting their teachers, setting and marking examination papers. They recognized no sufficient reasons for demonstrations, occupying buildings, or boycotting lectures.[23]

Thompson retired before the advent of massive faculty and student demands that roiled Canada, the United States, and much of western Europe after roughly the mid-1960s, and his thoughts on these developments are those of an elderly and sometimes perplexed academic. Frequently, in *An Academic's Progress*, Thompson returned to the problems of student activism which grew in intensity during the 1960s. These issues of student demands for a role in university policy led him to reflect on his own undergraduate years at Toronto. He recalled that the students then were not in the habit of objecting to university management and overall policies, although they did not hesitate to complain about weak or incompetent teachers or dismally weak presidents, as was the case with the 1895 "strike" against President Loudon. Thompson understood only too well such protests and that accounts for his agreement with contemporary activists that there had to be careful student evaluations of faculty teaching effectiveness. At times, Thompson expressed bafflement regarding student demands during the 1960s; on other occasions his view was one of dismay, notably about student demands for "parity" with faculty in all university decision making. Certainly Thompson had no patience with teach-ins, protest marches, or the seizure of buildings. Nevertheless, he believed that official views of student unrest had arisen in large part from the pervasive postwar "obsessive fear of communism."

During Thompson's tenure as president, the traditional university rules regarding male and female students remained almost unchanged.

Students continued to be separated according to gender in the residences, with the women in Saskatchewan Hall and the men in Qu'Appelle Hall. They often comingled in the Saskatchewan Hall dining room or cafe, until the cafe was replaced by a similar place in the Memorial Union Building. But men were forbidden to enter women's rooms and women could not go into Qu'Appelle Hall. Therefore, men taking their dates back to Saskatchewan Hall would frequently cluster uncomfortably in the foyer, especially on winter nights. And unless a woman had a special dispensation from the dean of women, she had to be in the hall by midnight. Students had no access to alcoholic beverages on campus, although many, especially students during the mid-to late 1950s, will remember that a prevailing slogan demanded "a pub in the MUB" – the newly opened Memorial Union Building, built 1953–55.

Thompson, however, was concerned about making the university congenial and intelligible to students entering right from high school, especially if they came from relatively isolated rural communities or farms. He met periodically with provincial high school teachers and then often continued discussions with them by mail. The issues on occasion concerned problems that some students from small rural and urban communities confronted when "projected into a city environment," where they felt very much alone. After discussing these problems at a university gathering with a number of high school principals, Thompson requested that one of them, the high school principal in Unity, Reg Cantelon, write him a letter expanding on the problems that had been discussed and Thompson would then bring it and other similar letters before the faculty. Cantelon responded, emphasizing that, unlike the returned veterans, many young, rural, and small town students were not yet mature when they began their university studies. They arrived at university from friendly, helpful high schools where they had been valued members in a community life. At the university, by contrast, they felt themselves to be cogs in an impersonal machine.

Thompson responded with understanding to such letters, noting that he had for some time "been concerned about our lack of guidance for students, [our] lack of help for students in becoming adjusted to university conditions and methods." He therefore wanted to show this letter to the whole faculty. Perhaps, he reflected, a partial solution would be the addition of "an expert to our staff whose whole duty would be to look after things in that area."[24] Thompson was as good as his word, for later in December 1956 the university council established a committee to give "serious consideration" to the matter of counselling and guidance for first year students. This committee presented an interim report on 18 April 1957 recommending a counselling service be set up, headed by a full-time director. In June 1957, the Board of Governors approved this proposal and declared that the director should be paid at a rate similar to an associate professor. Professor R.A. Rennie from Education was appointed the first director, with a full-time secretary. The scope of his office soon expanded beyond academic counselling to include more staff and to deal with very diverse issues, such as financial, marital, emotional, and other types of personal problems.[25]

Thompson also felt strongly that students needed to develop an "international sense." To that end he welcomed foreign students "who we know will help us," since, however many difficulties they confronted, they have "much more to contribute than our own native students," especially in fostering "international goodwill."[26] Thompson worked with several internationally directed organizations, notably World University Service of Canada (WUSC), for which he served as one of the national vice-presidents.[27] In particular, through WUSC, he gave a lot of time and thought to assist Hungarian students fleeing their country in the wake of the failed 1956 revolution. Many had significant problems with language and trauma, so fees were waived and board and room arranged for a brief period. One of the success stories was that of a woman who graduated from the medical college.[28] At Thompson's retirement, Lewis Perinbam, the General Secretary of WUSC, wrote thanking Thompson for his "warm personal support of the Organization" and all that he had "done to assist us locally and nationally for many years." WUSC had "profited immensely" to have had Thompson's "confidence in many of the difficult tasks and responsibilities that WUSC has faced."[29] It was also during Thompson's presidency that student exchanges with Germany and France were instituted and that first one and then two students from underdeveloped parts of the world were invited to the university, with their fees waived and room and board provided.

Even in his retirement, Thompson still retained his interest in students. Those attending a biology department summer party in 1967 recalled that Thompson was seated on a chair with a ring of students around him and emphasized that the former president was interested in what students were doing and was always very good at communicating with them.[30]

Faculty and students' roles in governance are now accepted features of university life. More contentious is the extent to which government and, increasingly, business or private interests, might interfere with academic freedom. One relationship Thompson cultivated particularly closely was his connection with the provincial government, which was, after all, the source of most university revenues. Throughout Thompson's presidency, the association between the Saskatchewan government and the university was close and constructive, for it was "a partnership that had shared aspirations." Although the two parties did not always agree, "each knew where the other's boundary line was and respected it."[31] Despite his respect and admiration for the CCF administrations of T.C. Douglas and Woodrow Lloyd, Thompson was emphatic in publicly proclaiming his political neutrality during his presidential years. Nevertheless, he often praised the policies of the government and the legislature.

When Thompson became president in 1949, the province was on the cusp of a "conspicuously" great improvement in "general economic conditions" that manifested themselves, especially by the mid-fifties. This development meant much larger grants to the university and that affected every member. Thompson reflected on his good fortune, from an economic point of view, in the timing of his presidency: "Finances were a nightmare to my predecessor," and hence J.S. Thomson was forced "to pare all expenditures to a minimum":

> Salaries couldn't be increased; equipment couldn't be purchased; expansion was impossible. Nevertheless large deficits were incurred ... The first time I went with a delegation of the Board of Governors to discuss our estimates we were told that the government would take care of the large deficit which had been incurred, but that there must be no more deficits. If necessary we would have to cut services and close colleges. The provincial treasurer told us that he expected our grant would gradually inch up to one million dollars, but it would not go beyond that.
>
> This year [1959] it is 2 ¾ millions.
>
> At the same interview we were asked seriously to consider closing Regina College in order to save money ... that was one of the first jobs I had as a president. The decision of course was to continue.[32]

Regina College was saved, but budget cuts needed to be made throughout the university. Addressing the members of the National Board of Federated Women's Institutes in June 1949, including members of Saskatchewan's Homemakers Clubs, Thompson informed the women that he was going "to say an unpleasant thing right at the start," namely that the university was in serious financial difficulty. This distressing situation was by no means distinctive to the University of Saskatchewan; it was nationwide, for "universities everywhere are having similar troubles ... even if there is no economic depression."

Some of the fiscal problems occurred because of the federal government policy on veterans. The universities received "about $300" for each veteran annually as direct income from the Department of Veterans' Affairs. By 1946–47, close to 34,000 veterans had taken advantage of this assistance, thereby approximately doubling the prewar 1939 enrolment figures. Anticipating the problem this influx of students would create, in 1941 the federal Liberal government planned to allow substantial fiscal benefits for veterans who sought to attend university. However, no similar financial assistance was provided for other potential students. This fiscal inadequacy would pose intolerable burdens on universities when they attempted to meet the needs of all those wishing to gain higher education but not qualifying as veterans.[33]

By 1949, however, the graduation of so many veterans caused financial difficulties of another kind, because they deprived the University of Saskatchewan of "about $600,000 a year." "Consequently, the budget of every department ... had to be cut." Although the board had made this budgetary decision before he became president, Thompson agreed with the members of the board that there was no alternative. Neither would he place the blame on the provincial government on which the university had "to depend for funds apart from fees and D.V.A. grants." Indeed, the CCF government that year had done "a great deal for the University" by "wiping out an accumulated deficit of $500,000" and increasing "our grant by $75,000."[34] In the first year of Thompson's presidency, the University of Saskatchewan received no federal aid and only $900,000 from the provincial government. At the time, Thompson was not aware that federal financial assistance would soon be an unprecedented reality, even though he knew that the universities had their own lobby with the federal government. In the meantime, however, even students received almost no federal help. Although some graduate fellowships for those in medicine and the natural sciences had been available through the National Research Council, "there were a few private scholarships for postgraduate study, in the arts and social sciences there were no government scholarships, and no loan funds ... Canadian governments contributed nothing to any of these grants or awards."[35] The president also regretted that the private sector contributed very little to Canadian universities. As late as 1958, "only 2.8 per cent of all tax-paying corporations contributed anything to Canadian universities, a situation that evidently changed little over the next several years."[36]

However, the situation with private donors was not entirely negative. Speaking to agriculture graduates in early 1952, Thompson praised past graduates, not only for their personal achievements, but also because of the

> quite remarkable goodwill and confidence of the public in the University [that was] in large part the work of our graduates ... For example during the two years that I have been in this job the university has received three quite large bequests ... One of the three bequests was for $325,000, one $220,000 and one $185,000. They came quite unexpectedly from persons who, so far as I now, had no connection with the University. But no doubt the general goodwill that is fostered by the graduates had a good deal to do with it.[37]

Despite those bequests, the university was largely dependent on the budget it received from the provincial government. Among Colb McEown's many duties, none was more valuable than helping to prepare and present the annual university budget to the provincial government. In 1946, the CCF administration was the first provincial administration in Canada to create a Budget Bureau and to place it "at the forefront of financial planning." By the mid-1950s Thompson, the chairman of the board, and McEown would meet in Regina for half a day with Clarence Fines, Woodrow Lloyd, deputy ministers Al Johnson and Allan MacCallum, and the Budget Bureau. After Thompson had made some general opening comments, McEown "would go through the details of the operating and capital budgets with such clarity that it drew the admiration of his audience and, I am told, gave the government reason to believe the University was well run."[38]

In 1958–59, the university began to negotiate for the first time with a private fundraising firm. In answer to a questionnaire, the university was able to inform the firm that during the "lifetime of the university and especially during the last ten years, the relations between the Government and the university on financial matters have been of the friendliest nature conceivable," adding "There are no particular skeletons in the university's closet."[39]

Thompson maintained cordial but always correct relationships with the CCF government. Thus, when another university president asked how Thompson managed such excellent terms with the government and wondered if he "cultivated them socially." Thompson replied that "we did nothing for them socially, that in fact only one minister has ever been in my house."[40]

It was true that Thompson was unusually successful in his negotiations with the Douglas-led CCF government. Their productive relationship says a good deal about the provincial government's consideration for the university's well-being and the civilized behaviour of the premier and his dominant cabinet ministers. Their association also shows just how much the government leaders trusted Thompson's competence, honesty, and careful judgment as the CEO of the university. The university was indeed fortunate that the CCF was in power all through Thompson's presidency. As the troubles of Thompson's successor were to demonstrate, government–university relations were far from constructive or cordial when President Spinks had to deal with the often high-handed demands of the Liberal premier, Ross Thatcher. In fact, they were often needlessly stormy.

II

The issues of creating a full medical school and an adjoining research hospital were two areas where the university and the provincial government had to work together carefully in negotiating the often blurred boundaries between vision, policy, research, and funding.

By the time Thompson became president in 1949, the congruence of three groups – the CCF government, many doctors in the province, and leading University of Saskatchewan scientists and administrators – grasped the imperative, if expensive, need to develop a university hospital and medical school. Even before the 1944 CCF election victory, T.C. Douglas had planned a medical college when he took power.[41] In a pre-election speech at Biggar, he promised that the CCF "would set up medical, dental and hospital services, available to all without counting the ability of the individual to pay."[42] Once in power, the premier authorized an extensive study of the health needs of the province. To that end, the government appointed Henry E. Sigerist, a well-known professor of medical history and public health at Johns Hopkins University, to direct a commission. The Sigerist Report was presented in October 1944 and recommended that the School of Medical Sciences at the university be expanded into a "complete Grade A Medical School," while also recommending the construction of a university hospital with at least 500 beds, on the University campus.[43]

Saskatchewan had "consistently led all of Canada in public health innovations and legislation, including twenty-nine firsts," and in two instances the province "led the entire world."[44] This has been attributed to two particular ingredients: the highly developed co-operative spirit of the people in the province and the presence of five important visionaries, including Douglas, who "possessed unusual wisdom and prudence." Among the others were Dr Allan Blair, for his pioneering work in radiation therapy for cancer patients, and physicist Dr Harold Johns, who developed the first cobalt bomb for the treatment of cancer – essential contributors to the distinctive development of medical care in the province and both university researchers.[45] By 1 January 1947, Saskatchewan had established the first successful hospital insurance plan in Canada. In tandem with this legislation, the major medical developments of Blair and Johns helped lay the foundations for development of the university's medical school.

In 1926, the university had established a four-year pre-med program. Students had to earn credit for two years scientific training in the College of Arts and Science, mostly in biology, chemistry, and physics. Since many more students applied for admission to the pre-medical program at the university than the twenty-four allowed entrance, their academic quality was very high. Those admitted then passed to the School of Medical Studies – unfortunately housed in a greenhouse because construction of the chemistry and physics buildings had devoured all the money available for new capital construction – where students spent two more years studying anatomy, physiology, biochemistry, and following that, students had to apply to major medical schools at other Canadian universities, mainly the universities of Manitoba, Toronto, and McGill, for their two clinical years.

One motivation to establish a full medical college was the fact that most of these students did not return: 75 per cent of Saskatchewan-born medical students relocated to other provinces or out of country once their medical training was complete. As was noted, "Unfortunately, these two-thirds include an undue proportion of the better students, and the loss to the Province is very serious."[46] Additionally, being dependent on other medical colleges in other universities posed significant problems for University of Saskatchewan students during the war, especially in the immediate postwar period. Manitoba and Toronto, in particular, said as early as 1939 that they were no longer willing to admit Saskatchewan medical students because they needed places for their own medical applicants.

Despite the clear need for a medical school, Thompson emphasized that the government hesitated until 1945 because of the great costs involved. A medical college would require the parallel construction of an "expensive hospital, and a nurses' residence, in addition to the greatly increased expenditures for staff and equipment."[47] Yet even after long consideration with experts, both Thompson and Douglas may have failed to clearly appreciate the costs of creating a first-class medical school. A later dean of the medical college, Dr Ian M. McDonald, carried this criticism of limited fiscal understanding further, stating that "both the founder of the four-year school, and President Thompson, did not have a very good idea of the complexities and cost of a medical college, and that the chronic underfunding of the college had made it vulnerable to intervention by government agencies." McDonald also faulted "generations of faculty, successive provincial governments, and university administrations for inadequate understanding of the financial resources needed for the College."[48] Clearly, both Douglas and Thompson could not have foreseen the enormous developments in the training of medical students, particularly, the rise in specialization among doctors who needed longer and more costly training to confront the extraordinarily expensive new medical technology, the increasingly rapid advances in drug therapies, and fresh initiatives in surgery.

By the time the medical college was constructed in 1949, it had cost $950,000 plus $250,000 for equipment. The University Hospital took eight years to complete, from 1947 to 1955. The story of its construction was one of delays, debates, and misunderstandings between the provincial government and the university, all of which led to a "halting progress to completion … ."[49] By the time the hospital opened in 1955, it had cost over $12,000,000, nearly $10,600,000 of which came from provincial coffers.[50] The hospital was a separate institution from the university and was paid for by funds that did not come out of the university budget. Nevertheless, the college and the hospital, of academic necessity, had to be closely linked. Various forms of "linkage" were tried, as mandated by the University Hospital Act of 1947: for example, medical students did their training at the hospital and interned there.

That legislation "set up the hospital as a separate institution with its own budget and Board of Governors, but with university representation." Dean Macleod, however, wrote to President Thompson in 1957 expressing anxiety that the relationship might not have ensured the dominance of the university's goals. Various modifications – reorganizing various departments and purchasing more advanced equipment and training physicians in their use – were instituted in the following years but they didn't entirely satisfy Macleod's and the university's concerns.[51]

Many faculty members welcomed the college and hospital whereas others lamented the costs incurred that prevented, or at least delayed, other university building developments, but neither the university administration nor the faculty had any real voice in the decision – the paymaster of the university was the provincial government. Douglas and his cabinet colleagues were dedicated to improving medical facilities in the province. Their decision was the reason why the construction of a proper library and an arts building was delayed once again. Despite the board's resolution of November 1944 asking the government for capital funding, with the "Arts Building to be the first choice ... to be erected," the medical college took precedence.[52] Thompson spoke of how this medical imperative affected aspirations for the creation of an Arts building, when addressing the university medical society in late 1945:

> This is a great year in the history of the medical school ...
> As a representative of another College, I congratulate you even though it probably postpones the equally-needed Arts Building to the very dim and distant future. Few people seem to know that the Arts Building fifteen years ago had reached the exact stage which the Medical Building has now reached. In fact I understand that the Medical Building is to use some of the very stones which had been assembled in 1929 for the Arts Building – which

> is I suppose symbolically if not literally significant. I cannot say that we are not envious. But we are happy in the good fortune of a sister college ... In the long run no college can profit at the expense of another. And in particular none can profit from the neglect of Arts and Science whose work is basic to that of all of them.[53]

Thompson has been severely criticized for not proceeding more rapidly with the building of the library and arts building. But, however much many of his other ideas were accepted by the provincial government he did not control that kind of directed capital funding for the university.

Thompson's support was instrumental in hiring the first dean of the new medical school, Dr Wendell Macleod. At his interview for the deanship in the Bessborough Hotel in Saskatoon early in 1951, Macleod met the three most influential men at the university in succession: chair of the Board of Governors, Arthur Moxon; Walter Francis, a senior member of the board with whom Macleod and his wife, the psychiatrist Jessie McGeachy, soon became very friendly; and the president. Macleod found Thompson "very friendly and impressive and open-minded. He pointed out that politics would not enter into the issue of any appointment." After all, "Moxon was a Conservative, Francis was a Liberal, and he [Thompson] was labelled as being very friendly to the government – a CCF man. He was determined that the new College of Medicine, like the College of Agriculture, would be a service to the people of Saskatchewan."[54]

In Macleod, the university found a vital, socially committed, left-wing dean. When he was twenty, Macleod had spent the summer of 1925 at a mine in Sudbury as a worker–teacher with Frontier College. Appalled by the unemployment in Northern Ontario, Macleod developed spiritually while pursuing a "growing commitment to the Social Gospel."[55] As a young physician in Montreal, he attended meetings of the League of Social Reconstruction in the 1930s, where he met and came to know some of Canada's leading social democrats and proponents of the "radical Social Gospel," especially the famous physician Norman Bethune; Frank Scott, a founder of the CCF; and the constitutional historian, and later senator, Eugene Forsey. Their ideas deepened Macleod's values and his beliefs in transforming medical education to render it more effective and humane.

Thompson and Macleod shared many political and social values. Like Macleod, Thompson believed in universal medical care. Both men admired J.S. Woodsworth, the founder of the CCF. Although Macleod believed, with Woodsworth, in the Christian dimension of the movement, Thompson was an atheist and did not share this part of the social gospel. Macleod's social democratic values were embodied in a belief in merit, not patronage, in government-funded medicare, in a trained, civic committed civil service such as Saskatchewan developed under T.C. Douglas, and support for the co-operative movement, and the British Fabian socialist tradition.

Thompson had taken the lead in hiring the dean and supported his appointment as effective from September 1951 so that Macleod could spend the year visiting medical schools, assessing methods of medical education, and exploring future candidates for Saskatchewan. Thompson regarded the report Macleod submitted in June 1952 as so important that he submitted it to the Board of Governors, who, in turn, "took the unusual step of incorporating it in full in their minutes."[56] In 1953, Macleod also formulated the only recorded mission statement of the college.

Despite failing to grasp all the complexities, financial and others, inherent in creating and sustaining the college, Thompson still understood a good deal about medical education. He and Macleod both admired the Flexner Report, a famous American medical report. In 1910, Abraham Flexner produced a report for the Carnegie Institute on medical education in North America, which significantly changed the education and practice of physicians. Flexner recommended replacing closing all proprietary medical schools (trade schools run by doctors for profit) and incorporating all medical education into universities and having a standardized medical curriculum. Many American medical schools followed Flexner's ideas. This policy led to a higher standard of medical care and a dramatic advance of medical knowledge, owing to the academic influence of universities. Thompson's admiration for the Flexner Report demonstrated his orderly nature and wide-ranging intellect as well as his respect for groundbreaking studies that rendered critical aspects of universities coherent. Thompson demonstrated these characteristics when he praised the royal commission of 1906 on the reorganization of the University of Toronto and in his orderly proposals delivered when he was chair of the1945–46 Survey Committee. As Thompson stated – rather bluntly – in 1952, "The general picture of higher education in Canada ... is not a pretty one. We need someone to do for university education what Flexner did a few decades ago for medical education in the United States. His famous report killed the great majority of proprietary medical schools."[57]

Thompson's determination that a new college of medicine must be of significant service to the province was attractive to Macleod because he believed that medical schools should not just teach medicine but offer community services as well. For example, Thompson recalled a meeting in Regina with the executive of the Cancer Society and then driving home with Dean Macleod while "carrying a cheque for $250,000." Thompson and Macleod met with the president and secretary of the National Cancer Institute where they worked out an agreement for "the N.C.I. ... to establish and pay all expenses of a cancer research unit" in the recently opened (1955) University Hospital. This agreement, Thompson commented, "became a model for agreements with several other universities."

Macleod saw his mission as that of "building-up a first-rate medical school with the best people we could get from outside and enough to do the work properly."[58] Perhaps not unexpectedly, this resulted in some tension with "town" doctors, who were concerned with the potential impact on their practices. Thompson described how he and MacLeod spent endless evening meetings with the senior professors and a group of local doctors in a determined effort to resolve the dispute.

> They still feared that their practices would be reduced and that the university men would form a large group-clinic which was almost a naughty word to the doctors in solo practice. They wanted us to restrict the number of full-time men to one in each main clinical department (four in all) whereas the dean and senior professors maintained that many more were needed for a first-class medical school. At one stage a delegation of practitioners delivered to me as president an ultimatum threatening that unless we stopped appointing full-time men, they would boycott the hospital and medical school – which would have been disastrous. Strong feelings were aroused almost throughout the local profession ... I did my best to be fair, to prevent the use of bitter words, and to find a compromise which they would accept and which would not sacrifice any important university interest. But very little progress was made as neither side would retreat an inch.

Eventually the conflict was resolved on terms that suited the university. And, despite some "irreconcilable differences," a good relationship developed with the local medical profession. "With time, however, the strongest feelings subsided and the situation gradually improved. The full-time men contributed towards building up the reputation of Saskatoon as a medical center, a reputation which attracted patients. The doctors slowly became reconciled to our plan when the number of their patients was maintained or increased."[59]

Thompson and Macleod also corresponded frequently about possible appointments, salary questions, and grants for various medical professors. The extensive exchange of letters between the two men is evidence of the significant amount of time and energy Thompson was willing to devote to building a good medical college. In addition to his own "perspicacity in selecting its dean and first staff and supporting them to the full extent of my ability,"[60] Thompson attributed the growing success of the new college to "the skill of the Dean in securing the implementation of his high ideals and by the intense loyalty and respect he inspires in all member of his staff." [61]

Yet the initial controversy left some local doctors with a distrust of Macleod, whom a number viewed as a "Red Dean" and a few even regarded as a communist.[62] On one "highly unpleasant" occasion, the downtown practitioners attempted to "discredit the Dean and called for his resignation ... Thompson and Dr Allan Bailey responded vigorously and put an end to that."[63] Despite the many difficulties Macleod confronted, the establishment of a modern, research-oriented medical college with a distinguished faculty must be reckoned as a major achievement, for Macleod especially, but Thompson's role should not be underestimated. Of all the faculty and administrators with whom Thompson worked, Macleod came in for the most praise.[64] In one of the last letters that Thompson wrote before his death, he reflected that he was "looking forward to having dinner this evening with Wendell MacLeod ... He is one of those about whose appointment I am very proud." Their relationship was "characterized by mutual admiration and respect";[65] "like a father and favourite son."[66]

Unfortunately, Macleod, who "shared the liberal ideas of ... Thompson," irritated Thompson's successor John Spinks. President Spinks feared that the controversy over medicare would damage the university's financial prospects with potential donors. Apprehensive about this prospect, Spinks "rapped Macleod's knuckles" and humiliated him by unilaterally imposing budget cuts.[67] Eventually, these actions led Macleod to resign in 1961. Thompson viewed Macleod's resignation as "an irreparable loss,"[68] and entirely "due to his support of the Government's Medicare program which the university authorities of the time thought unwise because of the attitude of the medical profession."[69]

Nevertheless, the legacy is clear. The university hospital and the medical college were both essential to the CCF government's medicare program, first advocated by Douglas, and embodied in legislation under his successor as premier, Woodrow Lloyd, in the summer of 1962. The coming of the medical college also staunched the flow of prospective MDs out of the province. And the medicare program provided a blueprint for the federal Medical Care Act of 1966 that paved the way for universal, free, accessible, and high-quality health insurance for all Canadians through separate but largely similar provincial plans.

6

Service

Thompson emphasized that in the early years, "the University only had two roles – teaching and extension."[1] In fact, the Department of Extension, established in 1910, was the first such university department in Canada. The traditional mission of extension work had been to act as an extra educational arm of the university, so academic experts could contribute their knowledge and training to help individuals and communities solve their own problems. According to Professor Lorne Paul, "the University of Saskatchewan owed much of its early popular esteem to its pioneering efforts in community work." Early Extension efforts focused on agriculture, or "sows, cows and ploughs," and included informal courses, sponsorship of 4H clubs, and homemakers' clubs. Members of the Extension Division sought not only to make farming more efficient, but also to help rural men and women become more effective citizens better able to contribute to society. In addition, educational activities were nurtured for immigrants, with lessons in English and continuing education courses at the university. There were programs in drama, poetry, ballet, and other cultural pursuits as well as courses on such subjects as welding and repairing farm machinery. During the 1930s, boys' and girls' summer camps became major projects. At a formal level, the university provided six-week co-educational agricultural courses. By 1953–54, the university was offering twenty-two short courses in everything from farm mechanics to beekeeping; rural electrification to general agriculture (heavily attended) and blacksmithing to farm building, both of which were practically filled to capacity. Additionally, the 4-H clubs remained active. In 1953 there were 476 4-H clubs in Saskatchewan, with 7,241 members enrolled.

These numbers still represented only 7 to 8 per cent of eligible rural youth, but limitations because of inadequate local leadership and numbers of Extension staff curbed the growth of more clubs.[2] Judging by the marginal notes Thompson wrote on every annual report from the Department of Extension, he read their documents carefully. For example, he added the following in his hand to the report of 1953–54. "In addition to the activities which can be included in a statistical summary, the following should be noted: Editing and distributing "Guide to Farm Practice," *Saskatchewan Farm Science* (a quarterly), publishing and distributing bulletins, providing a question-and-answer page for the *Western Producer* arranging a weekly broadcast over a group of Saskatchewan stations by members of faculty from all faculties."[3]" Thompson noted in 1957–58 that the university conducted "108 radio forums compared with 29 by the University of Alberta and 24 by the University of Manitoba."

Throughout Thompson's presidency, the university continued to sponsor many agricultural and 4-H clubs while continuing responsibility for correspondence courses and public service, and sustaining engagement in other volunteer agencies. In his first annual president's report, Thompson emphasized that whatever its fiscal problems, "this University is unique in its relationship to agricultural extension." Thompson was particularly concerned that the university continue to maintain responsibility for the 4-H clubs, for he believed that was "the most valuable and effective of the many kinds of work carried on by our agricultural extension service."[4]

Another service was the university's annual "Farm and Home Week," which, by 1958, then in its twenty-seventh consecutive year, attracted approximately 1,200 people. Such was its popularity and value to attendees that it was suggested the event be extended from a week to ten days, with more involvement from colleges other than Agriculture.[5]

Homemakers' Clubs were essential participants and Thompson gave these clubs a good deal of personal support and time. His respect for these clubs and for the farming community that they represented[6] was demonstrated one wintry day in Saskatoon when he stood on the steps of the College Building, greeting women as they entered Convocation Hall during "Farm and Home Week." Speaking to the "Associated Country Women of the World" in 1953, Thompson claimed, "The relations between this University and the organized country women are closer than in the case of any other university that I know of ... The association between University and Homemakers' Clubs has been very beneficial to the University and its work, and we hope the benefits have been mutual."[7] Marjorie Thompson hosted a tea for Homemakers at the president's residence, with her husband present, every year of Thompson's presidency.[8] Like her husband, she did not consider it at all onerous but, rather, thought it one of the highpoints of each year.[9]

In his unpublished history of Extension, Lorne Paul described the relationship the Homemakers' Clubs had with the university. In every other province, Homemakers' Clubs operated independently of any university support.[10] The distinctive association in Saskatchewan was carefully defined by the University and the Homemakers' Club leadership.

> It was organized virtually as part of the University. The Director of Agricultural Extension was the *ex officio* secretary and the managing director until 1913, when these duties fell to the newly appointed Director of Women's Work. From that time until the reorganization in 1952, women's extension remained as a separate unit, reporting directly to the president of the university. After 1952, its work was still carried on independently, but with a greater degree of integration with agricultural and adult education services. Unique in Canada was the Club's official association with the university, which provided the provincial secretary, secretarial staff, and extension resources to aid the development of the club and its programs.[11]

In 1950, almost immediately after becoming president, Thompson reorganized Extension into a formal department with the intention of enlarging the scope beyond agriculture and home economics to "include all suitable extension activities of all the colleges and departments" and giving it more of a research orientation. Both the department of Women's Services and Adult Education Services were absorbed into Extension, and Thompson described extension activities more inclusively: correspondence work, night classes and summer session; annual meetings of pharmacists, medical refresher courses and teacher institutes. Additionally, "Besides all these ... I estimate that between 15,000 and 20,000 letters go out every year from members of staff to citizens of the province who have written in to ask for information or advice on particular problems ... For some of the staff the most time-consuming activity is looking after visitors ... They know the experts that they want to see [and] won't be fobbed off with juniors."[12]

In defence of this revision, Thompson claimed it did not fundamentally alter the direction of Extension and it sustained the responsibility of the university for public service: "Critics of all these informal activities are likely to receive scant attention. This University ... had committed itself to the ideal of serving its community in every possible way. We would not draw back now even if we were so inclined ... We want every citizen of Saskatchewan to be fully aware of the University's capacity and willingness to serve him."[13]

Thompson reiterated this approach in his 1953–54 annual report, noting that the university must perform services beyond merely "teaching and research," for if the university were to "cut itself off from the public, it would be condemned to futility." There was, of course, tension between the "traditional" expectations of teaching and research, and the increasing number of enquiries from the public. Plant pathologist T.C. Vanterpool remarked on his personal extension burdens. "My predecessor had passed the duty on to me as if it were a commonly accepted third duty. Much as I liked doing this in my own particular field, it proved occasionally to be time-consuming and I think time and energy devoted to this job would better have been channelled into teaching and research. The answer to the problem is an Extension Bureau adequately staffed to answer what might be termed extension enquiries."[14]

The department of Extension was increasingly restricted during the 1950s by inadequate financial resources and, especially, too few staff members. The annual report of Extension in 1958 told the story: "No permanent additions have been made to the Extension Department staff since 1952 while the work load has increased tremendously. An additional problem is the increasing difficulty of securing help from regular College of Agriculture staff due apparently to their expanding research load."[15]

Thompson attributed the growing problems of Extension to the large increase in the undergraduates enrolled on campus. This increase made it more difficult for the staff to carry on outside work, given their increasing teaching demands and growing research requirements. Hence, many faculty members had been forced to decline Extension department requests. Without added assistance, Thompson worried, the public esteem in which the university was held would decline.

The tension Thompson experienced between supporting university extension and pure research was graphically demonstrated in his views and actions at the provincial government's decision in March 1952 to appoint a royal commission on agriculture and rural life. The decision to establish the commission "seems to have been the premier's personal idea,"[16] following "two decades of turmoil in Saskatchewan agriculture" in which accelerated mechanization had been responsible for part of the farmers' debts while rendering quarter and half-section farms no longer economically viable.[17]

When Premier Douglas announced the members and mandate of the royal commission, he predicted that their recommendations would be "a blueprint for the agricultural industry of this province for the next 25 years." Although the premier praised the rapid mechanization of agriculture, he pointed out that this had led to "fewer farmers tilling more land and producing a greater volume of farm produce than ever before in history." These developments made it increasingly difficult for young people to accumulate sufficient financial resources to "start up in what is now a highly capitalized business." Unless the problems resulting from these issues were addressed, "Saskatchewan may become a region of tenant farmers and absentee landlords."[18]

The mandate of the royal commission was comprehensive: to investigate the province's farm economy problems and make recommendations to meet the rapidly changing conditions of rural life in Saskatchewan. The government looked to the commission to offer policies that would assist young people to become established in agriculture while expanding the amenities of rural life.[19]

The commission was also to recommend better rural social services, new educational facilities, and ways to provide farm credit and capital while developing rural transportation facilities and electrification.

The provincial government selected W.B. (Bill) Baker, the director of the School of Agriculture at the university, as chairman of the commission, a person Douglas thought of "most highly." Premier Douglas "expected Baker's team to come up with a blueprint for rural revitalization as soon as possible.[20] Under Baker's creative leadership the commission pursued innovative research involving, for example, widespread rural participation by holding meetings throughout the province. The commission held some 200 hearings at a cost, as estimated by Baker, of approximately $225,000.[21]

Rural participants in meetings convened throughout the province repeatedly told commission members that there was a need for main market roads but that the current municipal structure "was incapable of dealing with it,"[22] for the municipalities simply lacked the funds. The need for increased adult education was also a major area of discussion as was the demand for greater rural electrification. Such services, of course, would have to be paid for by the CCF government.

From the outset of his work as chairman, Baker wanted to work through the university on many of the educational aspects of the commission. He believed that, should the commission's recommendations be left to the provincial government, political considerations would more likely get in the way of positive results. Instead, the university, "with its traditional independence from partisan participation in programs of rural development," was "ideally suited to the provision of the required services" including technical assistance for successful "community planning and social organization."

Thompson was sympathetic to the establishment of the royal commission and to Baker's requests for university assistance. At Baker's request, Thompson directed all department heads and deans to draw up a synopsis of the functions of their departments and colleges indicating the areas of strength and the places where more resources were needed to assist the commission. After these documents had been circulated to the commission, Thompson arranged for commission members to meet for up to three hours in sequence with each college and faculty.

Baker aspired to implement many of the royal commission's ideas through the establishment of a research centre "within the existing organization of the University," provided that such a centre avoided confusion with the special interests of existing colleges and departments, was distinct from the University Extension Service, and had a properly defined relationship with the "needs of the provincial government."[23] Baker also noted that a number of prestigious American universities in states with extensive agriculture, for example the Universities of Michigan, North Carolina, and Nebraska, had, with financial resources from their respective states, implemented the various kinds of technical services, such as rural electrification, a network of all-weather roads, and expanded and upgraded provincial telephone service, that the royal commission was recommending. Baker completed his report in March 1955 and sent copies to the provincial government and the university.

Thompson was sympathetic to many of Baker's requests and asked that the Board of Governors consider his memorandum. But the provincial government was unable to act as rapidly as Baker and Thompson wished. Minister of Education Woodrow Lloyd told Premier Douglas that the CCF administration itself had "not thought too specifically about the problem and certainly has no definite policy" that he could report to Thompson and other university committee members. In his lengthy letter to Douglas, Lloyd noted that both Baker and the president had raised the possibility of setting up some form of "independent" institute or commission. Lloyd noted that Thompson "saw no particular problems and some advantages" about locating such a body at the university. Both men agreed that as far as research was concerned, it needed to be "keyed to community needs." In contrast to Thompson, however, Lloyd believed that "such research" should be under the direction of the senior Saskatchewan civil servants Tommy Shoyama, the cabinet's chief economic advisor, and Meyer Brownstone, an economic advisor, rather than under university direction.[24]

By late 1956, Premier Douglas informed Thompson that the cabinet had studied the Baker memorandum with interest and had approved it in principle. The premier, to a greater degree than Lloyd, believed that the commission "has shown the need for a community development program in the province and there is much to recommend the idea of having it established on the University campus."[25] Thompson responded to the memorandum after discussing its contents with the Board of Governors and circulating it among faculty members.

Unfortunately, the differences between how Baker envisioned the proposed program and development differed significantly from how some board members and many faculty members construed the role of the university in society. The university community was split in its response. Some board and faculty members saw Baker's plans as "too primarily applied, rather than theoretical research," although Thompson was inclined to sympathize with some of the practical requests. Other faculty who held left-wing views tended to praise the Baker Commission. Carlyle King, a long-time activist in the CCF, a well-known pacifist and head of the English department, considered Baker's work "monumental."[26] Consequently, the requests the royal commission made to the university led to a series of often heated internal debates that extended well beyond Thompson's presidential years.[27]

The main difference was in the varying conceptions of the purposes of research. Most university people were not convinced that community work "of the type proposed by Baker is a proper university function." Curiously, perhaps, given the university's already extensive work in this area, many did not believe that they had a responsibility to assist local communities in developing specific practical skills in using farm implements and developing new harvesting techniques. There was also concern that projects arising from the royal commission's recommendations might be serious competitors for scarce funds from organizations such as the Carnegie and Kellogg Foundations.

As many at the university reflected upon Baker's recommendations, it was obvious the institution could scarcely deal with some of the practical recommendations of the royal commission, such as the oft-repeated popular need for roads or demand for greater rural electrification. Even modest recommendations for university support irritated some members of the Board of Governors, a disquiet shared by many faculty members. In contrast, the political needs and beliefs of the Douglas government required other recommendations of the royal commission to be implemented, as far as possible, by various forms of university assistance.

Thompson established a university committee to study Baker's ideas, since the board members thought that the proposal has "sufficient merit to warrant thorough study." The Board of Governors was "anxious that the committee decide whether a workable program can be developed and, if so, that it recommend a definite plan."[28] The dean of commerce, T.H. McLeod, agreed to become chairman, while Thompson would be an ex-officio member. In keeping with one of the areas of university involvement noted by Baker, McLeod's responsibilities would include visiting "certain universities in the U. S. to study their activities with regard to community planning agencies."[29] Baker also stimulated other ideas among members of this committee, notably the idea of concentrating the services the commission proposed "in a separate division of the University under the title of Bureau or Institute of Applied Social Science." After much discussion, this university committee submitted its proposal, as ratified by the board, to the provincial government.

Both the Douglas government and the university appeared to have reached a consensus on at least one of the Commission's recommendations: "the need for a community development program in the province ... established on the University campus."[30] The mandate of the program "was to accumulate and communicate tested knowledge about community phenomena, in order that the effectiveness of rural communities as contributors to social and economic development might be increased.[31]

This "program" became the Centre for Community Studies, established at the University of Saskatchewan in 1957. Thompson described the centre and the work it would undertake:

> The communities of Saskatchewan have been undergoing profound changes that have been well described and documented in the extensive reports of the Commission. The chief function of the Centre will be (1) to provide technical consultants to assist communities in self-development, and (2) to carry on social research to provide information for the consultants and to develop techniques for community improvement. The Centre has been established as a joint undertaking of the Government and University. It will function under a Board on which Government and University are represented. At the last session of the legislature a sum was voted for its expenses ... This enterprise promises to make important contributions to the life of the province.[32]

In July 1957, Baker was appointed the centre's director. The chairman of the Board of Governors and Thompson were selected to represent the university on the centre's board. Although Thompson welcomed the centre, after 1957, he developed reservations about some of the Commission's other recommendations involving the university. The centre's director and his colleagues sought a number of ambitious changes that led to considerable acrimony between Baker and Thompson, and ultimately, between the Board of Governors and the membership of the former royal commission. In particular, Baker and his staff wanted the university to develop a large department of social science to serve the province. But as early as July 1954 a gulf was beginning to open up between Baker and Thompson. In the early days of the royal commission, Thompson had told Baker that while he understood the value of a "course of a year or two's duration ... fitting students for social service work ... he saw no reason to implement such a program since such courses were already being offered at both Manitoba and British Columbia." Hence, Thompson informed Baker that he hoped that the university would do "all we can in the social sciences in general, such as economics, political science, history" while seeking a permanent appointment in sociology.[33] Thompson warned Baker that the university could not be fiscally responsible for a large number of new appointments and a departmental rearrangement.

In April 1957, the Baker Commission sent Thompson its list of recommendations for improvements of university services. The president was irritated and it showed in his reply.[34] He was annoyed by the commission's claim that "the University ... gives little evidence of serious interest in any great expansion of social science personnel and facilities [although] some faint credit for 'a limited development of economics and political science is given.'" Thompson was also annoyed by the commission's recommendation that the university take "immediate steps ... to establish a strong department of social science." This conflict between Bill Baker and the president illustrates how deeply the two men were thinking at cross-purposes. Baker's ambitious aspirations, influenced by the American universities where he had studied, envisioned a far more sweeping program of theoretical and practical social science courses, including social psychology and anthropology.

Thompson listed the areas and subjects that he saw as constituting the social sciences. He then went on to compare the numbers and academic credentials of the members of social science departments at Saskatchewan. There were nine permanent, full-time faculty members in the Department of Economics and Political Science as well as two others in agricultural economics and one other in the College of Commerce. In comparison, the University of Alberta possessed a complement of eight faculty members and two others in business administration. The University of Manitoba had five faculty members in economics, three in political science, and three in agricultural economics. Both universities taught "at least 1,000 more students than we." Even Queen's, long a national leader in political science and economics, possessed only nine faculty members in economics and political science and six in commerce. Without going into exhaustive detail, Thompson pointed out both the national and international reputation of at least five of the current members of the Department of Economics and Political Science, while at the same time noting by name two members of the history department, Professors Neatby and Simpson. Indeed, the university had moved significantly into the social sciences, given the faculty members in psychology and philosophy, and the teaching of sociology by one instructor, with plans then being studied by Council to hire two permanent faculty members. By 1955, the Board of Governors had agreed to the appointment of a "full-time and permanent sociologist" after the Department of Economics and Political Science had submitted a budgetary proposal for such a position. The sociologist in that department had previously devoted two-thirds of his time teaching political science and "one third instructing engineers in Political Economy 2."[35] Thompson remarked that, in contrast, neither Alberta nor Queen's had a single faculty member in sociology, whereas Manitoba had two – one was a dean and the other an economist. And neither of those universities yet had a department of sociology. Thompson argued that the only social science still not offered was anthropology. He concluded that had the "Commission limited its criticisms to sociology and not made reflections on all the other social science departments and the able men in them, I would have kept quiet." He reserved the right to publish his memorandum in the event the royal commission's report aroused too much criticism of the university.

Baker replied on 24 May 1957, stating that the "Commission has examined your memorandum with care and can find in it no basis for changing its statements within the context of the final report."[36] Thompson scribbled in the margin of Baker's letter: "I dealt effectively with the matter of quantity and what I said is ignored." Thompson also wrote on the last page: "The reply of the Chairman of the Commission to this letter [of 29 April] is reproduced below. No change was made in the final draft of the report as a result of my protest."

Thompson delayed sending his 29 April memorandum to the Board of Governors until 21 December 1957.

> In view of the criticism of the University's work in the social sciences, contained in the report of the Royal Commission on Agriculture and Rural Life, the Governors should have a statement from me about it. I have delayed making such a statement because I had hoped that little attention might be paid to the

> criticism. But since the matter had been taken up by the press (although favourably to the University) the Board should have my views on it.
>
> The best statement I can make is contained in a letter that I wrote to the Chairman of the Commission on April 29 last (please note date) when I was shown a mimeographed copy of one volume of the report. A copy of the letter follows.[37]

The Saskatoon *Star Phoenix* had copies of the Baker critique of the university and Thompson's 29 April 1957 rebuttal, since the documents were then in the public domain. In both a front page story and in a long editorial, the paper devoted extensive coverage to the conflict between the Baker commission's accusations that the university "was not pulling its weight" and the sharp refutations of this allegation by university spokesmen. The newspaper focused specifically on the commission's recommendation "calling for a new department of social science immediately."[38] The paper, under editor Eric Knowles, who was critical, indeed hostile to the commission, supported the university, emphasizing that a "new department of sociology had been set up" by a decision "long before the commission's report came out." In fact, the university had offered "classes in sociology for ten years." The editorial writer concluded:

> This is a University whose faculty members have attained national and international reputations in such fields as history, economics and political science ... It has sent out leading scholars in these and such other fields as literature, languages and philosophy.
>
> Likewise its handling of "vocational training" and extension services has been a matter of conscious policy. The commission, then, has seriously questioned University policy in general. It has ventured into difficult territory. We question whether it is on sound ground at any point in its references to the University.[39]

On 10 January 1958, Thompson named a committee of twelve members, made up of eleven faculty members and one lawyer, to examine the commission's recommendations for the university. He included himself as one of the members and named as chair, Board of Governors' member Mervyn Woods, a well-known Saskatoon lawyer. In his letter appointing this committee, the president included an eight-page copy of the royal commission's recommendations as they involved the university. The board directed Thompson to send the Woods Committee the memorandum that he had submitted to the board at its last meeting. They also directed the president to inform the faculty committee that they fully approved and endorsed Thompson's letter of 29 April 1957 to the board, which formed part of the memorandum. The first meeting of this committee was scheduled for 21 January.[40] It asked Thompson to prepare comments on two of the Commission's recommendations in particular. Thompson noted, first, that:

> The University has expanded its personnel and equipment in the social sciences and humanities as fast as its resources have permitted. During the last four years 12 men have been added in those subjects and the Board of Governors have authorized the addition of 19 more during the next three years, if resources are available. At the same time library facilities essential for their work have been greatly enlarged. The personnel of those departments, both in numbers and distinction, compare favourably with those of comparable institutions in Canada. There may be differences of opinion in regard to the relevant expansion of different divisions of the University. But this is under constant review by the administration and Board of Governors, assisted by a Forward Planning Committee, and the decisions reached represent the considered judgment of those bodies.

Second, Thompson made a point of exploring the definitions used – which in turn had informed the Report and its conclusions:

> This recommendation [Recommendation 3] and similar statements elsewhere in the report are likely to give a very erroneous impression. There are many social sciences such as economics, political science, psychology, etc, but apparently the Commission is using the term "social science" to mean sociology (and possibly anthropology). At any rate the other social sciences are well provided for. It is unfortunate that the Report gives the impression that the University has no social science departments. And last year by action of the Senate and Board of Governors a separate department of Sociology was established which will also provide for the related subject of anthropology. It was

established before the Commission's report was published. A department of Geography has also been established and appointments to it will be made next year.

The president sent the committee's report to Douglas on 28 April 1958, and received acknowledgment a few days later: "I think [your committee members] have done a very thorough job of examining the recommendations of the Royal Commission as they affect the University ... this material will be of great assistance to us in assessing the value of the Royal Commission's recommendations and what steps should be taken toward their implementation."[41]

The creation of the Centre for Community Studies did, however, become connected with the university decision to establish an independent sociology department. Thompson, Lloyd, and Bill Baker were the major members of a committee formed to appoint members to the centre. By coincidence, two candidates, Harold Baker and Richard DuWors, flew from Toronto to Saskatoon. Harold Baker was offered the position as head of the centre's consulting division. DuWors was instead asked to create a sociology department. As early as 1946, under Thompson's decanal authority, sociology had been added to "the list of subjects offered by the department of Economics and Political Science" with the appointment of an Instructor.[42] With the exception of McGill, which had established sociology in 1925, sociology in Canada had a limited history. By 1960, only three universities had established "independent departments of sociology," Carleton, McMaster, and Saskatchewan.[43] It was not until 1963 that the University of Toronto established a department of sociology, although courses were offered through other departments. In contrast, by the academic year 1952–53 Saskatchewan was offering three sociology courses.[44]

Nevertheless, funding for sociology and a sufficient number of courses in the Department of Economics and Political Science had been uncertain. The head of the department, George Britnell, urged Thompson early in 1950 not to sacrifice sociology at a time of severe university budgetary constraints because it was "widely recognized as an essential part of a well-rounded course in the social sciences" since its introduction three years previously. Approximately sixty students took the introductory course each year and seven or eight had taken each of the advanced classes that had been given. Majors in social work needed Sociology 1 as a prerequisite whereas other students took it as an "adjunct" to professional courses in nursing, education, and business administration.[45] Britnell's arguments prevailed, and a full-time sociologist was hired in 1951. But the creation of a separate department was delayed by continuing financial considerations. In 1954, Thompson was troubled by the high costs of the day, stating that the "University is at present unable to do many things which a good University in our position should do. For example we should have a veterinary college ... a dental college ... departments of sociology, geography, anthropology, and archaeology which we now lack."[46] By 1957, the university budget had increased sufficiently to create at least a sociology department.

Such fiscal improvement is why Thompson could refer to the forthcoming appointment of DuWors in a letter to the dean of education, J.B. Kirkpatrick. On 16 December 1957, Kirkpatrick had requested that the president allow him to meet Bill Baker with a view to instituting a course on "rural sociology" that would be of particular interest to students in education and could be offered by a member of the new Centre for Community Studies. Thompson replied the next day: "I think your idea of a course in rural sociology is an excellent one and I see no reason why you should not discuss it with Mr Baker." However, because the university was about to appoint a head for the new sociology department, Kirkpatrick should "bring the new Head into the picture no matter who gives the course."[47] In any case, the Board of Governors passed a budget for a department of sociology for 1958–59.[48]

Courses, workshops, and seminars for undergraduates at the Centre for Community Studies began in 1958 when Dr Darwin Solomon took over the training division and Arthur K. Davis took over the research division. One of the more important tasks of the Centre was to host workshops on subjects pertinent to rural life, such as the role of the church, the problems of population migration, and the partnering of six communities in the province that differed in nature and history. These gatherings must have gone a long way toward supporting Kirkpatrick's aim of gaining a rural sociologist.

Unfortunately, according to Davis, who was a neo-Marxist scholar, "the Centre was riven with conflict between its research wing which often wished to undertake 'politically sensitive research,' and a community development wing that favoured 'the sacred myth of gradualism,' so dear to the heart of 'second area liberals.'"[49] Another cause of bitter discord was the ideological differences between DuWors and Davis.[50] Whereas DuWors was influenced by the ideas of the American Harvard sociologist Talcott Parsons, who attempted to see society as a "holistic entity," Davis saw Marx as crucial to sociological theory. Moreover, there were personality differences between DuWors and Davis. Conflicts within the sociology department also plagued relations with the centre. Professor Ed Abramson was the second full-time faculty appointment in sociology.[51] Soon, however, Abrahamson and DuWors quarrelled bitterly, a dispute that eventually led to DuWors being relieved of the headship. In the meantime, Abramson's wife, Jane, along with Helen Buckley, soon became active members of the centre.

What then was the impact of the recommendations of the royal commission on the university? It has been argued that its recommendations jolted the president and the university into accepting the Centre for Community Studies and "various training programmes for municipal officials and others," and that the Baker recommendations accelerated university policy both in redeveloping counselling "to help prevent drop-outs" and in hiring more faculty members in the social sciences and humanities. "All in all, the report of the royal commission marked a turning point in the history of the University of Saskatchewan; it brought the social sciences and perhaps teacher-training to the university."[52] As Thompson's documents demonstrate, however, almost all the social science disciplines were available before Baker's recommendations, matching the other prairie provinces and equalling Queen's.

In a number of vital ways, Thompson and Baker viewed the issue of the social sciences at cross-purposes. Thompson, a realist who had to consider the overall needs of the university, could not possibly meet the royal commission's demands for additions to these fields on the ambitious scale recommended. Baker was concerned with "the needs of the rural economy over the next quarter century"[53] and saw the university "deficiency" as one "of quantity and not of quality." He claimed that the commission did not mean to imply that current faculty in social sciences were failing to perform their duties competently. Quoting from a UNESCO book on the social sciences, Baker argued that his commission was concerned with "the need for all of these disciplines ... economics, sociology, political science, social anthropology, and social psychology" to be developed and gathered together for administrative purposes. He was against merely tacking on "any single discipline such as sociology." Baker conceived of a large interdisciplinary grouping at a time when "interdisciplinary" had not become the byword it is today.

However much Bill Baker and Thompson differed on this social science issue, they continued to get on well together. Professor McCrorie, a retired sociologist and one-time research fellow at the centre, recalled: "From what I learned from Bill Baker and others, Thompson was both supportive of the Royal Commission on Agriculture and Rural Life and the establishment of the Centre. Bill, who was always discreet and diplomatic, would often recall, over coffee with the staff, fond memories of his association with Thompson. He seldom spoke of [later president] Spinks and when he did, his comments were always cautious and non-committal."[54] However, Harold Baker, who reported to President Spinks for a decade, believed that Spinks supported the centre and various forms of university outreach. Baker saw the president's dilemma as that of faculty politics and limited influence on overall direction.[55]

The diverse effects of the Baker commission and centre were, in many ways, constructive and groundbreaking. The commission, after all, "sponsored eighty community forums and nearly sixty public hearings" while surveying "hundreds of rural residents." The commission's findings and studies undertaken by the centre "provided a comprehensive snapshot of a society undergoing fundamental change."[56] The Douglas government acted with dispatch on some of the recommendations even though neither the provincial government nor the university had the powers and financial resources to implement many of the commission's recommendations. For example, the CCF implemented a program of crop insurance to help "stabilize" farm income.[57] The government also acted to improve roads and attempted to finish the rural electrification grid. On occasion, the centre seriously embarrassed the provincial government, especially its "Northern Study" that "documented, in chilling detail, the unwillingness of a social democratic government to challenge ... the constraints imposed on northern development by capital."[58] The centre accomplished much despite the fact that the research staff at the centre "did not share a common theoretical orientation to their work and their interests ... were diverse."[59]

The centre survived for only seven years after Thompson's retirement. The organization had always been viewed with scepticism and even outright hostility by certain individuals and groups in the province as "socialistic," and outside, as a distraction from the university's legitimate obligations and proper functions. In particular, the centre incurred the animosity of the one person in the province with the greatest potential to destroy it. Ross Thatcher, the leader of the provincial Liberal party after 1957 and premier from 1964 to 1971, despised the centre as ideologically socialist. While he was leader of the Opposition, Thatcher declared that when the Liberals came to power, he would cut the centre's budget allowance "to one dollar."[60] As premier, he abolished the centre in 1966.

Thompson regretted Thatcher's action. In his history of the university, Thompson wrote of the establishment of important research institutes that promoted co-operation between university departments and organizations "in the same or related fields." Good examples, he suggested, included "The Centre for Community Studies [as a] valuable institute which did excellent work but unfortunately lost its government support" because of Ross Thatcher's antipathy to it.[61]

President Spinks also came to view aspects of the centre sceptically, although he strongly supported Harold Baker's Extension activities. Baker undertook a number of important university initiatives, many of them after Ross Thatcher had dissolved the centre. For example, as director of university extension from 1963 to 1973 and then as the administrator of the Community and Rural Development Program (1974–94) he initiated the interdisciplinary Masters of Continuing Education degree program out of the College of Education and created the Saskatchewan Committee for Rural Area Development.

Persistent problems with DuWors had soured some members of the College of Arts and Science on the Centre. So had the demands of Bill Baker and Arthur Davis's Marxist ideology. The dean of medicine, Wendell Macleod, was a member of the centre's board. When he and Bill Baker approached Spinks to "negotiate the position of the CCS on campus, the president was anything but enthusiastic ... In a letter written in the summer of 1961, he objected to some of Macleod's remarks ... suggesting that some of them 'were the same as the German views leading to communism and then Hitler [and could] lead to the loss of our medical centre.'"[62]

Spinks' remarks may have resulted more from his dislike of Dean Macleod than any antipathy toward the centre, but Harold Baker remembered Spinks with regard and affection.

During the 20 years of his tenure, ten years as dean of arts and science, and ten years as president, Thompson created many courses and departments, with a new emphasis on research. He introduced and nurtured foreign student programs. He believed student rights should not be constrained by the university, as shown by his firmness in advancing women's rights on campus. He fostered a cordial relationship with the CCF government, thereby ensuring a steady increase in university funding. His Extension department highlights his commitment to the citizens of the province. Thompson reinforced the ideal of the institution as the people's university.

7

Unfinished Business

I

Closely related to the future of farm life in Saskatchewan was the need for professional services beyond those provided through the College of Agriculture or the university's agricultural extension program. Recognizing this, in 1909 in his first president's report, Dr Murray had called for a college of veterinary science decades before it became a reality. But it was not until 1963 that an agreement was reached between the four western provinces and the federal government to build a college to serve those provinces. Although courses in veterinary diseases were being taught in the College of Agriculture by 1913 and an animal disease lab was established in 1924, and there was public support for a veterinary college, it could not override the disastrous effects of the Depression. Yet the University of Saskatchewan had one of the leading veterinary scientists in Canada, Dr J.S. Fulton, head of the veterinary sciences department from 1930 where among other discoveries, he gained fame by developing vaccines to prevent western equine encephalitis. With sounder economic conditions emerging by 1944, the western universities, their provincial governments, and the federal government realized that the veterinary colleges in Ontario and Quebec were not supplying the West with enough graduates. Representatives from the provinces and the federal government held an interprovincial conference to discuss the possibilities of situating such a college at the University of Saskatchewan. The university, however, believed that it was imperative to fund a medical school, an arts building, and a proper library before undertaking the expense of establishing a veterinary college.[1]

The issue of whether or not to establish a veterinary college at Saskatchewan to serve all four western universities only came to the forefront during Thompson's presidency, particularly in his final three years. The prolonged debates over the proposed college graphically illustrate the depth and intensity of the conflicting demands, and the differing priorities that an especially active president like Thompson confronted.

In February 1951, Thompson told the Saskatchewan Cattle Breeders' Association, a powerful lobby in the province, that nothing had altered since the university senate resolution of November 1946, which stated that the "needs of Saskatchewan do not justify the establishment of a Veterinary College at the University." Moreover, the Board of Governors was "unable to place the Veterinary College in a position of high priority," especially before "such needs as a Library have been met."[2] All the same, the veterinary college issue was soon to lead to many meetings and often heated debates.

On 4 September 1956, the Board of Governors passed a resolution reversing the negative approach of five years earlier. Board members resolved "that a study of the establishment of a College of Veterinary Medicine at this University be approved and that the president be asked to name the persons to make the study." Thompson appointed Dr V.E. Graham, dean of agriculture, to make a study of the needs of local veterinarians and to obtain any necessary technical assistance from them. Graham went about his task thoroughly and reported to the board and to the senate on 9 May 1957.

What had changed the minds of the members of the Board of Governors between 1951 and 1956? There were three factors. A major cause of the shift in opinion was that it had become clear that Saskatchewan confronted serious problems because it had too few veterinarians. About fifteen had left the province in the previous eight years, presumably for higher salaries elsewhere. Second, although Saskatchewan had fifty practising veterinarians, investigators discovered that twenty organized veterinary service districts were unable to obtain their services. Third, the province was richer in livestock than generally assumed. After Alberta, with $310,000,000 worth of livestock, Saskatchewan followed with $200,000,000, in other words one veterinarian for each $4,000,000 worth of livestock on Saskatchewan farms.[3] In contrast, the US was much better provided for: Maryland, for example, had one doctor for every $906,000 worth of livestock. Graham estimated that the western provinces needed about 350 veterinarians to cope with animal diseases, seven times the current number. His arguments led the senate to mandate the forward planning committee to analyze the Graham report further, and to study resolutions from the Alberta and Canadian Veterinary Associations. However, after three meetings, on 20 November 1957 the University Council rejected the planning committee's recommendation as too expensive.

In December, Thompson entered the debate once again. After noting that the senate had appealed to Council to reconsider the question of founding a veterinary college, he appointed a committee from the executive council, chaired by Balfour Currie, head of Physics, to do an additional study.[4] Currie was an able negotiator and an academic Thompson trusted fully. In the president's estimation, Currie was a stronger personality and his judgment more acute than Graham's. At meetings of Currie's committee on 31 December 1957 and 31 January 1958, discussion ranged widely for and against the proposed college. They ended with general agreement that the new college should only be proceeded with if the university was assured that no priorities for existing colleges for facilities and staff would be adversely affected.

Late in January 1958, President Andrew Stewart of the University of Alberta convened a meeting in Edmonton of representatives of the four western universities, the four provincial departments of agriculture, and the four western veterinary associations to investigate the need for a western veterinary college. The arrangements for this meeting had been negotiated during a telephone conversation earlier in January 1958 between Thompson and Stewart.[5] The meeting concluded that there was "immediate need" for such a college and that "the need will continue to increase."[6] Such an increase was inevitable, particularly since the research needs of western Canada could not be met by increasing the facilities of the Ontario Veterinary College in Guelph, where enrolment was already "considerably above the averages for colleges in the United States and Great Britain." Yet, as Currie noted at that time, each western provincial government "seemed determined to let another absorb the capital and maintenance costs."[7]

Then, on 28 April 1958, at the suggestion of Alberta's minister of agriculture, Thompson met with Stewart and representatives of the veterinary associations. Thompson encouraged Stewart to take the initiative, since the Council at the University of Saskatchewan had rejected the proposal for a veterinary college in Saskatoon. Inter-university discussions continued and on 12 December 1958, Thompson asked Currie to continue as a representative despite the fact that it would be "a long time yet before anyone can give definite commitments. We could not give them on behalf of the Board of Governors until the matter is taken up with the government and they give us the green light. While we have informed the government in a general way that consideration is being given to the establishment of a veterinary college, we would need to have definite details before we could ask them for a commitment."[8] Currie then attended another veterinary college meeting in Edmonton on 30 January 1959.[9] Once again, the arrangements for this meeting had been negotiated during a telephone conversation between Thompson and Stewart.

Thompson called a special meeting of the Council on 12 March 1959 to discuss Currie's report of the Edmonton meeting. By this time, the issue of where to situate a veterinary college had come down to Alberta or Saskatchewan. As Thompson informed Council, "Manitoba and British Columbia were not interested in establishing a Veterinary College."[10] In his last annual report in 1959, Thompson stated that the question of establishing a veterinary college at Saskatchewan, for which "there appears to be little doubt about the need," would not proceed at this time "in view of other pressing needs of this university."[11] Premier Douglas must have told Thompson at the time that it was impossible to build a veterinary college. In a letter to the president on 27 July 1959, Douglas acknowledged "the urgency of the need for such an educational facility in the interests of the livestock industry of Western Canada." Nevertheless, the government of Saskatchewan "did not feel that at this time the College should be developed on our own campus," particularly since the premier believed "that the Alberta authorities have indicated a readiness to proceed in this matter."[12] Douglas must have been unaware that both the University of Alberta and the Alberta government hoped that Saskatchewan would undertake the project.

Only in early 1962, after Thompson's retirement, did the universities of Saskatchewan and Alberta reopen the question of whether to press for a veterinary college and where to locate it. By this time, the Honourable Alvin Hamilton, minister of agriculture in the Diefenbaker cabinet, favoured locating the college in Saskatchewan. President Spinks wrote to Colb McEown, then in England, that the veterinary issue was "quite a hot topic, here." But federal government financing was essential.[13] With Hamilton's influence, Ottawa provided $100,000 to start up the college at the University of Saskatchewan. Since both Diefenbaker and Hamilton's parliamentary seats were in Saskatchewan ridings, they may well have been predisposed toward helping with the financing.

In 1963, a committee of three specialists, led by the dean of the prestigious veterinary college at Washington State University and two other men, one from the University of British Columbia and the other from the University of Manitoba, decided that the college should be in Saskatchewan. The keys in arriving at this judgment were the assistance of the federal grant and the fact that Saskatchewan would have the complete school under one roof, whereas Alberta would divide the facility, "with the clinical teaching at the University Farm that would be half a mile from the main University where the buildings for the basic and pre-clinical sciences would be located. This consideration was critical in the decision of the committee." Moreover, the premier of Alberta, Ernest Manning, rejected the idea of a veterinary college in Alberta, alleging that the cost could possibly make it a "white elephant."[14] After the federal government promised capital support of 25 per cent and the Saskatchewan government offered to commit $1 million if the other three provinces agreed to share the operating costs, the university had the authority to begin recruiting staff for the Western College of Veterinary Science.[15] The first classes were held in 1965. Although the college did not begin its work until after Thompson had retired, he had played an essential role in getting it started.

Another sphere of professional training, and Thompson's one great frustration, was the failure "to see the training of all teachers transferred to the University during my administration."[16] Although the academic side of teacher training echoed all the same issues Thompson had with scholarship in the humanities, he laid the groundwork for the development of a four-year education degree for all prospective teachers. The College of Education was founded in 1928 to train teachers for the province's high schools. Its "dual mandate was to prepare university graduates to teach in secondary schools and to conduct research in education."[17] Elementary school teachers were trained in what were called normal schools, or "teachers' colleges," as they were designated after 1953. This dual tradition co-existed until 1964.

Previously, if a student with a degree from another college, usually arts and science, wanted to teach, he or she could enroll in a one-year university program for training in the "methods and practice of teaching with a minimum of educational theory, history, and psychology."[18] Significant changes were introduced in 1947, when a four-year program was started to train students for all grades up to and including Grade 12. Yet much time was still spent on teaching methods and practice teaching rather than academic courses. The lack of a full academic program aroused much criticism, not only from Thompson but from many other faculty and students, who lamented the program's lack of intellectual rigour. The education curriculum led to the prevailing belief, held by Thompson, many other academics, and members of the public, that education degrees were of secondary quality and that teachers were weak academically. Thompson explained his reasoning in a 1959 address, when he argued that "teachers perhaps more than other professions, require the broad education which can best be acquired in university. In addition, it would bring teachers in training in close contact with other kinds of students and it might give the profession needed prestige."[19]

Thompson's failure to transfer teacher training to the university was not the result of any lack of interest on his part, for he immersed himself in the politics of the issue and in the literature about teacher training. At the College of Education dinner in February 1953, he commented:

> Educational literature is ... repetitious, [full] of platitudes, clichés, and slogans. The usual procedure is that someone proposes an idea or criticism or pronounces a fine sounding phrase, and then everyone rushes in and kicks it around for a year or two, when it is forgotten. A slogan is a godsend to an educator who is to make a speech or write a paper – and today they do an immense amount of both. During the last couple of years the most fashionable kind of educational writing has been violently critical. In fact the amount and violence of the criticism of education have become disturbing.[20]

The president went on to list the kinds of "faults and shortcomings" of teacher training in the province, criticisms that led to "a whole page of articles in the *Star Phoenix*" and then listed what he saw as the replies of educators, which were "equally numerous and varied." Finally, he concluded:

> One of the deplorable results of the controversy is the widening of the gulf between the professors of pedagogy and the professors of academic subjects. These two groups have always been at war. In some places and at some times a truce is declared. But the truce generally takes the form of a nasty kind of cold war to which we have become accustomed to in other circumstances. And too frequently it flares into a violent, shooting war. The chief bone of contention is the old one of methods versus content.[21]

Thompson recalled his frustrations over the lack of proper educational research in a letter to his heir apparent, John Spinks, when commenting on a draft speech Spinks was preparing to deliver.

> You are likely to be criticized for referring only to the state's needs of professional people, and not making a bow in the direction of general liberal education ... You might refer specifically (before that audience) to the need of research in professional education. I have been much impressed in my search for a dean of education (twice) at the nearly complete absence of educational research in Canada. And in the Quance Lectureship Committee I have tried every year to get the other members (who are professional educators) to name a good research man whom we could get to lecture. And they never are able to do so, with the exception of Jackson of Toronto, and we couldn't get him. Educators do a lot of writing but it is never based on original studies. (My own assessment of the reason is that there are very few real scholars in professional education.)[22]

Thompson recalled these debates in his history of the university, published early in 1970. Most teachers as well as the Teachers' Federation supported the proposal whereas the staffs of the normal schools and most officials of the department of education opposed it. Woodrow Lloyd, the minister of education, as well as the deputy minister Allan MacCallum, were firmly against transferring all the training to the university. Lloyd had found his time in normal school one when "he blossomed socially and intellectually." Moreover, Lloyd believed that Hilda Neatby's criticisms in *So Little for the Mind* (1953), which poured ridicule on modern educational ideas and educators, were profoundly disturbing. Why, he argued, train teachers under faculty who espoused such old-fashioned ideas?[23] So, despite Thompson's ambitions for teacher training, this responsibility was not transferred to the university until 1964.

II

One of the most significant and controversial decisions Thompson made came at the end of his presidency. In July 1959, he pushed through Council and the senate the decision permitting Regina College to establish a full undergraduate degree program. In so doing, he completely reversed the university's hitherto adamantine refusal, previously reinforced by his own persistent opposition, to grant the college independent authority. Why exactly Thompson made this decision is still debated today. Now, with some new evidence, his reasons are reasonably clear.

What was but dimly grasped by university leaders in Canada and elsewhere in the mid- to late-1950s, after the veteran enrolment phenomenon had passed, was the inexorably rising tide of future university enrolments. Nineteen-fifty-five was the beginning of startling, largely reliable enrolment projections with the coming of age of the Canadian postwar baby boom – a boom developed in the United States earlier.[24] That year, Dr Edward F. Sheffield, from the education division of the Bureau of Dominion Statistics, published an analysis that dramatically demonstrated the extent of the future crisis facing Canadian universities. "This report, commissioned by the National Conference of Canadian Universities, the Sheffield Report, linked public-school enrolments to the future of higher education, and warned that enrolments could double in the next decade."[25] Even this forecast proved too low, and Sheffield soon extended his statistics through 1962–64 and then to 1974, and showed that enrolments would quadruple by that time.[26] Thompson immediately understood the significance of Sheffield's projections for the 1960s and commissioned him to do a special survey of Saskatchewan that was published for the university two months after the national report. As Thompson digested the study, and examined a further letter from Sheffield, he wrote an additional sentence: "It is evident that the projection was much too conservative."[27] Thompson thereafter remained deeply troubled by the significance of the Sheffield Report. Sheffield's projection was borne out: from 1956 to 1965, university enrolment increased nationally from 64,200 to 178,200 as a consequence of the baby boom, and the increasing conviction among young people and their parents that higher education was a birthright, not a privilege.[28] Despite the obvious problems associated with increased enrolment, because of limited budget increases Thompson believed "no part of Canada compares favourably with the United States." In the US, one student out of seventy went on to higher education. In contrast, Saskatchewan boasted only a single student for every 358 persons of university age in the province. In fact, Saskatchewan had fewer university students than any other province except Prince Edward Island and Newfoundland. In Canada as a whole, "the ratio is one to 232." The president noted that if Saskatchewan had the same ratio of students as the United States did, the enrolment would be 10,000 rather than "a few hundred more than 2,000." Though he was confident that the achievements of Saskatchewan's graduates were "not excelled elsewhere," Thompson lamented the small number of students at the University of Saskatchewan. Barely half of those eligible to go to university attended, compared with students in the rest of Canada. Part of the problem was that, while there was "much evidence of esteem and goodwill for the University ... there is also much evidence of ignorance regarding it."[29]

Pressed by sharply increasing enrolment projections that the University of Saskatchewan could not accommodate, expanding Regina College now seemed sensible, especially since by the late 1950s both the premier and the minister of education had come to that conclusion too. Other provincial opinion leaders were also aware of Sheffield's alarming projections of rising enrolments, which meant that the problems of inadequate faculty and facilities would "far outweigh those accompanying the veteran deluge."[30] These projections "jolted the academic community and the Government into recognizing the magnitude of the problems awaiting them in the 1960s."[31] Thompson emphasized the new situation in his 1958–59 annual report. He noted that "conditions have changed greatly since 1954," with the most important development being the projected "great and continuing increase in the number of students and the resulting decision to limit the size of the student body at Saskatoon" to 7,500 students by 1964–65, with an additional 400–500 graduate students.[32] For the academic year 1958–59, full-time enrolment was approximately 4,110, an increase of nearly 500 over the previous year, despite the fact that the the 18–21-year-old age group was not increasing. Moreover, "enrolment has increased nearly 15% *each year* for the past five years."[33] In spite of this enrolment increase, the population of Saskatchewan remained static, and the creation of a four-year program in Regina was, arguably more a political decision than an educational need. After peaking at 931,000 in 1936, the population fell until the mid-1980s, when it barely passed one million, before slipping back below a million. Only by 2011 did the population, barely, surpass one million. In contrast, British Columbia has reached four million and Alberta over three million; even Manitoba has increased its population to over one million people.

The relationship between the University of Saskatchewan and Regina College had always been fraught, starting with the board decision in 1908 to favour Saskatoon as the site for the university, rankling many in Regina. In 1911, the Methodist Church established Regina College as a one-year institution, and in 1925 the college became affiliated with the University of Saskatchewan as a junior college, This status meant that the college could offer students the first year of the three-year bachelor of arts program before they transferred to Saskatoon to finish the degree.[34] During 1929–30, Regina College developed plans to present courses that would proceed to a full BA, a proposal that was rejected by the university. The new premier, Anderson, stated that in time the junior colleges could receive degree-granting authority, even though Regina College, the largest, was in chronic financial difficulties. However, all plans for junior college expansion were suspended during the Depression, and Regina College fell badly into debt to the point of bankruptcy.

This fiscal crisis led to extended negotiations between the college and the university, resulting in the university taking over the entire assets of the college in 1934 and assuming all its debts.[35] A grant of $50,000 from the Carnegie Foundation enabled the university to acquire Regina College, thereby ensuring central control of higher education in the province and temporarily appeasing Regina citizens still angry over of the decision to put the provincial university in Saskatoon.

The RCAF took over Regina College's buildings from 1940 to 1944, but under the aegis of the university the institution survived, adding first-year engineering in 1945 and first-year commerce in 1947. In

1952, a Regina College Citizens' Committee was formed to lobby for a full degree program. Any such degree would have to be granted in Saskatoon, because the University Act of 1907 gave the University of Saskatchewan sole degree-granting power in the province, except for theology. Earlier, in 1952, both Woodrow Lloyd and a prominent member of the university Board of Governors, Regina lawyer E.C. Leslie, told Thompson that they did not see "much of a threat ... in the agitation."[36] Both men were wrong. On 19 March 1954, the Regina College Citizens' Committee launched its campaign for a full arts program. Lloyd asked Thompson how the university viewed the request. Thompson replied that after an intensive study, both "the Board of Governors and the Senate voted unanimously that approval not be given" and enclosed a memorandum explaining the university's reasons.[37] There were three. First, the college had not been underfunded since 1934 as many Regina citizens claimed, but had actually received more than its share of provincial and federal grants. Second, the young people of the province were better served by a single strong university than by several small weak colleges around the province. If Regina had a full program, other cities in the province would also want one, thereby wrecking the ideal of one first-class university. Finally, Regina residents were well served by the kind of college that they already had. Despite this decision, the Regina Citizens' Committee was determined to continue its campaign and in the fall of 1954, Regina's mayor Leslie Hammond, on behalf of the committee, lobbied the CCF cabinet, arguing that Regina College needed and deserved to be a degree-granting institution.[38]

The situation worsened on 28 April 1955 when Dean Leddy mishandled a public debate in Regina on the full-degree program issue. Leddy, whose position as dean of arts and science also made him the university spokesman for the provincial junior colleges, expressed the university's position that Regina and other out-of-town students were not unduly "out-of-pocket" by having to pay room and board in Saskatoon. Unfortunately, that claim, plus Leddy's allegation that his debating opponent made "reckless and irresponsible statements," served only to weaken the university's case. Some present believed Leddy's remarks had angered the audience, although Leddy's memory was quite different: "On one occasion I was delegated to attend a public meeting in Regina to withstand the local pressure for a full degree program, a rather gruesome assignment in which I did the best I could, but changed no minds."[39]

In fact, the unrest was much more intense than Leslie and Lloyd had stated, as the dean of Regina College, William Riddell, warned Thompson on 2 August 1955. Riddell told the president that the Trades and Labour Councils of Regina and Moose Jaw, representing groups "whose opinions counted with the CCF government," supported creating a degree program in Regina, going so far as to send briefs to the premier. The briefs argued that paying board away from home unduly burdened students who were not economically privileged. Impressed by such claims, Douglas underlined this sentence and other statements in his copy.[40]

Such economic arguments carried greater weight with many CCF politicians and others involved in the controversy than the arguments of University of Saskatchewan's advocates for a single provincial campus offering unrivalled provincial library and lab opportunities. What good were such facilities, the Trades and Labour Councils countered, if students could not afford to leave home to attend the university in Saskatoon? Moreover, as the prospects of much larger enrolments loomed from the pressures of the baby boom, the opposition to a degree program in Regina became increasingly unsustainable. There was also the argument that by the 1950s many people throughout North America had come to see that a university education had become far more attractive to young people than ever before, whether as a road to the middle class, as a means to advance in science and technological pursuits, or as a necessary requirement for employment in the expanding white-collar world. Finally, there was the fact that other provinces were establishing new universities in new urban locations. Through all the discussions and concerns over the need to create new universities, Thompson consistently urged that duplication be avoided and that cooperation, not rivalry, was the best way to proceed. According to Willson Woodside, a knowledgeable assessor of Canadian universities, this argument against duplication met "with a magnanimous attitude on the part of other Western universities."[41]

Late in 1956, Thompson attempted to mollify advocates of the expansion of Regina College when he addressed an alumni group in the city. He claimed that he was not going to speak about the dispute. Indeed, "his great regret in the whole affair" was that the controversy had "deprived the University of that goodwill ... on the part of a number – I hope a small number – of the citizens of Regina." Instead, he intended to focus on the degree to which Regina College was an "integral and important part of the university." He noted that six of the fourteen board members lived in Regina whereas only five lived in Saskatoon. In addition, he praised the two deputy ministers who sat on the board as "remarkably able and devoted," both graduates of the University of Saskatchewan. Thompson went on to extol at great length the university's recent achievements, achievements that he believed redounded to the benefit of Regina and the entire province. He praised the new medical college and hospital and noted that *Science,* the leading peer-reviewed scientific journal in North America, had ranked the university eighth on the continent in 1954 "among the 1,860 institutions ... in its production of distinguished scientists."[42]

However enlightening to the Regina alumni, Thompson's speech did nothing to stem the demand in the city and surrounding area for a full degree program at Regina College. In early 1957, Regina alderman Alex Jupp claimed publicly that Regina "is the only city in Canada of comparable size without a degree course for its young people," many of whom could not afford to pay for board and room in Saskatoon. This became an oft-repeated theme by the city's lobby groups, disregarding the fact that students from elsewhere in the province had to pay those expenses.[43] By late 1958 and throughout the spring of 1959, it was becoming clear that influential people at the university and in the provincial government, however reluctantly in many cases, had recognized the political reasons for accepting a full degree program in Regina.

At the same time, Thompson and others on the Board of Governors were considering the problems of funding. The impetus for this came from "the inability of the province to provide the extra funds" for a five-year building program "valued at approximately 14 million dollars." For example, late in 1958, the provincial government refused to accept the Board of Governors' request for an additional $750,000. The board had requested these funds to meet the university's "urgent needs" for capital grants to upgrade – ironically – "engineering extension, physical education, food services, and residences, rooms and laboratories at Regina College."[44] The unprecedented student enrolment also had an effect on the Saskatoon campus buildings and infrastructure. The university was forced to shift its priorities for capital construction from a proposed auditorium and residence "in favour of teaching buildings," when even the 1954 enrolment forecast for 1957–58 of 2,681 full-time students had been proven low: "the actual enrolment was 3,637."[45]

Thompson turned to the president of the only fundraising company in Canada, George A. Brakeley. The company had been formed in the United States as World War I was ending and had begun its fundraising with a successful campaign for Harvard, launching the era of large-scale fundraising in America. Brakeley founded a subsidiary in Canada in 1950, the first such organization in the country. In 1951, Brakeley had written Thompson asking him to provide figures on the university's endowments because the company was gathering data on all Canadian universities.

In January 1957, the Board of Governors received a letter from the Brakeley Company "offering its fund-raising services to the University."[46] Despite the growing reputation of the company in Canadian university circles, the board moved cautiously. According to a letter from the vice-president of the Brakeley Company, early in June 1958 the director of the alumni office, Frank Lovell, asked the company to submit a proposal for a "study or survey" for the University of Saskatchewan Foundation. That led the company to contact Thompson directly on 6 November 1958.

Lovell appears to have acted so proactively because sometime during late 1958, McEown left the university for two months, leaving Lovell as his temporary replacement as secretary to the Board of Governors. According to Lloyd Barber, former president of the University of Regina, the board had commissioned McEown to assess the University of California system of universities and the New York system to evaluate just how effectively a state-wide university system worked. His roving commission results led the board to conclude that two universities of 10,000 students each was a better educational design for the province than a single university with 20,000 students.[47]

However accurate Barber's assessment is, there is no doubt that for a time late in 1958 and early 1959, Lovell was closely involved in considering the wisdom of inviting the Brakeley Company to assist the university in raising money. On 5 January 1959, he reported to the board that he had sent a questionnaire to twelve Canadian universities and presented a chart distilling their replies: whether they had conducted a fundraising campaign recently and whether they recommended and had employed a professional organization to carry out their campaign. Lovell's results demonstrated that several universities had employed Brakeley to carry out a pre-fundraising survey and pre-campaign planning, to manage the fundraising campaign and the University of Toronto was preparing to employ them.[48]

The Board of Governors was already preparing for a fundraising campaign. At its meeting of 10 December 1958, the board created a seven-man fund solicitation committee with specified terms of reference. Herb Pinder was chairman and Frank Lovell the acting secretary. Among the committee's recommendations was a strong suggestion for a capital campaign. Second, the committee urged the board to establish building priorities. Third, the committee recommended that the Brakeley Company be invited to assess, plan, and manage the jubilee year capital campaign, an effort to raise funds for a new library and arts building, the first time the university had ever fundraised through a private firm. The committee noted, "The Brakeley firm. ... is the only firm considered to have the necessary Canadian university and industrial knowledge and experience required."[49]

After returning to his position at the university in mid-January 1959, McEown quickly began negotiating with the Brakeley firm "to discuss ... a proposal for a capital campaign this year." The company outlined their policy – to carry out a preliminary survey to "determine the basis for a campaign"[50] – which was agreed to, "for the fee to be $5,500 including expenses." A meeting was set for early February;[51] in the meantime, Brakeley sent fifteen copies of its detailed, thirteen-page questionnaire to the university.

While these discussions were underway, both the provincial government and Thompson himself began to suggest expanding university programs beyond Saskatoon. On 30 December 1958, Woodrow Lloyd sent a memo to the premier suggesting that, because of the large projected increases in enrolment at the University of Saskatchewan, the time had come to discuss with the president the matter of expanding university facilities at Regina College. Lloyd wondered "if we ought not to be discussing it with the President. I have not put this idea forth to anyone else."[52] A few months later, at an alumni banquet on 7 May 1959, Thompson alluded publicly to the need for expansion, reflecting that, given the doubling of the enrolment at the university over the past six years, it might be desirable to "develop branches in other centres. There will no doubt be strong differences of opinion about when that stage is reached."[53]

Early in May 1959, the Board of Governors received the preliminary Brakeley report and met with Brakeley representatives. The

Brakeley company stated that "there was a reasonable chance for success for a capital campaign for an objective of $2,500,000 provided the four following conditions were met."

First, there had to be proper timing. November 1959 was best, for then the impact of the jubilee year on "Saskatchewan and Canada" would be evident. Second, the university would have to provide appropriate leadership. Third, the provincial government's commitment had to be sustained over five years to provide financial resources "as generously as in the past" and match the money raised in the fundraising campaign dollar for dollar. Finally, "the Brakeley Company stressed very strongly with regard to the timing of the campaign that a strong statement regarding the policy for Regina was needed at this time."[54] The company emphasized this point. "The University's arguments will probably never be accepted since the Regina proponents' main argument is: Regina is bigger than Saskatoon therefore Regina should have a university of its own so Regina citizens are spared the burden of sending their sons and daughters to Saskatoon for University study beyond the first year."[55]

The company's clear meaning was that it was essential that Regina College be granted a degree program if more revenue for both the University of Saskatchewan and the Regina Campus was to be raised. This assessment showed that for the fundraising campaigners to be successful, the university would need resources not only from Regina but also from the south of the province. The Brakeley assessors also commented favourably on the university in general, including the shift in emphasis in Saskatoon over the past decade "from undergraduate teaching to graduate teaching and research," and listed the seven major research institutions sited on the campus. In addition, the assessors highlighted the "impressive" physical facilities, emphasizing that the campus was "the second largest in Canada, [after the University of British Columbia] comprising some 2,650 acres fronting along the Saskatchewan River for two miles."[56]

With such a significant recommendation at hand, the board decided that the related questions of "the limit of enrolment at the Saskatoon campus and the development of Regina College be referred to the Forward Planning Committee," to report its conclusions as soon as possible. After meeting on 20 May, then on 15 and 16 June, the forward planning committee proposed the following measures. The recommended optimum enrolment for the Saskatoon campus should be 7,500, which would be reached by 1964–65. This would mean that significantly increasing residence capacity, better food services, and expanding the facilities and programs of many of the departments would be essential. Finally, the committee also recommended that a three-year degree program be instituted at Regina College.[57] Thompson noted these recommendations in his annual report.

The Board of Governors meeting on 17 June 1959 decided on a number of these important issues, deciding first to proceed "with a fund solicitation campaign with an objective of $2,500,000 and that G.A. Brakeley and Company Limited must be employed as professional counsel ... to appraise the situation."

Board member Justice E.M. Culliton was chosen to chair both the university jubilee and fundraising committees. He was ideally suited: he had been active in assisting the St Thomas More College fundraising campaign, had practised law in the south of the province, was highly regarded in Regina as a Liberal, and was a former cabinet minister who was a good friend of Premier Douglas. By this time, the University of Saskatchewan planners had set their sights on far more money than the $750,000 requested from the government. The jubilee fundraising campaign set certain precedents for the university. It was the first such venture to be carried out by an outside professional company and the goals were much greater in scope than in any previous campaigns. For example, the Memorial Gates, opened in 1928, raised $40,000, largely donated by students and alumni. Although the 1947 fund-raising drives for the Murray Library and the Memorial Union Building suffered because of "confusion and conflict" between the two campaigns,[58] the Murray Library campaign had raised $225,000 from the general public, industry, and business.

Finally, the board resolved that, given the high enrolment estimates, it appeared desirable "to offer a three-year degree course in Arts and Science at Regina as soon as possible." The board then decided to call the above-mentioned senate meeting on the morning of 8 July to consider the recommendation.[59] It was also announced at the same meeting that the provincial government had agreed to match "dollar for dollar" contributions to the university fundraising campaign without reducing its "usual support for capital expenditures at the University." This assurance, to be backed up in a formal letter from Premier Douglas, may have been an aspect of the *quid pro quo* between the government, which now desired the expansion of Regina College, and the University of Saskatchewan, which had for so long opposed a degree program in Regina.

First, however, the board's recommendation had to be considered and voted on by Council before taking the resolution to the senate. As Dean Riddell recalled, "the announcement of the special meetings of council and senate to consider the extension of University work in Regina came as a complete surprise to the Regina College faculty." Since even Riddell had not been told what the board was planning, he expected "little in the development of the new program in Regina." Nevertheless, the subject of both the council and senate meetings was "exciting both for the vigorous discussions and because of the expectation of new developments in Regina ... Naturally, a significant number of the faculty in Saskatoon objected," for they feared there would be "wasteful duplication."[60]

On 6 July, with Thompson chairing the meeting, council approved the board's recommendation, despite the fact that there was no quorum, a point raised by George Britnell.[61] Two days later, on 8 July, the senate met, with McEown helping to explain the policy issue. The senate was required to "receive the advice of Council" but it did not have to accept it. Riddell has provided the only account so far found of the nature of the Senate debate that day.

Rusty Macdonald, executive editor of the *Western Producer* and a respected senate member, questioned Thompson as to why he, while previously "adamantly opposed to any expansion ... beyond the first year Arts and Science" had "now reversed his position." Thompson replied with "his pipe cocked up to the highest point possible and he quietly but very firmly pointed out that when new information or new needs arose, he could and would change his position and hoped it would always be so."[62] As Riddell recalled,

> The Recommendation was forwarded to Senate for approval and the discussion there was one of the best ever heard by members of that body. Normally the meetings resulted in perfunctory discussions because members lacked information about the issues being considered, nor did they understand the implications. To a large extent they merely provided a rubber stamp of approval to the requests of Council. However, in this case there was a wide-ranging consideration of the implications for students, the province, and society at large, as well as the attitude of government.[63]

Again, according to Riddell, "the earlier [fundraising] campaign[s] ... had produced very little response from the citizens and corporations in Regina. The emphasis on this aspect engendered in the minds of many people in the academic field both in Saskatoon and Regina a belief that the decision [to grant Regina College a full degree program] was based on political necessity rather than academic need."[64]

Thompson believed that it was necessary to proceed at once. He called for a vote to support the resolution allowing Regina College to develop a degree program. According to the senate minutes, "during the discussion, the question was raised concerning two universities ... It was pointed out that Regina College was part of the University of Saskatchewan and would not be a separate university under the proposed expansion program."[65] Students from the Regina campus continued to receive their degrees from the University of Saskatchewan until 1974, when the establishment of the University of Regina created two separate universities in the province. But in his annual report of 1958–59, Thompson never speculated about the eventuality of two separate universities. "Expansion beyond a full arts course at Regina is not at present contemplated ... Possibly in time a full southern branch or the university will be developed but that is not likely to take place soon."[66]

Thompson's motives for recommending the adoption of a degree program at Regina College are not difficult to surmise. The Brakeley firm had noted that Regina in 1959 was wealthier and more populous than Saskatoon. In their report, the Brakeley assessors noted that in the spring of 1959 the population of Saskatoon was approximately 75,000 whereas Regina's was about 90,000. Furthermore, they commented that "Saskatoon is not noted ... for giving to community campaigns" and hence "*Saskatoon's level of giving will have to be raised.*" By contrast, Regina "has a much more impressive record of philanthropic support ... A substantial measure of support for the University will, understandably, be sought in Regina."[67] This disparity in wealth and traditions of philanthropy has been noted by Herb Pinder, who in 1959 was a member of the Board of Governors in Saskatoon and a highly successful businessman who understood the financial realities of the province.[68] A committee composed of the forward planning committee, the Board of Governors and a faculty council committee met on 6 July 1959 and were informed "no Regina, no money."[69] Regardless, the Brakeley report listed a tentative objective for personal gifts at $40,000 from Regina, and $60,000 from Saskatoon contributors.[70]

Writing many years later, Leddy commented on Thompson's sudden change of policy. "Throughout the early years of the Presidency of W.P. Thompson, he and others in Saskatoon were adamantly opposed to any development of Regina College beyond the junior years ... Not long before his retirement Thompson abruptly reversed his previous stance ... His announcement, to that effect, was a shock to all of the administrative officers in Saskatoon.[71]

Leddy was away and therefore unable to attend the Council meeting on 6 July 1959 and the subsequent senate meeting on 8 July 1959 to discuss the question of a degree program for Regina.[72] The dean protested that the Regina College "overall situation has not changed substantially" since 1955 when the government and the board at the University of Saskatchewan had rejected the appeal for a full degree program. He warned that a "number of the ... Faculty of Arts and Science have spoken to me expressing their anxiety about what they regard as an unexpected and an abrupt reversal of policy ... on rather short notice." Leddy concluded that, in his opinion, "expansion was not a practical or desirable development for some years to come." Furthermore, Leddy was responsible for the junior colleges. "As the relevant Dean, with academic jurisdiction over Regina College, I was astounded to learn that without reference to me, or to other appropriate academic advisors, W.P. had gone ahead, on his own, and made decisive commitments in 1959 on future developments in Regina."[73]

Thompson's reversal of his former position on Regina College dismayed and exasperated the Faculty Association. Members expressed their irritation in their "Report of the University of Saskatchewan Faculty Association Committee on Faculty Participation in University Government," written by the Association chairman R.N.H. Haslam, completed on 16 March 1960, and submitted to the new president, John Spinks and to former president Thompson.

> Members will be aware of the ... despatch with which Council executed a major reversal of policy towards Regina College in July 1959. This action was taken without full information at Council's disposal (much less a study by a committee of Council), without more than a few days' notice of motion of the proposed change, and – in view of the date of the meeting – without the possibility of all Council members being free to attend. As this example shows, Council is weakened by lack of knowledge of its past procedures and by inattention to

procedure, if only because it is often impelled to deal hurriedly with topics that deserve full study.[74]

As noted earlier, in the margins of this document Thompson had written many critical comments. On the Regina College issue, he made the following observation: "For reasons which I can't explain here delay in 1959 would have been a fatal mistake. And reasons for the reversal of policy (not the same reasons as for hurry in making it) were quite sufficient."[75]

Thompson never elaborated on the reasons for his decision. In his history of the university, he merely stated that "The irony of the events may, however, be pointed out here. The man who had to bear the brunt of the refusal to yield to the agitation for independent status for Regina College – myself – ten years and 3,000 unexpected students later took the lead in making the decision to grant the virtual equivalent of that status."[76]

Just why Thompson stated that "delay in 1959" would be "fatal" is not known. Since Thompson seldom used hyperbole, his emphatic word must have meant the imperative he believed the university faced. The historian of the University of Regina, James Pitsula, speculates that by a "fatal mistake" Thompson meant that rejection of expansion would be perceived by the government, people in Regina, and even some in Saskatoon as demonstrating just how "hopelessly out of touch" and "self-serving" the university would appear.[77] If this were true, such an image would have been calamitous for the university, especially on the eve of a fund-raising campaign.

Thompson had grasped the nettle. Perhaps his reasoning was also, in part, driven by the realization that, although his forthcoming retirement was public knowledge, he still had the prestige to carry such a contentious measure through the board, the council, and the senate. If Thompson took the responsibility for an expansion in Regina that was, in any case, probably inevitable, then the decision would not fall immediately on the new president-elect, John Spinks. Moreover, Thompson had always understood the necessity of good university relations with the provincial government. He gave succinct advice to Dr Spinks when he warned "don't forget where the money comes from."[78] Nevertheless, as he recalled, "While the governors were presenting our annual budgets, members of the government sometimes suggested that the University undertake particular enterprises or withdraw from others ... In every case the matter was put in the form of a request for consideration. In every case the University authorities made the final decision."[79]

But provincial government leaders clearly placed pressure on the senior University of Saskatchewan administration, especially Thompson and the Board of Governors, to accept a program for Regina College leading to a degree program. Maybe these politicians could have been persuaded that Regina should focus exclusively on arts and a four-year BA program and eschew the "carbon copy" expansion that occurred. Yet how they might have done so, without significantly increasing government interference in university affairs, is uncertain.

Rather than relieving his successor, it has been suggested that Thompson's decision on the expansion of Regina College placed his successor in an intenable situation, leaving Spinks with "the impossible job of making the two campuses work as one university."[80] Were there other alternatives that could have been pursued between 1959 until the establishment of the University of Regina in 1974? Spinks' ideal system was the "California model": one president of the university and one central board over the entire system, and a separate board, senate, and principals or chancellors for each of the campuses. Other American universities attempted to adopt this system, with disappointing results. Even as late as 1966, when he was chairman of a commission to study the future of graduate education in Ontario, Spinks was determined to copy the California model. But his main idea was unacceptable to the commission co-sponsors, the Council of Ontario Universities (COU) and the Ontario Commission on Post-Secondary Education (CPUO). Spinks proposed a centralizing model whereby all graduate studies would be directed by a province-wide University of Ontario. Each Ontario university president condemned the idea as "unnecessary" or, for various historical reasons, "unworkable."[81] One way Spinks could have resolved the difficulty he faced at Saskatchewan in the autumn of 1959 was to immediately recognize Regina as a separate university. He might thus have avoided the "ultimate ruination of his influence with the Government and the faculty."[82] Alas for Spinks' distinguished administrative career, he tried to maintain his position as the single university president in the province. And in 1974, when two new presidents were appointed in Saskatoon and Regina, he was simply rendered redundant.

8

Retirement and Medicare

I

Thompson retired in October of 1959, accompanied by many tributes. The CCF government hosted a dinner in his honour at which Premier Douglas spoke. The Board of Governors also gave him and Marjorie a warm dinner and reception. On 15 September 1960, the new biology building was ceremoniously opened and quite properly named the W.P. Thompson Building. On the south and west exterior walls is a mural of mosaics depicting the four main stages of cellular mitosis, as a tribute to Dr Thompson's research as a cytogeneticist in the genetics of wheat. His daughter and son and their families were proudly present, as well as a large number of his former graduate students, now distinguished scientists in their own right. Among those who gave addresses were James Jenkins from Berkeley, Edward Britton from Davis, and Peter Larkin from the University of British Columbia. Thompson was especially pleased that his first graduate student in genetics, Lillian Hollingshead, was there. The main speech was given by the rising CCF cabinet minister, Allan Blakeney.

Thompson's retirement had been preceded by the question of who should succeed him and then the subsequent search. The Board of Governors had appointed Thompson with ease and without controversy, and the members had wished him to remain past 1959. Indeed, as Thompson related to his daughter Mary, the board "begged me to stay on indefinitely." Thompson rejected the kind offer, claiming that "70 is old enough for that. I have seen too much of men hanging on after they should have quit. And I realize better than anyone else that I am not the man – intellectually – that I once was."[1]

The board met on 10 May 1958 and formed a search committee, composed of Walter Francis as chair, Judge Culliton, Allan MacCallum, deputy minister of education, and Dr Thorvaldson. Some months later, when Thompson again wrote to his daughter about the certainty of his decision, he noted that "They have appointed a committee to look for my successor. I declined to act on it, but I met with them for two hours because they wanted my advice – general and particular."[2]

No evidence of the deliberations of the sub-committee has been found, but J. Alexander Corry was the primary candidate. He was a University of Saskatchewan graduate, who had earned both a BA and a law degree. In 1923, he was Saskatchewan's Rhodes Scholar, and later taught for some years at the university in the College of Law. By the late 1950s, he was a well-known scholar in political science and law. He moved to Queen's in 1936 as the Hardy Professor of Political Science and in 1951 became vice-principal. The Archives at Queen's University contains two letters from Walter Francis to Corry, offering him the presidency of the University of Saskatchewan and stating that Thompson warmly supported the offer. Some years earlier, when the university bestowed an honorary degree on Corry, Thompson had expressed his high regard for him as "one of our graduates ... and the best political scientist in Canada."[3]

Corry asked for three months to decide. He had already turned down invitations to become president from two other universities but the Saskatchewan offer, he found, "was the most tempting." Corry ultimately rejected the offer, partly because the Board of Governors at Queen's offered to make him principal after three years had passed (and did, in 1961).[4]

Although Francis Leddy, the dean of arts and science, had been the favourite to succeed Thompson after Corry refused the offer, he was not selected. On 12 November 1958, the search committee recommended that John William Tranter Spinks be appointed president, with the same salary, benefits, and allowances as Thompson, as well as a leave of absence from 1 July 1959 until Thompson was "desirous of relinquishing his duties."[5]

Spinks was a formidable candidate: an internationally known chemist, a successful dean, and a highly cultured academic. He had also earned much respect for his pivotal role in bringing Dr Gerhard Herzberg to the University of Saskatchewan in 1935. Spinks was awarded an MBE for his work developing search and rescue procedures during World War II and was distinguished for his post-war pioneering research on radioactive isotopes.

However, the decision by the Board of Governors to select Spinks was controversial because it was widely known that he and Leddy were the prime candidates. In a speech in 1963, Thompson stated that he couldn't "tell you anything about the appointment of my successor as president, because I declined to have anything to do with it," except to, unsuccessfully, urge the Faculty Association to name a representative to the search committee. Since the Association would not allow their representative to "act as an individual" rather than serve exclusively as the representative of the Association, no faculty member was present for the decision.[6]

Dr Leddy's papers at the University of Windsor provide important information about the succession to Thompson in 1959. Leddy became president at Windsor in 1964 and retired in 1978. He knew a great deal about the University of Saskatchewan, and the culture both of Saskatoon and the province as a whole. Hence, his letters reflect some of the issues that he believed led to the decision against him. The correspondence also sheds light on a number of controversies surrounding Thompson's apparent alienation from him.

Leddy had begun as a member of the classics department in 1936, and had been appointed by Thompson in 1942 as director of the summer school. He was a close colleague of Thompson's on the survey committee of 1945 and had been promoted to dean of arts and science when Thompson became president in 1949. In a letter to his daughter in 1951, Thompson went out of his way to praise Leddy as "a vigorous young man of sound judgment and high scholarship as indicated among other things, by his election to the high office of President of the Humanities Research Council of Canada. He is also a first-rate administrator ... I suppose the Alumni association owes more to him than to any other man."[7]

In 1954, Thompson was even more generous in his praise. At the time, he was president of the NUCU so happened to meet with the prime minister and significant cabinet ministers. He assured his daughter that she would enjoy seeing Francis Leddy ("he is full of fun") despite the fact that Marjorie Thompson "has never liked him very much because she can't shake the old-anti-catholic atmosphere in which she was raised. Of course she is not alone. There is already considerable fear that he might succeed me and a good many people are preparing to block it if they can. But he is the brightest young university administrator in Canada ... I am taking no sides for or against him re: the succession and doing nothing to advance him. My only fault with him is that he is educationally conservative."[8]

Thompson and Leddy had disagreed over whether or not a veterinary college should be established at the university. Their disagreement became clear when professor Kenneth Buckley presented an economic study to the University of Saskatchewan Council that, according to his colleague, Edward Safarian, "tore apart the basic assumptions" of the veterinary college supporters. Buckley argued that because Saskatchewan had dairy cattle, it had minimal need for such an expensive investment. According to Safarian, after the Buckley report was presented to Council, many members were upset by the analysis. Leddy then incurred some criticism by arguing that the proposal for the veterinary college "would have to be rethought."[9] Safarian believed Thompson was "extremely annoyed" for "he had put himself behind the proposal." The motion to create a veterinary college at Saskatchewan was discussed by Council on 15 and 20 November 1957 but was defeated.[10] The second Council meeting is probably the one Safarian remembered. There is no mention of the Buckley report in the Council minutes. They merely note that the recommendation was rejected.

Leddy also stated that from 1957 onwards, Thompson had stopped consulting his senior administrators as he had earlier. This alleged personality shift led Leddy to speculate that Thompson "might have suffered a small stroke, in the silent areas [of the brain]" and hence "experienced a marked diminution in judgment."[11]

One can conjecture about any number of reasons why Leddy did not become president. First, he and his family were leading Roman Catholics in Saskatoon and in the province. How much of a role that played in choosing Spinks is not known, since the discussions of the Board of Governors on this question have never been published. As early as 1953, however, Thompson had apparently said to Leddy that his religion would, indeed, be a barrier.[12] Second, Leddy was not a well-known classics scholar, whereas Spinks was a distinguished scientist, and, despite being a highly educated man, Leddy did little research. Thompson may have mistaken Leddy's skill in making often important speeches for scholarship, or perhaps as a young man Leddy had displayed great promise as a scholar, a promise that was not fulfilled. Leddy also believed that Thompson told Walter Francis that he preferred Spinks, for Thompson seemed to have viewed Leddy as "too political."[13] Thompson said to his daughter that he was "very glad to have him [Spinks] as my successor ... Perhaps I should add that the selection of him [Spinks] was the work of the committee and Board – not mine."[14]

Thompson already had a high regard for Spinks's administrative and scholarly abilities well before he appointed him dean of the graduate school in 1949. He also knew Spinks as a deeply cultured man in literature, music, and art. While he was president, Thompson had even had more opportunity to assess Spinks more deeply and more positively. For example, in the spring of 1957, he wrote to Spinks, praising him for his "work as chairman of the Committee on Departmental Organization ... It was a difficult assignment and you handled it excellently."[15] To his daughter, Mary, who had long viewed Spinks as an individual who "rubbed people the wrong way," Thompson replied: "His work as Dean of Graduate Studies has been absolutely first-rate ... He is recognized everywhere as one of the top chemists in Canada. And he has built up one of the best chemistry departments in Canada – if not the best."[16] He did differ with Spinks on one important judgment: recommending Professor McCallum as head of chemistry. Thompson doubted McCallum could "do what you and Thor[valdson] have done in building up the department, putting it on the map." But if Spinks and Leddy agreed about McCallum, then Thompson "was prepared to go along with you" and authorize the appointment.[17]

Retiring from the presidency not only meant leaving an office, but leaving the "President's Residence," a home provided on campus. Thompson wrote to his son of the "recent rather hectic doings":

> I moved out of the office yesterday and left it quite bare except some documents which Spinks will need. It was a heck of a job going through the files....Until the new Biology Bldg (W.P. Thompson Bldg!) is completed I have been give[n] a room in Field Husbandry Bldg. At present it is all cluttered with cartons of books, papers, etc. ...
>
> We are going over to the big house [President's Residence] now for the last time to pick up a few odds and ends.
>
> Love Dad
>
> I think it is going to be all right to be an ex.[18]

II

Thompson's last role as a leader on public issues in Saskatchewan was his participation, as chairman of the advisory planning committee, in the medicare crisis of 1959–62. His work, unfortunately, has largely been ignored in the voluminous writings on the subject. The fact that he devoted only two pages to the controversy in *An Academic's Progress* may simply reflect his tiredness. He completed his memoir in late 1969 and early 1970, just before his death. More likely, the brevity of his account reflects his disillusionment both with the hostile behaviour of three of the six medical doctors on the advisory committee and with many of the doctors in the province who often, as their leader Dr Barootes later admitted, "dreamt up the most god-awful things to say. The cartoons and things we put out were, well, immoderate."[19] Barootes repeated this self-critique in a symposium convened in Saskatoon in 1993 to celebrate the fortieth anniversary of the first full medical class. The doctors' political intervention, he admitted, was "amateurish, clumsy, aggressive, and ineffective." At the same time, Barootes blamed both sides "for the breakdown" of negotiations between the eight-person majority of Thompson's committee and the minority of three doctors and one businessman.[20]

The idea of a comprehensive health insurance program for Saskatchewan had been studied in detail as early as 1949–51. After a 1948 federal initiative provided funds to each province to examine current health services, the provincial government created a committee to carry out the survey. Ottawa had provided Saskatchewan with $43,506 for this purpose. The committee of twelve members consisted of members from provincial organizations involved in health services. After two years of study and twenty-five meetings, the committee, with Fred Mott, Malcolm Taylor, and Clarence Houston playing major roles, arrived at 115 recommendations. The first was the need for a provincial comprehensive health insurance program.[21] In 1951, however, there were not enough financial resources in the province for the CCF to implement it.

Well before the medicare crisis, Thompson had been sympathetic to the progressive left generally, and to Premier Douglas and Education Minister Woodrow Lloyd, specifically. Medicare had been a campaign promise of the CCF in the election of June 1944. The Douglas government had stated in its election platform that socialized medicine was its aim, but that the implementation of such a massive program could only come about after "considerable time and with significant federal financial support." By 1947, the CCF had managed to establish a hospitalization plan, but its 1944 promise of prepaid medical care was beyond the provincial government's resources and Saskatchewan received no support from Ottawa until many years later. Only after the Diefenbaker administration in 1957 committed itself to sharing the costs of any provincial plan that offered universal coverage could the CCF proceed with serious planning for medicare.[22] Douglas was further encouraged when Diefenbaker succeed in winning enough Conservative seats in the 1957 federal election to form a minority government. Soon after the election, the Diefenbaker government passed the Hospital and Diagnostic Services Act (1957) in which the federal government agreed to finance 50 per cent of hospitalization costs, with the provinces paying the other half of the costs. "This made full medicare financially possible for Saskatchewan." [23]

In a byelection speech at Birch Hills in April 1959, Douglas announced the government's decision to further fulfill the CCF's 1944 election promises of universal healthcare. On 18 December 1959, in a radio broadcast, the premier reiterated the cabinet's decision and outlined the five principles that would guide the government: prepayment of costs, universal coverage, superior quality service, government sponsorship by a public administrative body responsible to the legislature, and service acceptable to both providers and receivers of the medical care. Douglas also said that an advisory planning committee would be appointed to represent the government, the medical profession, and the citizens of Saskatchewan.

In between the premier's two speeches, Thompson wrote to Douglas on 20 November 1959, telling him that "(a) I am in agreement with it [the plan] ... and would like to see it implemented, and (b) I have been in a specially favourable position ... to learn the views and attitudes of a cross section of the profession – and they are far from being unanimous." Thompson urged the premier to consult reliable members of the university medical school staff, particularly Dr Hilliard and Dean Macleod, whom he considered to be a "medical statesman." The premier was "most happy" to receive Thompson's letter because "I have been planning for some time to talk to you about a medical care program for Saskatchewan."[24] Thompson had earned respect throughout the province and had both the stature and the requisite executive abilities to lead such a committee. On 23 November 1959, Douglas asked him to serve on the proposed planning committee, citing the "general confidence in his objectivity" and his "experience with the Medical College."[25]

Thompson told his son and daughter-in-law a few days later that he "was going to do it, though I suppose my medical friends will all be down on me. But it is going to come and we should try our best to work out the most acceptable scheme."[26] By 30 December 1959, the provincial minister of health, Walter Erb, congratulated Thompson for agreeing to serve as the chairman of what popularly came to be called the "Thompson Committee."[27] The minister had sent the registrar of the provincial College of Physicians and Surgeons the terms of reference for the committee – it was to consist of twelve people, three of whom would represent the interests of the College of Physicians and Surgeons (Dr E.W. Barootes, Dr J.F.C. Anderson, and Dr C.J. Houston), three to represent the government (deputy minister of health Dr F. Burns Roth, Dr V.L. Matthews, and former health minister T.J. Bentley), three representatives of the public (Thompson, Beatrice Trew, a former CCF MLA, and Cliff Whiting, a farm and community leader), one representative of the University College of Medicine (Hilliard), one from the Chamber of Commerce (Donald McPherson), and one from the Saskatchewan Federation of Labour (Walter Smishek).

The announcement of the members of the committee and its terms of reference was delayed for months by the College of Physicians and Surgeons. As Thompson informed his daughter Mary on 18 April 1960:

> The Government still is held up in naming the committee on medical care – or state medicine. Two of the bodies to be represented haven't named their representatives. I know all the others and it is a good committee. And we have a fine research and secretarial staff, already appointed. There has been a terrific fuss about the plan, with doctors/or many objecting strenuously ... We expect to start to work as soon as the full membership is announced. It will keep me busy for a year with an immense amount of homework to do.
>
> We are to have a provincial election in June [1960]. My friends ... say the CCF is likely to be beaten. If so, I'm glad I

> am no longer president, as it would be dreadful to work with the others ... I don't think it will interfere with the work of the medical care committee. The others wouldn't dare stop it.[28]

It was not until 25 April 1960 that the names and terms of reference of the committee were finally announced. The delay resulted from the lengthy negotiations between the government and the College of Physicians and Surgeons, because the College objected to the advisory committee restricting its mandate almost entirely to the medical care plan. After months of negotiation, the government agreed to broaden the terms to include various phases of health, but only in relation to the plan. Unfortunately, despite Thompson's efforts to maintain the committee's focus, the "broadened terms" of the planning committee gave the two doctors adamantly opposed to any public plan, Barootes and Anderson, the opportunity to digress on many other aspects of health problems. Douglas had initially been sanguine about the provincial doctors accepting medicare. He held this optimistic view despite the fact that the College of Physicians and Surgeons, at its annual meeting in October 1959, "had stated its opposition to any government-controlled, province-wide medical care plan."[29] Thompson, too, at first believed that the medical profession would agree to the medical program. Thompson noted to Dr Roth on 28 December 1959 that in meeting with doctors "who speak to me freely," he found "widespread goodwill towards the general plan or at least recognition of its inevitability."[30] As late as April 1960, Thompson remained optimistic about the outcome of negotiations with the doctors and convinced of the importance of the advisory committee's task. Before the planning committee began its deliberations, he expressed his optimism about the prospects of success and described the significance of the planning committee's task to his daughter. "We have an opportunity to do a [good deal of good] it will spread to all the other provinces and maybe even to the U.S.A!"[31] Both Thompson and the premier, however, were to be proven profoundly in error with these optimistic hopes, not grasping the adamantine resistance of the College of Physicians and Surgeons.

When he accepted the appointment as chairman of the planning committee, Thompson could not recall any public criticism directed at him personally from the College, although the Liberal leader, Ross Thatcher, complained that there were too many government appointees and civil servants on the committee. By November 1960, however, members of the Saskatoon medical profession were angrily recalling their opposition to Thompson at the time University Hospital was being established. The doctors had threatened to boycott the hospital unless the medical staff was chosen from the ranks of the Saskatoon doctors. Thompson and Dean Macleod had refused to accept this demand, insisting on the university's prerogative to decide on its own employment policies. As the discussions over medical care became more heated, many doctors in Saskatoon and throughout the province became increasingly hostile to Thompson, perceiving him as having long been unsympathetic to their interests.

The committee began its deliberations on 9 May 1960, the beginning of sixteen months' work in which twenty-three meetings were held for "a total of forty-three days," with thirty-three public and seven private hearings, 1,226 pages of documentation from forty-nine briefs and fifty study documents, "submitted by ... interested professional organizations, community agencies and individuals."[32]

Thompson, with the help of advisory committee secretary John Sparks, began reading all this material widely and sending on references to the other members of the committee.[33] In August 1960, Thompson sent a memorandum to Sparks to circulate to the committee. It contained a long list of subjects that he believed the entire committee would have to study, including psychiatric services, chronic diseases, the distribution of labour in hospitals, methods of paying doctors, private insurance plans and medical care in other countries, as well as plans to visit some of them.[34] The readings and the answers to Thompson's memorandum led the committee to engage in a number of study sessions before plunging into their interviews.

Thompson pushed his committee members hard and was irritated when some of them sought to avoid visitation obligations. For example, he thought it was "essential" that the four on his committee who were opposed to the idea of medicare should visit the United States. These were Donald McPherson, representing the Chamber of Commerce, and three of the doctors, Barootes, Anderson, and Houston, who represented the College of Physicians and Surgeons. From this committee, Roth, Anderson, and Whiting visited Australia and New Zealand for three weeks, while Houston made a separate tour of the Scandinavian countries.[35] Thompson knew that Dr Houston's "conscience [was] bothering him" about whether or not to take the Australia trip and, as Thompson and Sparks knew, Houston had "a well-developed conscience." In contrast, Thompson was well aware that "Drs Anderson and Barootes have no intention of modifying their views and no interest in seeing the European plans in case they might have to modify their views."[36]

Four members of the committee – Smishek, Trew, Matthews, and Hilliard – went on a month-long visit to examine health plans in Norway, Sweden, Denmark, Holland, and, for the longest period of their investigation, Britain. Before their departure, they prepared extensively on research materials prepared by Sparks. The committee members who travelled to Britain met with two important experts on health care, Richard Titmuss and Brian Abel-Smith, both professors of social administration at the London School of Economics. Both men were noted scholars and influential but independent-thinking supporters of the Labour Party on such issues as the relatively low costs of the National Health Service, poverty, and child poverty in particular.[37] The members also consulted Graham Spry, the agent-general for Saskatchewan, who was later essential in recruiting British doctors during the Saskatchewan doctors' strike of 1 to 23 July 1962, and Lord Stephen Taylor, a Labour Party peer and physician, who later was the arbitrator who settled the strike.

The representatives from the College of Physicians and Surgeons "took every opportunity to delay the committee's work," and other doctors and their supporters throughout the province organized rallies against the plan, using "nearly $100,000 raised by the Canadian Medical Association" to attack the plan and to traduce the government and Thompson himself.[38] The provincial Liberal Party supported the medical profession, arguing against any form of medical insurance and urging that the question be submitted to a plebiscite. Yet the Liberals never stated just what question ought to be put to the people. Primarily because of the medical profession's delaying tactics, the advisory committee had still not been able to hold hearings by November 1960, although for eight months the members held "study sessions" to acquaint themselves with the issues involved.[39]

Clearly, the optimistic hopes of both Thompson and Douglass were misplaced. The doctors were not willing to consider the medical plan with goodwill. Thompson later told the legal historian of the medicare crisis, Professor E.A. Tollefson, that two of the medical members of the planning committee, Drs Barootes and Anderson, were "Deliberately going over as much ground, not related to the Medical Care Plan, as possible, partly to simply put off the consideration of the Medical Care Plan, partly in order ... to scare the government and the public off ... Now this went on for a long time and we had almost no consideration of the ... Plan for months after the committee started to work ... I objected strongly to this ... so I told the committee ... that I was seriously considering resigning."[40]

Thompson's statement to the advisory committee about wishing to resign prompted the one female member of the group, Beatrice Trew, a leader among the homemakers' clubs, to appeal to Thompson to stay, believing that his "ability as a leader [was] needed." His chairmanship had her "complete confidence" and was essential in helping the government in its plans for a comprehensive medical care program.[41] The CCF cabinet was also alarmed about Thompson's desire to resign. Douglas knew that "he could not put health insurance into law without an Advisory Committee report."[42]

After consulting Douglas, Thompson agreed to remain as chairman. To the planning committee, he said that "a good deal more was said on both sides but I am not at liberty to repeat it ... But I am permitted to say that he urged me strongly to continue in the hope that the committee will endeavour to reach some definite conclusion on our main task as expeditiously as possible.[43]

The persistent acrimonious slurs directed at Thompson angered him considerably. He was especially rankled by the rumour put about by some doctors and their supporters that he was senile. He later wrote to the deputy minister of finance, A.W. Johnson, "I knew that I was being called many uncomplimentary things – prejudiced, unfair, crooked, a lackey of the government, etc. But the senility was new ... it was those charges some made to and in the committee which prevented me from following through with my desire to resign, expressed in the letter to Mr Douglas. I couldn't run away in the face of them."[44] When the biology department celebrated his fifty years at the university, Thompson remarked sardonically that "the medical profession claim that they have already seen evidence of senility."[45]

Thompson had been prompted to resign not only by what he viewed as the intransigence of Barootes and Anderson but also by what he saw as a lack of support from Dr Roth, the deputy minister of health, and John Sparks, the secretary. Writing later to Al Johnson, Thompson remarked

> I think now that Burns [Roth] sincerely believed that we should study all phases of health first and meticulously. But at the time I thought he did not want to antagonize the doctors and didn't want a row. He may still have had hopes of a satisfactory settlement. Sparks' general method of work as well as his correct secretarial attitude played right into the doctors' hands. With no support from these two I felt completely frustrated and hopeless. Shortly after I wrote Mr Douglas several incidents made it impossible for me to resign without running away in a cowardly fashion. The outcome proved that I was right and that there was no hope from the beginning of any kind of satisfactory compromise ... You will understand that in all this, while in my opinion the basic aim of the College's representatives was to prevent a public program at all costs, one of their methods was to delay a real study of it as long as possible and hence to insist on the prior study of all sorts of health problems, most of which had nothing to do with such a program. [46]

Walter Smishek, the Labour representative on the advisory committee recalled that "Dr Thompson always had proceedings in hand, despite the difficult times in many sessions, because of the opposition of the doctors, particularly Dr Barootes ... [who was] the most articulate. Nevertheless, Thompson never lost his steady disposition, despite the fact that some members of the College of Physicians and Surgeons publicly demanded his resignation."[47] Smishek elaborated on what he saw as Thompson's qualities as the chair. "He went out of his way to accommodate and listen to the views of everyone on the Committee and was a consummate listener."[48]

A colleague of Barootes, Dr John Leishman, claimed that "the Chairman of the Advisory Committee on Medical Care is prejudiced and biased, with his mind made up, and in my opinion is there to implement the policy of the government and collect his $35 a day." In his interview with Tollefson, Thompson later suggested that the College was determined to name doctors to the committee who were "violently opposed" and they "couldn't have gotten two men more violently opposed than Dr Barootes and Dr Anderson."[49]

Thompson complained that "nearly all the time of the committee was being used in consideration of other phases of health, there was little on the Medical Care Plan proper which I regarded as our job, the reason we were appointed." Finally, after all the debates and delays by the doctors on the advisory committee, Thompson met with a committee of the cabinet. Because of months of "fruitless discussions" within the advisory planning committee, stalled mainly by Drs Anderson and Barootes, Thompson was convinced that the "discussions might go on forever."

The obstinacy of those two representatives on the planning placed the premier in a dilemma. Douglas believed that he could not put health insurance into law without a report from Thompson's committee.[50] Therefore, at a cabinet meeting on 2 June 1961, the ministers decided they would require an interim report.[51] The case can be made that Thompson's threat to resign was the catalyst that brought about the demand for what became the majority report, the report that provided the essence of the medicare legislation. Thompson believed that Barootes and Anderson, in particular, were so implacably opposed to tax-financed health care that he saw no point in continuing any discussions, much less hoping that the doctors would sign any report authorized by him. Right up to the signing of what became two reports, however, Thompson still hoped that at least one representative from the College of Physicians and Surgeons would sign what became the majority report.

> That was Dr Houston I'm referring to. Dr Houston is a very fine man and I have the greatest respect for him. All through he was obviously trying his best to be judicious and to get the best possible scheme. As I say, I was hoping until the end that he might sign the majority report. In fact he was the one that moved several, what I regarded as important parts of the Medical Care Plan – individual recommendations, you know. But in the end he went along with the minority report.[52]

Although Thompson and a majority of the committee found the cabinet request for an interim report entirely reasonable, four members of the committee did not accept the proposal. As a result, the majority interim report was submitted to the cabinet on 25 September 1961 together with a minority report signed by the three physicians on the advisory committee representing the provincial College of Physicians and Surgeons and by Donald McPherson, the committee member from the Chamber of Commerce. The four men submitted their minority report, which opposed any universal, compulsory plan. Thompson informed the cabinet that the majority report was "the best he could do, given the college nominees' lack of co-operation."[53]

Premier Douglas wrote Thompson a complimentary letter soon after receiving the majority report.

> I think you have good reason to be satisfied with the report of the Advisory Planning Committee on Medical Care. Like yourself, I agree with some of the views expressed by Walter Smishek but I have learned over the years that "politics is the art of the possible" ... Of one thing I am sure and that is that you have made a major contribution in the field of providing health services on an insured basis. You and your colleagues have helped make history and when a comprehensive system of health insurance has been established across Canada many will point to the basic work you did as being the first important step in that direction.[54]

Apparently, College representatives had been promised an opportunity to study the Medical Care Insurance bill in advance, but unfortunately, this did not occur before the bill was introduced in the legislature by Minister Erb on 31 October 1961. Perhaps this failure arose because of the late date of the receipt of the interim report or maybe it reflected the cabinet's conviction that it already knew just how unyielding the College's refusal would be and did not wish to delay the legislation any longer. However, "tactically" the government made "a grave mistake" by leaving the College with the conviction that its views had been assessed with "callous disregard."[55] Thompson believed that the government had made an even more grievous error earlier by deciding not to appoint all members of the advisory planning committee. In confidential discussions with Badgley and Wolfe in the fall of 1965, Thompson was emphatic in his belief that the entire planning committee should have been appointed.[56] Had the CCF done so, though, the crisis might well have been even worse, for the opposition would have had no voice until the medicare plan was presented to the legislature. The medicare bill followed "closely the recommendations found in the majority report of the Thompson committee."[57] By holding the advisory committee together under extraordinary circumstances and managing to produce a majority report that became the heart of the medicare legislation, Thompson had done Saskatchewan and Canada an enormously important service.

A little earlier, on 5 October 1961, Thompson had outlined to his daughter the main recommendations, noting that there were "two major features which in principle I don't like – administration by a commission instead of Department of Health, and fee-for-service instead of salaries for doctors ... As expected the representatives of the medical profession ... objected to the universality and the compulsory features, ostensibly on the basis of cost. But they were so thoroughly discredited at the election campaign that it won't have any effect."[58] Thompson noted that he was "reasonably satisfied with the substance of the report," although he agreed with Walter Smishek in thinking that "user-fees" were unfortunate. Thompson would have preferred doctors to be paid by salary, not by fees. Although Smishek signed the interim majority report, he also appended to it his own minority report, with two resolutions. One advocated that the medical scheme be administered directly by the department of public health and the second that remuneration should be on a salary or capitation system. But Thompson thought that he had to accept fee-for-service to gain "even the minimum amount of cooperation from the doctors ... essential to make the plan work." Smishek later succeeded in getting the Saskatchewan Federation of Labour to persuade the New Democratic Party at their founding convention in November 1962 to abolish "user-fees," thereby "saving Canadians billions of dollars."[59] In his 1964 book on medicare, *Medical Care: Programs and Issues,* Thompson argued from extensive data that "in comparison with the other methods, the advantages of the fee-for-service method of paying doctors are smallest and most doubtful, and the disadvantages greatest and most certain ... It was allowed in Saskatchewan and ... a mistake was made without attaining appeasement."[60]

As the battle for medicare entered a new phase, Douglas resigned as the CCF provincial leader and in November 1961 was elected leader of the newly formed federal New Democratic Party. Woodrow Lloyd succeeded Douglas as premier and carried through the implementation of medicare for Saskatchewan on 1 July 1962. Before Douglas left he had successfully solved an important and difficult internal issue within the CCF by appointing William G. Davies, a trade unionist and a resolute politician, as the successor to the ineffectual Walter Erb as minister of health.

The Saskatchewan Medical Care Insurance Act received royal assent on 17 November 1961 with a proposed implementation date of 1 April 1962. The members of the Medical Care Insurance Commission slated to administer the Act were announced publicly on 5 January 1962. Premier Lloyd and Davies, the new minister of health, attempted, unsuccessfully, to convince the provincial medical association to accept the plan, even extending the implementation date to 1 July 1962. On 1 July, medicare became law. In defiance, doctors went on strike in Saskatchewan from 1 to 23 July, when they finally capitulated. Lord Taylor, the British Labour Party peer, was the skilled man who acted as the arbitrator to settle the strike. The so-called "Saskatoon Agreement" was signed between the medical profession and the government, enabling medicare to function thereafter. Among other things, the agreement allowed doctors to opt out of medicare. However, few doctors actually did because for the first time, they had a guaranteed income.

The strike not only alarmed many lay people in the province; it also frightened the new dean of the medical college, R.W. Begg, who had succeeded Wendell Macleod when he resigned late in November 1961. Begg wrote to all deans of medicine in Canada arguing that the "dispute could be disastrous" and asking each dean "how many students you could accommodate on transfer ... [and] could [you] assist with the provision of staff on a short term basis until we reorganize?" Luckily, the strike never remotely jeopardized the university's medical college.[61] In its aftermath, Thompson told his daughter that, while

> My Committee has finished its work ... the secretary (Sparks) and I have a lot of work to do in editing the final report. It includes 16 chapters and will probably run to 250 pages. In addition there will be one or two volumes of documents – briefs submitted to us, and special studies which we got various people to carry on for us, mostly the secretariat. The full committee has been over a draft of the report and approved it, but it needs a lot of editing ... Mother sent you the full statement of the agreement between government and doctors, which has since been translated into legislation at a special meeting of the legislature ... But essentially the government secured what it wanted (and what we recommended) – a universal (both for all persons and all sickness) – compulsory, tax-supported, government-controlled plan.

Thompson believed then and for the rest of his life that the doctors had disgraced themselves by their strike. "The violent reaction and criticism of the doctors' strike everywhere outside Saskatchewan and to a large extent within the province finally made most of the doctors ashamed. And the government and particularly the premier behaved excellently throughout, showing an obvious willingness to compromise wherever they could but maintaining complete firmness on essentials." He noted that private plans, like Blue Cross and Blue Shield, here "run by the doctors" will survive. "But they will be really nothing more than post-offices receiving doctors' bills and sending them to the Medicare Commission, receiving the money from the commission and passing it on to the doctors ... It is not much more than a face-saving device for the doctors, as it enables them to say that they are independent of the Commission."[62] Former premier Allan Blakeney remembered the confrontation between Thompson and some of the intransigent doctors.

> The doctors representing the College of Physicians and Surgeons had a line that they didn't deviate from, and you couldn't argue with them ... Dr Thompson felt they should engage in the intellectual argument about whether their position was a good position or not, and I don't think he thought they did ... Thompson felt that that's how you arrived at the right solution, at the truth if you want to use that term: if we talk about what can engage our minds. He did not exude an ideology; the issue he exuded was the rational man's approach to the world.[63]

Thompson also pointed out that "the public seems to have overlooked all the work the committee did on other subjects and ... the very important recommendations which we made," notably "mental health, dental care, a drug program, rehabilitation of the sick and injured, home care, medical education, medical research, and several other subjects."[64]

After Thompson had submitted the majority interim report, he reflected to Allan Blakeney that "it has been quite an experience, and so important to everyone in the future that it has been very stimulating and challenging. There is tremendous interest in it all across Canada and also in health and social science circles in the States ... The American Medical Association has such a tight grip on politics in the States and such a powerful lobby that it will be later there."[65]

At a dinner the CCF government gave in honour of the advisory planning committee on medicare on 28 January 1963, Thompson recalled that "when our report was published I made a vow that I would not take any part in the controversy that was sure to take place" despite being "sorely tempted," especially by people "who took the lofty and superior attitude; 'A plague on both your houses,' for in a democracy important issues must be decided by public debate. It should be debate and restrained." Despite his decision not to intervene in the immediate post-medicare debates and propaganda, Thompson's concern for medicare made him vigilant in watching for public criticisms of the legislation, especially if it came from weighty members of the university community. For example, Otto Lang, then recently appointed dean of law, gave a speech to the Hanley Liberal Association blaming the CCF for administering medicare by a commission. Lang claimed that the CCF method was dictatorial in that the commission "handed over ... arbitrary power ... to persons who were not elected."[66] In an angry letter, Thompson replied that "from the beginning" the medical profession claimed that if medicare came into being, "it should be administered by an 'independent commission.'" So, Thompson stated that "while your friends the doctors are, like you, opposed to the medical plan, they are in complete disagreement with you about whether it should be administered by a commission." Thompson believed that there was a place for "commissions such as the CBC, Cancer, Workmen's Compensation as well as numerous crown corporations."[67]

In 1964, Thompson published *Medical Care: Programs and Issues*. He concluded that, after a lengthy review of the evidence and arguments, the evidence "strongly favours governmental over private control, administration and financing of the program."[68] As evidence, Thompson addressed in detail much of the material and many of the ideas and debates that the members of the advisory planning committee had discussed. These were debates that could not be developed properly in public during the charged atmosphere of the doctors' rebellion and their subsequent strike. Thompson's data came almost entirely from the research the planning committee gathered in many countries, on which they based much of the analysis in their interim majority report. He prefaced his account by allowing that though he supported the recommendations of the Saskatchewan government, he wanted to deal fairly with the opinions of those who did not agree with the majority.

Thompson began his analysis by claiming, often sharply, that most North Americans were sadly ill-informed about government health care plans in western societies. He was blunt about what he saw as the causes of this ignorance.

> Until a short time ago most people on this continent were under the impression that Britain was the only country which had adopted a government-sponsored program. And thanks largely to the efforts of the master propagandists of the American Medical Association and of their somewhat more restrained and scrupulous confreres in Canada, even well-read people were under the impression that Britain, in a moment of socialist aberration, had embarked on a fantastic, unworkable, and harmful scheme, and that sensible people there would get rid of it tomorrow if they could. But it is gradually becoming known in Canada and the United States that a great majority of Englishmen, including a substantial majority of their doctors, are happy with the British National Health Service and indeed proud of it. It is gradually becoming known too, that Britain is not alone, that in fact every European country has a program of medical care in which the government participates and people in these countries are well satisfied with the general nature of these programs.[69]

Thompson reflected on the new respect and even "glamour" accruing to the medical profession because of advances in health care over the past half-century. He hastened to add, sarcastically, that the medical profession had little to do with these improvements; they were largely the result of a "fraction of one per cent of the members usually working on salary in university laboratories and hospitals, and in research institutions." Such scientific possibilities were a dominant reason why the president and Dean Macleod worked so diligently and purposefully to bring research physicians into the new college of medicine.

Thompson also mentioned that the heightened degree of public interest in medical care resulted from the increase in health-care costs. After reviewing the costs in the United States and Canada and in Europe, he concluded that some form of government participation brought better and cheaper benefits to citizens than private systems. He also argued that, in all modern societies, some compulsions are accepted with little or no objections. For example, all of us must drive on one side of the road, pay for snow shovelling, send children to school, observe quarantine regulations, and pay taxes to support public libraries and parks. Thompson dismissed as minor or irrelevant the doctors' fear that working under government programs would lead to loss of prestige or diminution of their personal incentives to carry out good work or take initiatives. As for payment of doctors, Thompson argued against fee-for-service plans as bureaucratic, cumbersome, costly, and leaving the system open to abuse. He believed that either payment by capitation, which would involve less paperwork for doctors and give them a regular, predictable income, or remuneration by salary, would be far more equitable. Thompson rejected as ridiculous the objection to salaries – that they would destroy doctors' initiatives or lead to "under-service." So many other professions paid by salary, such as research scientists, were often exemplars of devotion to duty and high achievement. Thompson believed the "operation of all agencies and facilities concerned with health care" should be administered by a department of government, equipped with the necessary fiscal resources. For him, "the underlying philosophy of government-sponsored provision of medical care is that society has the responsibility of ensuring all citizens receive adequate health protection," a right "like the right to education."[70] Until Prime Minister Pearson's national program of health insurance became law in 1968, wealthy North America stood in "unsplendid isolation."[71] Just before this, Thompson remarked on a law passed by the United States Congress that provided some degree of financial assistance to sick citizens. Medical coverage for all Americans would come in time, he believed. He noted optimistically that "Ontario and B.C. have now enacted medicare laws. They, too, are very small steps. One of these days our federal government will get around to doing something and then there will be hope for the rest of Canada getting something like Saskatchewan's."

In an otherwise positive review of Thompson's "splendid" book, *Star Phoenix* reviewer Jean Swanson wondered if those "scores" of English doctors who came to the "rescue of Saskatchewan residents" were not guilty of deserting their own patients, perhaps for more money here?[72] Thompson's publisher, Clarke, Irwin & Company, sent Thompson clippings from international periodicals that had reviewed his book, offering him the chance to send excerpts to his family.

The *Canadian Reader* says that he "writes clearly and gracefully. He puts the case ... very powerfully and he treats the opposition's case with objectivity ... Dr Thompson reveals himself as a thorough gentleman who is concerned to apply the dictates of his conscience to the problems of human suffering and to do so with as much respect for the views of those who disagree with him as possible." Even the *Canadian Hospital Association Journal* calls it "this very readable book."

"I hope their readers pay attention," Thompson concluded.[73]

Thompson continued his inquiries into doctors' perceptions of medicare. On 12 February 1965, three years after medicare's implementation, Thompson sent out an article with a covering letter titled "Saskatchewan Doctors' Opinions of 'Medicare': A Questionnaire Survey."[74] Altogether, of the 809 doctors who received the document 225 answered particular questions, and 72 per cent of them said that now they would vote "to continue the present medical care program of that province." There were corresponding positive figures for other questions. At the top of Thompson's copy of the document he wrote: "Even the doctors are coming around."[75] To his daughter he commented: "After all the fuss the doctors made with their strike and prediction that everything would go to pot," the "results are amazing"[76] The College of Physicians and Surgeons, however, was "in a big stew" about his questionnaires:

> They sent a circular letter to all doctors less than a week after the questionnaires were mailed, saying that the questions are biased, useless, that I am prejudiced and results will be invalid or purposely distorted. They also wrote to Spinks and while they didn't ask for it to be suppressed, that could have been their only purpose. Also sent a delegation to see me to 'persuade' me to desist. They are scared because they have a good idea of what the results will be, and that it will show them to have been asses. Nearly 200 replies have been sent back before the College's letter reached the doctors. Have about 240 now – quite enough for a good sample.[77]

Thompson feared that the College of Physicians and Surgeons would attempt to prevent publication of his results.[78] Ultimately, his apprehensions were allayed when the results of the questionnaire were published in *The Canadian Medical Association Journal* on 30 October 1965.[79]

Thompson deserves substantial credit, more than he has received, for chairing the advisory planning committee. He kept an extraordinarily discordant group together, led a majority of them to carry out vital investigative trips to gather the necessary data, and requested that the cabinet demand an interim report before the recalcitrance of Drs Barootes and Anderson, in particular, could bring about the committee's collapse. Most significantly, the majority interim report included the recommendations ultimately contained in the bill implementing medicare.[80] The passage of medicare also increased Thompson's already high regard for Woodrow Lloyd. On a Christmas card that he sent to Lloyd after Ross Thatcher's victory in April 1964, Thompson wrote: "I was always aware that I was very fortunate to have you as Minister of Education and Premier. Recent events have demonstrated it abundantly."[81] In May 1965, Thompson saw Lloyd as further vindicated for his courage and leadership in the medicare controversy when Thatcher also threatened to take over the university and administer it as a government department. The horrified reaction of the faculty, the NDP opposition, and much of the general public, caused him to withdraw his threats.

In 1961, the Conservative prime minister John Diefenbaker had appointed the Conservative justice of the Supreme Court, Emmett Hall of Saskatchewan, to chair a commission of inquiry into the feasibility of a national medicare scheme. Canada's medical establishment was elated, thinking Hall would condemn the idea. They were wrong. In 1964, Hall sent his report to the new Liberal government of Lester Pearson, recommending a far-ranging national medicare program. Thompson explained to his daughter the importance of the Hall Report:

> The [Emmett] Hall federal Royal Commission on Health Services has made a huge report (900 pages). It recommends a plan almost identical with ours in Saskatchewan for the whole country. In fact they go further than we did in regards to drugs, dentistry etc. The doctors are sore about it. It looks as if we are in for the same kind of contest for the whole country that we had in Saskatchewan. But I fear that the federal Liberals haven't the courage or skill or humanitarian ideals of Woodrow Lloyd.[82]

He was to be pleasantly surprised. The Liberal government of Lester Pearson did have the qualities to enact a national health care act along the principles of Saskatchewan's medicare. As Justice Emmett Hall wrote to T.C. Douglas:

> I think your greatest and enduring accomplishment was the introduction and putting into effect of Medicare in Saskatchewan. Without your program as a successful one in being, I couldn't have produced the unanimous report for the Canada-wide universal health recommendations in 1964. If the scheme had not been successful in Saskatchewan, it wouldn't have become nation-wide. Generations to come will be your debtors. The fact that the two leading figures in the crusade ... came from Saskatchewan ... suggests something quite fundamental about the political culture of that province.[83]

Saskatchewan provided the blueprint for universal, free, accessible, and high-quality health insurance for all Canadians. It wasn't only Thompson's chairmanship of the advance planning committee that led to the first government funded medical care plan in Canada. His efforts to create the university hospital and the medical college also helped create medicare: both institutions were essential to the CCF government's medicare program. Since Thompson deserves significant credit for the coming of medicare to Saskatchewan, he must also be credited with helping to bring in a national health services plan.

9

Last Years and Legacies

I

As the Thompsons got older, they reduced their duties and began to lead a more relaxed life. Thompson reflected on this shift in tempo to Mary in letters of 9 May and 27 June 1965. "As you can gather we don't do anything very exciting. I suppose that is to be expected at our time of life. But we find it interesting to watch the world go by." In late June, Thompson noted that he and his wife "have learned a lot about Saskatoon in our daily drives. It is very beautiful now ... I don't know where all the people are coming from. Population is now supposed to be 110,000." Because Marjorie Thompson was not in good health from 1960 on, Thompson sometimes had to engage in occasional recreational activities on his own – activities that had been difficult to fit in when he was president.

Despite the slower pace, the former president remained active, especially with the advisory planning committee on medicare. Another appointment, which he took up in the autumn of 1959, was as a member on the provincial Oil and Gas Conservation Board. He wrote to Mary in April 1960:

> Our chief duty is to look after the interests of the public from the conservation standpoint and not let the big companies gouge the little man. It is a very big job – 50 million barrels of oil were produced in the province last year ... As you can imagine the two boards have kept me busy and I am looking forward to finishing the health one and easing up ... She [mother] gets more tired than I do and more worried about the medical care business.[1]

> It is very interesting and important work ... The essence of it is that Saskatchewan has very advanced legislation from the conservation standpoint, and the Board tells the numerous companies what they must and must not do in order to prevent waste and get the greatest amount of oil and gas out of each field.[2]

Nevertheless, Thompson found this work taxing, especially for his wife. "Consequently we keep pretty much to ourselves and go out very little," Thompson wrote with relief to his daughter. "It is wonderful to be able to stay at home by ourselves and not feel that we have social obligations which pressed us so hard during the presidential years."[3]

In April 1962, Thompson went to eastern Canada to attend meetings of the National Cancer Institute in Toronto, and then went on to Montreal to receive an honorary degree from McGill, along with the new governor general, Georges Vanier, and the physicist Harold C. Urey, a Nobel Prize laureate for his discovery of the isotope deuterium. Thompson admired the accomplishments of both men, but did not consider this honorary degree particularly special, for McGill "hands out a heck of a lot of them, particularly to wealthy business men, royalty etc."[4]

Thompson had also embarked on a steady routine of writing on diverse subjects that sparked his interest. The NCCU had also asked him to take on a survey and study of graduate education in the sciences in all Canadian universities.

In the survey, Thompson wrote that until about 1900–10, all graduate work for doctorates and almost all study for MAs in Canada was carried out at McGill and the University of Toronto. One of the reasons why there was so little graduate work, besides limited funding and equipment, was that "no need for it was felt. Few posts were available for which graduate training was a prerequisite." Many years passed before an undergraduate degree became insufficient for a university position. In 1946, Saskatchewan became only the fifth university in the country to create a college of graduate studies. The Saskatchewan decision reflected the impetus the war had given to graduate work, especially in science in 1948. That year, Saskatchewan became the ninth Canadian university in Canada to announce it was offering doctoral studies and, in 1952, was the eighth to award its first doctorate. Then, in 1954, the National

Research Council established a "considerable number" of post-doctoral fellowships available to Canadian universities.

Thompson presented evidence that in the postwar period the MSC had declined in importance, whereas the PhD had become the focus of university support and student interest, dramatically demonstrating the rise in the numbers of doctorates completed between 1946 and 1959–60. Incidentally, the University of Saskatchewan came out rather well, standing sixth in Canada over that period.[5] Using and critiquing the projections of the Dominion Statistician, Dr Sheffield, Thompson estimated that the number of graduate students in Canada by 1970 in all fields would be approximately 12,000. (His prediction was correct.) He addressed the fear expressed in many quarters that the United States, with its vastly greater financial resources and opportunities, would entice many Canadian PhD students away. Thompson showed that by 1959–60, 788, or one quarter of the total number of Canadian science students, were studying in American universities, but only about 10 per cent of those students then took employment in the United States.[6] Also, the number of Canadians taking degrees in the US was almost completely offset by the 760 foreign students attending Canadian graduate schools in science. Thompson's conclusion was optimistic as he argued that, "The defects and shortcomings in our Canadian graduate work in the sciences ... must not be allowed to blind us to the great progress that has been made."[7]

In retirement, Dr Thompson was also able to devote more attention to his granddaughters, to whom both he and Marjorie were devoted. As soon as they were able to read, Thompson sent books to them each year. Both Lucy, born in 1944, and Marcia, born in 1948, knew "that he read a lot ... Gramp seemed to especially enjoy biographies and history."[8] For her part, Marcia recalled the "very important contribution that he made through the books that he and Gram gave me each year. They were always signed by Gramp, and I'm sure he selected them as well. So yesterday I went through my personal library and created a list ... I believe it started when I was in high school – as birthday and Christmas presents. I think the poetry collections and the biography probably came first."[9]

Thompson also sent Marcia Winston Churchill's four volume *History of the English-Speaking Peoples*, and *The Tragedies of Shakespeare* for her nineteenth birthday in 1967. For Christmas that year, Thompson sent Marcia "all Shaw's plays." She recalled receiving

The Complete Plays with Prefaces of Bernard Shaw that she "was sure ... was a result of my enthusiasm for Shaw.[10] Her grandfather sent both granddaughters many other books, including dictionaries and complete volumes of American literature, American biography, and *The Oxford Companion to English Literature*.

Because he had been at the centre of university policy-making so long, Thompson noted – somewhat ruefully – early in his retirement his exclusion from the inner circles of power. He experienced this inevitable erosion of his authority both at the senior levels of the university and at the support staff level. As he wrote to his family in Raleigh late in 1961, "Fortunately for me (and I would like to think unfortunately for the university!) I have not been consulted about a single thing since I left office – I mean by administrators."[11] Thompson also experienced the evanescence of his fame at a clerical level, according to his daughter, when on 18 December 1963 he went to the bursar's office "to cash a check" and "no one knew him in the outer office" until "eventually someone came out and identified him."[12]

In the autumn of 1963, Mary hastened to Saskatoon. The quiet retirement of her parents had been suddenly curtailed in November when Marjorie Thompson suffered the first of a series of heart attacks. Mary stayed in Saskatoon for nearly two months to help her parents. Marjorie's illness was compounded by a sustained anxiety so extreme that Mary and her father had to watch John F. Kennedy's funeral on 25 November 1963 with the volume turned as low as possible on a "nearly portable" television set.[13] The next day, Thompson spoke frankly to Mary about her mother's and his own finances for their last years. Mary told her husband that her father had stated that "it now looks as if he will not be the one to go first. Absolute calm acceptance and reasonableness, *as always* [italics added]." In fact, Marjorie managed to stay alive for two more years. One incident in particular suggests Marjorie was as calm, accepting, and rational as her husband. Barbara Chaney, visiting her in hospital, found Marjorie reading Lucy Maud Montgomery. "If I am going to die in the University Hospital," she announced resolutely, "first I am going to read *Anne of Green Gables* again!"[14] She died at the end of the first week of December 1965. Her funeral service was conducted in the Emmanuel College Chapel on 9 December. Her eulogy read in part: "She loved people – so they responded by loving her – and I think, and I believe, that because of her we learned to love people a little more too."

His wife's death left Thompson bereft and lonely. They had shared many happy, mutually helpful years together. He had relied on her when he was stricken with severe gout and she had quietly helped to nurture his career. He was devoted to her and provided as much support as possible, whether by companionship or by providing her with essential household help to ease her duties, especially when he was dean of arts and science and, later, president. Thompson encouraged Marjorie's interest in world affairs, evident in her long-time participation in the University Women's Club and the Local Council of Women, which later joined the Canadian Federation of University Women.

Thompson also remained interested in public affairs and politics. His commitment to the collectivist measures and political philosophy of the CCF made him hostile to the Republicans in the United States. He was not deeply anti-American, but Thompson found many American politicians to be bombastic and their ideas crude and simplistic. Yet he was constrained in his criticisms since his daughter and two grandchildren had settled permanently in Raleigh, North Carolina where his son-in-law was a professor of botany at North Carolina State University. Still, his daughter and her husband must have been sympathetic to the Democratic Party, given the freedom with which Thompson criticized the Republican Party leadership.

Thompson's comments about the American political scene demonstrate his strong support for the Democrats. In June 1952, Dwight D. "Ike" Eisenhower and Senator Robert Taft were the main contenders for the presidential nomination. After reading "Eisenhower's speech and the verbatim report in the *New York Times* of his press conference," Thompson concluded: "he is more conservative than Taft! But I suppose we Canadians should want him to be elected because of his views on foreign policy."[15] Thompson was even more alarmed by the American right when Barry Goldwater was the Republican nominee for president in 1964.

Commenting on the American political scene in August 1952 as the campaign heated up after the two nominating conventions, Thompson, like so many Canadian progressives, praised Adlai Stevenson: "I listened to the Democratic Convention for three nights. Was very much impressed with Stevenson. He sounded the most literate of them all. But I suppose the slap-bang methods of Truman may be more effective with the mass. Nevertheless Ike is going to have his work cut out to beat him ... I hope Stevenson wins. Ike is too conservative for me. Perhaps he had to be if he were going to get the Republican nomination."[16]

Thompson was almost as gloomy about the federal Conservative party victory in Canada in 1957 when John Diefenbaker defeated the Liberal party of Louis St Laurent, ending twenty-two years of Liberal governments. Thompson had disliked Diefenbaker ever since he supported the four malcontent faculty members in the 1919 university crisis, remarking that Diefenbaker never spoke except in a bombastic rant. After the Conservative victory, he wrote in some astonishment to his daughter and her family. "Have you heard our election results? It was a complete surprise to everyone including the conservatives. How Diefenbaker's mouthing of platitudes could convince anyone – let alone a whole electorate – to vote for him, I don't know. I despise the man. You will remember the awful performance when he introduced me to the alumni dinner the day I was inaugurated."[17] Thompson predicted that, as a result of the loss, Louis St Laurent "will undoubtedly retire soon and I hope the liberals have sense enough to elect Pearson in his place."[18]

Thompson read Kennedy's *Profiles in Courage* and "was greatly impressed by it." Thompson also remarked that he had "'made' the Canadian edition of *Time* – in its account of the Sask. Medical Care Plan." To Mary, Thompson observed that that in North Carolina they would be amused to see that [in] all the newspaper accounts (and the papers are full of it), editorials, speeches etc, the committee is always referred to the Thompson Committee."[19]

Thompson complained about American–Canadian trade conflicts, especially in light of the 1963 Canadian bumper wheat crop – "the biggest on record." The government arranged to sell $500 million dollars worth of wheat to Russia (239 million bushels) and 150 million bushels to China. But there is "great annoyance at the American attitude,"[20] for one American senator "branded the Soviet–Canadian deal as 'an inexcusable case of trading with the enemy, for the enemy's benefit, in our cold war with the Soviet Union.'"

> First the prominent people and papers blamed us for dealing with Russia at all. Then when they realized what a good thing it is and that the Russians want more than we can supply, they want to come into the deal. Then they raise cain because Canada sold at the present world price for the next 18 months – thought we should have boosted the price in view of the

scarcity. But our Wheat Board (which handles the whole crop and has 30 years experience) wants to retain the good will of customers and not have them feel they were gouged. We can't charge the Russians more than our other regular customers and we must supply them."[21]

A year later, Thompson was even more discontented politically. He commented to his daughter:

> Our [provincial] election is over and the government got licked ... All our friends are very disappointed. The farmers' vote did it ... The farmers are very sore about the union of CCF with labour to form the New Democratic Party, largely because of labour strikes which held up the movement of wheat. I suppose the union was necessary if the CCF was to go anywhere nationally, but I am afraid the party will gradually die in Saskatchewan, except the urban labour vote – which is very uncertain.[22]

After twenty years of CCF government, Saskatchewan confronted a new political outlook in 1964. Thompson hoped that the new Liberal provincial government of Ross Thatcher would be temperate about medicare. Fortunately they had campaigned on a promise "not to change the Medicare plan," although, since they had tried "to strangle it in 1961 and 62," Thompson did not "trust them." Moreover, in Thompson's estimation, the Liberal government soon began "playing very dirty" for they had "fired several top-notch civil servants, all the members of the Hospital Appeals Board which was established to look after the interests of the Community Clinic doctors who were being harassed by the regular profession."

In 1966, the Liberals also "closed out Bill Baker's Centre for Community Studies," which had been established in 1957. Thompson was so disgusted by the Saskatchewan Liberal party policies that he judged "Thatcher ... to be nearly as far right as [Barry] Goldwater." Hence, he was "glad I am retired and don't have to deal with him on university affairs. I was very lucky to have Douglas and Lloyd during my whole administration."[23] In 1967, Thompson expressed further reservations to his son and daughter-in-law about Thatcher, who boasted that he would closely monitor the university's budget: "The staff are very worried about Thatcher's decision to visit the university every month, as well they might be. The Faculty Association sent a delegation to interview Spinks about it. Later he [Spinks] sent a letter to every member of the staff that attempted to be reassuring. I don't know what he really thinks."[24]

On the federal level, Thompson reflected on the April 1963 election, when Lester Pearson's Liberal party defeated Diefenbaker's minority Conservative government. Contrary to expectations, Pearson and the Liberals failed to win an overall majority and hence were dependent on NDP support.

> We are sorry Douglas and the New Democratic Party didn't do better – just held their own. They have far the best men and for small-l liberals the best ideas. But the desire for a majority govt – "stable govt" – worked strongly against them also the feeling that they are eggheads. Diefenbaker has definitely resigned and Pearson will form a government this week. The prairie vote was amazing. Every single seat in Saskatchewan went Tory as did nearly every seat in Manitoba and Alberta. All because so much wheat was sold at such high prices.[25]

II

If many university developments and numerous societal changes in the western world during the 1960s had left Thompson adrift, much that he had instituted or played a dominant role in bringing to fruition remained. His seminal ideas, embodied in the amendments to the 1907 University Act, which had been incorporated from his ideas on the 1945–46 Survey Committee, had enabled the University of Saskatchewan to function effectively for decades after World War II. Thompson lifted the morale of the university community and was an exemplar of quiet decency and personal probity. His curriculum changes in the College of Arts and Science demonstrated prescience about vital new directions in intellectual inquiry and pedagogy. Thompson's aspiration to create a department of comparative literature, although unfulfilled in the 1940s, foreshadowed by at least four decades what occurred much later throughout North America.

Thompson accelerated advances in graduate research at Saskatchewan and in Canada as a whole. The success of the university's students, particularly in the sciences, was clearly evident. As Thompson was able to tell an audience of alumni, "There are far more Saskatchewan graduates on the staff of the NRC ... than from any other western university ... Only two universities in Canada have more graduates on the staff of the Council."[26] By 1958, so useful had a degree from the University of Saskatchewan become in securing top positions, for example at the federal department of agriculture, that Thompson observed, humorously but with satisfaction, that the direct road between Saskatoon and Ottawa had almost "become a standing joke."[27] Thompson's contributions to cytology to determine the chromosome conditions in wheat hybrids arising from various crosses were still vital in understanding the underlying causes of sterility and linkage. Then there was his supervision of graduate students who went on to have outstanding scientific careers in Canada.

Thompson had accomplished a great deal. He was a university president during a decade characterized by many outstanding leaders in Canadian universities, notably F. Cyril James, principal of McGill from 1940 until 1962, whose publications in economics were admired by American and Canadian scholars. He was a leader in the NCCU and, as the author of a white paper that mapped out Canada's postwar economic strategy, a prominent voice in educational reconstruction issues in Ottawa. William Alexander Macintosh, principal of Queen's from 1951 to 1961, was a leading economist and political scientist who, even more than James, was a dominant presence in Ottawa during World War II in finance and postwar reconstruction. Thompson knew both men well and admired them. Yet neither leader, despite his academic achievements, was in the same rank of world-class scholars as W.P. Thompson. Indeed, no other Canadian university president in the 1950s had such a distinguished research record. Among the four western Canadian presidents of his time, no one achieved Thompson's scholarly status. N.A.M. "Larry" MacKenzie of the University of British Columbia achieved longevity as president from 1944 to 1962 but his biographer described him as "never quite" at home "in the world of professional scholarship."[28] None of Thompson's presidential peers could claim the combination of honours and achievements he had: twice president of the NCCU, in 1954 and 1955; chairman of the National Research Council; president of the Royal Society in 1948; winner of the Flavelle Medal in 1949; member of the National Research Council from 1948 until 1959; vice-president of the Tenth International Genetics Congress in 1958; and president of the Eighth International Botanical Congress in 1959. None had supervised as many MA students who went on to important careers in academic, government, and private sector life as Thompson. In his handwritten notes of the International Genetics Congress, Thompson counted eight former students presenting papers at the meetings.[29]

Thompson pioneered the establishment of genetics as a critical form of intellectual inquiry in Canadian universities in 1915. The University of British Columbia did not even establish a doctoral or master's field in genetics until 1954.[30] The University of Alberta was also slow to develop a genetics field. In 1956, Dr Stephen Threlkeld, now a retired geneticist at McMaster University, asked a senior wheat geneticist at the University of Alberta about the chemical basis of genes and was told "you're wasting your time worrying about that – a gene is just an abstract quantity."[31] The geneticist Dr Len Shebeski joined the University of Saskatchewan to work with and learn from Thompson in 1947 after taking his PhD at Minnesota, because there was no genetics course at Manitoba. A genetics course was only introduced at the University of Manitoba in 1953 when Shebeski left Saskatchewan and returned to Manitoba, where he had received his undergraduate degree, to set one up. Apparently, the first botanist appointed at Manitoba, A.R.H. Buller, did not believe in genetics and so the path he chose in 1912–14 "affected the University of Manitoba for a very long time."[32] In contrast, genetics had been a major part of the curriculum in both biology and agriculture at Saskatchewan since 1915.

Thompson's success in nurturing scientific research at Saskatchewan attracted the attention of the well-known news analyst Willson Woodside. In his book on Canadian universities, he praised Thompson as president of an "institution [that] holds an exceptionally high rank in research on this continent, in relation to its size."[33] An example of the university's excellence in science was the recognition by the National Research Council for 1940–41 in its awarding of postdoctoral fellowships. Usually, McGill and Toronto won most of the awards. It was "worthy of special note that 15 of the 63 awards in 1940–41 were to graduates of Saskatchewan," whereas McGill took 26 and Toronto 11.[34] *Science* concluded that "among all the hundreds of institutions of higher education on this continent," the University of Saskatchewan ranked "eighth ... in its production of distinguished scientists." Among those in Canada, Saskatchewan was second, while "the next [Canadian university] stood 21st."[35]

Upon learning of Thompson's decision to retire, Premier Douglas wrote:

> You have succeeded not only in establishing harmonious relations within the university itself but also with the Board of Governors, the government and the people of Saskatchewan. No words of mine can fully express my admiration for the splendid leadership you have given but I would like you to know how much I appreciate the fine work which you have done and to say what a great privilege it has been to work with you.[36]

At age seventy-five, Thompson began to experience symptoms of the heart illness that was to kill him in 1970. In hospital in November 1966, he received many cards and notes wishing him a speedy recovery. Thompson's brief replies revealed his deepest priorities. To Eli Bornstein, Thompson reflected "It may seem strange but the things of which I am proudest about my presidency are not administrative and curricular changes in which I have had a hand, nor the new ventures such as the medical school nor all the buildings but the fine men whom I was able to appoint to the staff. And I think of such men as Wendell Macleod, Murray Adaskin, Ed Safarian, Roger Graham, Irwin Hilliard and yourself."[37]

Despite his ailments, Thompson continued to write. At the urging of many friends and motivated by his own forty-six years at the university, he decided to write "a personal history." He had known or knew well almost all of the main people in the institution, including past presidents, many members of the Board of Governors, many leading provincial politicians involved in university policies, and most of the deans and department heads. In particular, he had known most of the leading academics, indeed had often played a role in hiring them. Moreover, he had participated in many of the important policy decisions, learning, as he said, that "the real reasons ... were not always the same as the stated reasons, for decisions and actions."[38] In November 1967, he was pleased to announce to his family that "The University of Toronto Press is going to publish my book on the history of the university, provided the university will bear some of the cost. That is only fair since there won't be much sale apart from people connected, past or present, with the university. I haven't much doubt that the Board will agree to put up a subsidy [and] indicated they were quite pleased with the manuscript and complimentary about it."[39]

Thompson's history was written in his characteristically clear and unadorned prose style. His intellect, evident in his earlier writings, had lost none of its lucidity as he aged. His sources were based both on the full records of all the constituent bodies of the university and on personal recollections. The time frame of his work did not go beyond 1959, since that was the year that he retired. That year was the university's jubilee anniversary and it marked a definite break in his own close involvement with the university.

In the book, he discussed World War I and its impact. Although many faculty and students joined the military and served overseas, Thompson never seems to have considered enlisting despite being only twenty-five years old in 1914. He never mentioned any reasons for his failure to engage in the war effort as a recruit. Perhaps his marriage, just as war broke out, coupled with his intense desire to begin his research, explains his decision. In any case, his work as a cytogeneticist was of national importance during the war. Nevertheless, he was uniformly gracious and helpful to veterans at the university both after 1918 and after 1945.

He believed that "the crisis of 1919" was of general interest and importance, because it involved a near civil war within the university and the close involvement of the provincial government. Thompson was certain that the dismissal of the four disgruntled, rebellious faculty was essential both to the survival of the university and to the rescue of President Murray, for Murray's subsequent administration was "characterized by great ability, vision, and resourcefulness that was recognized throughout the province and far beyond."[40]

His discussion of the "post-war explosion" and the creation of a number of important new departments and disciplines is key reading, as is his chapter on the creation and development of the various colleges, not least for the modest explanations of his own constructive work as dean of arts and science. There are fine brief character sketches of such prominent faculty members such as Vernon Fowke, J.W.T. Spinks, Thorbergur Thorvaldson, and the prominent engineering leaders, C.J. Mackenzie and Arthur Porter. Nowhere does Thompson seek to place blame on others for any failures or disputed policy changes, not least the issue of the development of a degree program at Regina College, for which he takes full responsibility.

On 23 October 1968, Thompson was among the first group of Canadians to be invested, by Governor General Roland Michener, as a Companion of the Order of Canada, the highest rank in that firmament. In 1921, Thompson had been one of the first academics elected to the Royal Society of Canada. And in 1968, he was among the first group of Canadians to be so invested in the Order, after his colleague Hilda Neatby who had been honoured in 1967, the first year of the Order.

Thompson recalled that Convocation Hall was "jam packed. Spinks made it into a kind of Convocation with a platform party in academic dress, consisting mainly of vice-presidents and deans."[41] Thompson noted that many of those at the ceremony were

> old friends, especially ones whom I had appointed or for whom I had done something special – men like Eric Nanson and Louis Jaques for whom I had fought the battle with the doctors in 1955 and who reminded me of it ... Most of the people must have gone over to the tea which the Spinks put on in Marquis Hall, and a lot of additional people were there ... For the first time in years I had to take a sleeping capsúle. But I was very pleased that I had come through the day with much standing and walking and excitement without chest pains or nitroglycerine.[42]

A year later, in October 1969, however, he was hospitalized in Toronto soon after moving there to be near his son and daughter-in-law. He wrote reassuringly to Mary, claiming that the problem was caused by all the emotional involvement of moving.[43] He kept on working, noting on 22 October 1969 to his former student, and later colleague, J.G. Rempel, that he was "correcting page proofs of my history of U. of Sask ... I have now been in my house [66 Glenridge Avenue] for some days and like it very much." Soon after, he wrote again to Rempel that he had been "keeping in touch with Saskatoon news because the Horlicks [Medicine faculty member Louis and his wife Ruth] were kind enough to give me a six-month subscription to the *Star Phoenix*."

On 1 January 1970, Thompson wrote to his son and daughter-in-law: "*An Academic's Progress* could be called my memoirs or autobiography, if those terms were not too pretentious. It really consists of some recollections of the academic life that I have written down to occupy leisure time. You have read parts of it some time ago and are therefore familiar with its general nature, but I hope it has improved through recent revisions."[44]

By the time Thompson left the university, the city, and the province that he had known for over half a century for good, Canada had changed profoundly. During the 1950s, the Canada that had been characterized, however loosely, by homage to a British imperial past, by hopes for English–French collaboration, and a diffuse but liberal Protestant set of values in English Canada, had vanished forever. Thompson was one of the few university presidents of his era who did not defer to the British connection and was not a Christian, even in the general sense of his contemporaries, such as Claude Bissell of Toronto, Norman MacKenzie of British Columbia, and A.E. Kerr of Dalhousie. Yet he had been successful as a scientist and administrator within that loose, undefined sense of Canadian identity. His emphasis on the primacy of research in universities had anticipated the academic world that developed in the 1960s. But, by contrast, the wholesale student freedoms in deportment, mixed residences, and the erosion of presidential authority concomitant with the greater faculty autonomy of the 1970s represented a university world that was evolving in a different direction.

Thompson's last letter was written to his daughter and her family on 6 March 1970. He contrasted the efflorescence of the North Carolina world with Toronto's, especially when he looked out his window at the "1 ½ feet of dirty old snow." Still, he placed a table near his front window with African violets, tulips, amaryllis, and begonias on display.

Near the end of March, Thompson suffered a serious heart attack. He was taken to hospital, where he died on 30 March 1970, a few days short of his eightieth birthday. His ashes were flown to Saskatoon. The letters of sympathy sent to Thompson's daughter and son after his death were revealing, particularly from those people who had worked with Thompson or known him for many years. Dr Margaret Newton wrote: "I was very grief-stricken when I learned of the sudden death of your father ... He was one of Canada's most outstanding scientists, and I always felt so happy that I was privileged to work with him for over five years. I was sorry to leave him when I had to go to Winnipeg to take charge of the work on the cereal rusts ... Your mother and father were extremely kind to me and I spent many happy hours with you, Jim and your parents."[45]

Two other testimonials also sum up much of Thompson's personality and career. President Leddy wrote from the University of Windsor. "In terms of personality, he was one of the most dominant and forceful men whom I ever encountered, on which account he very properly earned the deepest respect of all those who came to know him well and who had the privilege of working with him."[46]

Earlier, writing to Sam Wynn, the editor of the *Yorkton Enterprise,* historian Charles Lightbody described Thompson "as no publicity seeker" but a "man of great distinction of mind and character, and has claims to be regarded as Canada's leading educator," and surprisingly, perhaps, "a reserved, rather shy man."[47]

Students' respects for his contributions had been expressed in a November 1959 edition of *The Sheaf,* where the editor praised Thompson's scientific achievements, and reflected that, as president,

> Dr Thompson's greatest contribution has been the building up of the morale of the University through his faith in the institution and by spreading his faith to others. By his personal qualities of fairness and consideration for students and staff, and by working for conditions in the university such as increased salaries and better facilities, he has made people happy and more willing to do their best. In regard to student affairs, it has always been Dr Thompson's policy to give the Student Representative Council the greatest possible freedom in the management of student affairs.[48]

Two faculty members spoke at Thompson's memorial service in Saskatoon on 3 April 1970. J.G. Rempel reflected that "Dr Thompson had many qualities that go with greatness ... But if there was one quality that above all else characterized him, it was his complete integrity."[49] Hilda Neatby remembered him from her own student days when she addressed his inspiring impact as a teacher.

> My personal memories go back to the early 1920s when in the very small university of those days he was known by sight to everyone – tall, strikingly handsome, and even in the eyes of a seventeen-year old, still young. In those early days he always taught the freshman class. He was not a showy lecturer. The first impression given in his lectures was an intensity of concern almost amounting to severity. Then, as one lecture after another

unfolded with superb precision and exactness, revealing a kind of flawless and inevitable pattern, every member of the class realized that he was unusually privileged. Some will remember the class as having provided an intellectual appreciation of a matter which, otherwise, they knew little. Others were captured for life.[50]

APPENDICES

APPENDIX ONE

A Key Example of Thompson's Chromosome Work

In 1916, Thompson had turned the direction of his research to chromosome research because a great deal of work was necessary "on rust strains and chromosome behaviour before any practical solution could be expected."[1] He began to make crosses between his two resistant lines, tetraploids with 14 pairs (28 chromosomes), and non-resistant bread wheats, which are hexaploids with 21 pairs (42 chromosomes). However, it proved difficult to combine rust resistance with the desirable characters of bread wheat, since the problem of sterility in the hybrid resulted from the difference in the chromosome numbers in the parents.[2] As one example, Thompson, with his MA student Lillian Hollingshead, crossed emmer wheat, *Triticum dicoccum*, and *Triticum vulgare* (a bread wheat [n=21]), but again there was "no conjunction of chromosomes."[3]

He and his students also crossed an emmer wheat, *Triticum dicoccum*, (n=14) with *Aegilops speltoides* (n=7), a species of Middle Eastern goat grass, and doubled the chromosome number by using the drug colchicine. The result was a wheat strain resembling prehistoric bread wheat.[4] It was not entirely successful in producing bread wheat, although Thompson actually came very close to recreating it, and in fact was one of the first scientists to make such a cross. This lack of success was largely because of Thompson's difficulties in finding and obtaining a sufficient variety of plant strains he could cross. Bread is made up of the D genome (the entire genetic material of an organism). The donor of the D genome is *Aegelops squarrosa*, known today as *Triticum tauschii*. Thompson created a rust-resistant hybrid, but not edible bread. Nevertheless, Dr E.B. Babcock, head of genetics at Berkeley, and Dr Roy Elwood

Clausen, professor of genetics at Berkeley, viewed Thompson's work on chromosomes as important enough to cite in their 1927 influential text on genetics.[5]

In his 1930 study, Thompson crossed einkorn, *T. monococcum*, (n=7) and emmer wheats (n=14), specifically *T. durum* and *T. turgidum*, and examined both gametes and the first (F_1) and second (F_2) generations of plants. He noted that in screening the most common pollen mother cells, which had 5 bivalents (homologous pairs) and 11 univalents (unpaired), meiosis at F_1 showed that 55 gametes out of 2,048 studied would have had 14 chromosomes, the number in the gametes of the emmer plant. The chromosome numbers of the F_2 plants showed that the great majority of F_1 gametes that functioned successfully must have had 14 chromosomes.

In their 1994 paper proposing a targeted genetic mapping strategy for wheat, the distinguished and prolific wheat geneticists, K.S. Gill and B.S. Gill cited Thompson and Robertson's 1930 work. The University of Saskatchewan geneticist Dr G. Rank has commented on the paper by Gill and Gill and their citation of Thompson and Robertson's work as follows:

> Bread wheat has a large genome of 16,000,000,000 base pairs – roughly five times the size of the human genome. Genome complexity is further complicated by the presence of an allopolyploid structure of three related genomes (A, B, and D). This intricate structure results in difficulties in the classical mapping of genes by recombination frequencies. Early cytological observations of Thompson and Robertson (1930) laid the foundation for mapping genes based on later cytological and molecular technology. Their 1930 publication showed that chromosome pairing between wheat varieties decreased with the evolutionary distance between varieties. This contributed to the subsequent identification of chromosomal regions exhibiting high genetic recombination and the potential to reduce the effective genome size for genetic mapping.[6]

APPENDIX TWO

Thompson's Work on Endosperm

Dr Margaret Steeves has demonstrated Thompson's continuing influence as a major international scholar in wheat rust research, examining how his work, notably in two papers published in 1930 and 1949, has been cited throughout the 1990s and even as recently as 2003 and 2006.[1] Thompson's publications on plant endosperm attracted the most attention. Writing in 2006, V.A. Sokolov reminded readers that 99 per cent of human food is derived from 24 cereal species.[2] Since the main commercial species is grain and 90 per cent of that grain is endosperm, we can easily grasp why Thompson's study of the academic and applied problems of wheat was so significant.

The main focus of Professor Thompson's research and that of his students was the study of chromosome behaviour, both paired and unpaired, in interspecific crosses (crosses between species) in the genus *Triticum* (wheat) as well as in hybrids (crosses between different genera) and the accompanying sterility often resulting from these crosses. This same problem exists today in the cereals as well as in many other genera (1, 3, 5 4, 8) and is the result of chromosomes not pairing. The mechanism that governs the success or failure of crosses between plant species of different ploides (number of sets of chromosomes in a cell) remains elusive and may result in dysfunctional endosperm and aborted embryos and fruit.

Professor Thompson was one of the earliest researchers to cite endosperm dysfunction as a cause of seed failure. He concluded that on the female side there was almost no pre-fertilization breakdown, because nearly all embryo sacs were capable of fertilization. The most important cause of sterility was abortion of the endosperm, which caused the death of the embryo. Thompson found that when two species that differ in chromosome numbers are crossed the cross is usually much more successful if the species with the larger number is used as the female parent than if it is used as the male parent. Thompson concluded that the reason was the genetic constitution of the endosperm itself.[3] Thompson's work is cited in many recent research publications. Some of them, in addition to Sokolov's historical review, will be noted here.

Thompson demonstrated the exact relation between chromosome numbers, shrivelling of the endosperm, and elimination of hybrid types in crosses between 21 and 14 chromosome wheats *Triticum vulgare* (n=21) and the emmer series (n=14), by assessing the vigour of the seeds of the F_1 generation.[4]

Because the number of chromosomes in the offspring does not give the number in the endosperm, it was necessary to backcross, that is, to cross one pure parent with an F_1 offspring. This is done because the number of chromosomes in the pure parent is already known, so the number in the F_1 offspring is calculated by examining the pollen mother cells and counting the number of univalent chromosomes. In every case in which *vulgare* was the female parent the majority of the seeds were plump. The results were the same for all three kinds of F_1 backcrosses; *vulgare* × *dicoccum*; *vulgare* × *durum*; *vulgare* × *persicum*. Thompson concluded that the condition of the endosperm depended on chromosome content and emphasized the advantage of using the parent with the larger chromosome number as the female.

Thompson also compared the chromosome numbers calculated in the endosperm with the physical condition of the seed; plump, wrinkled, shrivelled, large, or small. Furthermore, he reiterated that endosperm conditions played a large part in the non-appearance of many types of the F_2 and later generations of ordinary crosses. From genetic analysis of these crosses, Thompson urged that special care be taken in the selection and culture of seeds, so as to isolate shrivelled seeds, since they represent genetic types not found in the plump seeds. Special efforts were also urged by H.C. Sharma in his paper on "wide crosses," crosses between crop plants and wild relatives. Sharma found that wide crosses were a source of desirable characteristics for genetically improving crops. Wide crosses where female parents contribute lower chromosome numbers have also been successful. Thompson found the same results in crosses of *Aegilops* (n=7), various species of wheat, and with rye (n=7).

In a companion paper to determine whether the rule that holds in interspecific crosses in wheat – that the best results are obtained when the parent with the larger chromosome number is female – would hold in other plants, Thompson published the results of a wide variety of crosses from a survey of the literature. As a rule, the results were similar in other genera of plants: *Nicotiana* (tobacco), *Brassica* (turnip), *Limum* (Flax), *Digitalis*, and others. An apparent exception was *Frageria* (strawberry) where Thompson postulated that the seedlings were maternal and parthenogenetic (an embryo developing from an unfertilized egg cell).

Thompson concluded from the number of cases reviewed as well as the work on wheat that success or failure was due to the difference in the condition of the endosperm chromosome. When the species with the larger number is female, "the excess of the chromosomes over other species are doubled in the endosperm, whereas when it is male they are single."

Endosperm is formed when two polar nuclei, derived from each end (pole) of the embryo sac, fuse with a male nucleus at the centre of the sac. The resulting ploidy is 3n in many angiosperms – though depending on how the embryo sac develops, ploidy may be 5n or even 2n. Sokolov has shown that the polar nuclei number in 13 per cent of species is not equal to 2, and the resulting ploidy is 2n, 1 maternal: 1 paternal genome, not 3n.

The endosperm nourishes the embryo and its successful development is crucial in producing viable seed. It has been suggested that the normal development of the endosperm usually requires a parental genomic ratio of 2m: 1p (maternal/paternal genomes) or 3n. Deviation from this ratio by crossing plants of related species but different ploidies levels is associated with non-viable seed. It has also been proposed that the underlying requirement for this ratio is genomic or parental *imprinting*. This is the process by which a gene is expressed differently in offspring depending on the parent of origin. Bushell et al. state that the term *imprinting*, as proposed by Haig and Westoby, represents a struggle over resource allocation to offspring between maternal- and paternal-derived genomes.[5] The use of the term *imprinting* has returned thinking about endosperm dysfunction to qualitative differences, as Thompson had postulated, rather than to numerical ones.

In a discussion of imprinting, scientists have pointed out that the 2m: 1p rule isn't always successful. This is because the strength of the imprinting signals in different species lies in being unequal, the results of a long, independent evolution, as seen in wheat and oats.

To quantify the strength of the imprinting signals, the term EBN (endosperm balance number) was introduced and it is this effective ploidy, rather than the actual ploidy, that must be in a 2m: 1p ratio. Furthermore, from this work on *Datura* (a genus of nine widely cultivated species of flowers with hallucinogenic properties), it was concluded that only 2 chromosomes, 19.2 and 1.2, i.e., less than a genome, may be involved in determining the EBN (endosperm balance number), or effective ploidy, in the endosperm.

On a different, but slightly related, note, Sharma has reviewed the success rate (seed set) in about 100 wide crosses (crosses between species of the same or different genera) of wheat and its relatives, oats, barley, *Aegelops*, and the *Agropyron* (wheat grass) complex.[6] Evidently, wide crosses have attracted significant attention: between crop plants as well as with their wild relatives to improve yield or to find sources of resistance to disease. Wide crosses are not new. They have been practised since the early 1900s by Thompson and other researchers. What is new is that post-fertilization barriers to wide crosses can be overcome by various technologies, embryo culture for example. After all, wild species that cannot be crossed with the crop species are of no use for crop improvement. Though finding answers to sterility problems is essential to the production of viable seeds, it also permits the erection of hybridization barriers to control gene flow in the deployment of genetically modified crop plants and contain their spread.

It is a credit to the calibre of the research undertaken by Professor Thompson, his associates, and his students that their work has been cited in these current worldwide research journals.

APPENDIX THREE

Recent References to Thompson's Wheat Rust Research

1 Bushel, C., Spielman, M., and Scott, R.J. 2003. "The Basis of Natural and Artificial 1 Postzygotic Hybridization Barriers in Arabidopsis Species." *The Plant Cell* vol 15: 1430–42.

2 Haig, D. and Westoby, M. 1991. "Genomic Imprinting in Endosperm." *Philosophical Transactions of the Royal Society of London: Biological Sciences* vol. 333: 1–13.

3 Johnston, S.A. and Hanneman, R.E. Jr. 1999. "Nature of the Genetic Control of Endosperm Balance Number based on Aneuploid Analyses of *Datura.*" *Sexual Plant Reproduction* vol. 12, no. 2: 71–5.

4 Mont, J., Iwanaga, M. Orjeda, G. and Watanabe, K. 1993. "Abortion and determination of stages for embryo rescue in crosses between sweet-potato, *Ipomoea batatas* (2n – 6x = 90) and its wild relative, *I. trifida* (2n = 2x =30)." *Sexual Plant Reproduction* vol. 6: 176–82.

5 Sharma, H.C. 1995. "How Wide Can a Wide Cross Be?" *Euphytica* vol. 82, no.1: 43–64.

6 Sokolov, V.A. 2006. "Imprinting in Plants." *Russian Journal of Genetics* vol. 42, no. 9: 1043–52.

7 Gill, K.S. and Gill, B.S. 1994, "Mapping in the Realm of Polyploidy: The Wheat Model." *Wheat Genetics, Resource Center,* Kansas State University, Manchester, Kansas, 1310 Essays, 16, 841–46.

The following three articles remain the most cited of Thompson's work:

Thompson, W.P. 1930. "Causes of Difference in Success of Reciprocal Interspecific Crosses." *American Naturalist* vol. 64: 407–21.

Thompson, W.P. 1930. "Shrivelled Endosperm in Species Crosses in Wheat, Its Cytological Causes and Genetical Effects." *Genetics* vol. 15: 99–113.

Thompson, W.P. 1949. "Some Problems in the Cytogenetics of Cereals: A Historical Review." *Transactions of the Royal Society of Canada*. V. XLIII: Series III: 35–44.

APPENDIX FOUR

Bibliography of Papers and Books Published by W.P. Thompson

ON MORPHOLOGY

"The Origin of Ray Tracheids in the Coniferae." *Botanical Gazette* vol. 50 (August 1910): 101–16.

"The Origin of the Multiseriate Ray of the Dicotyledons." *Annals of Botany* vol. 25 (October 1911): 1005–14.

"Ray Tracheids in Abies." *Botanical Gazette* vol. 53 (April 1912): 331–8.

"Artificial Production of Aleurone Grains." *Botanical Gazette* vol. 54 (1912): 336–9.

"The Structure of the Stomata in Certain Cretaceous Conifers." *Botanical Gazette* vol. 54 (1912): 63–6.

"The Anatomy and Relationships of the *Gnetales* I. Ephedra." *Annals of Botany* vol. 26 (October 1912): 1077–1104.

"Is the Vesselless Secondary Xylem of Certain Angiosperms a Retention of Primitive Structure?" *Science* no. 53 (March 1915): 1105 (with I.W. Bailey).

"Preliminary Note on the Morphology of *Gnetum*." *American Journal of Botany* vol. 2 (April 1915): 161.

"The Morphology and Affinities of *Gnetum*." *American Journal of Botany* vol. 4 (April 1916): 135–84.

"Are Tetracentron,Trochodendron and Drimys Specialized or Primitive Types?" *Memoir New York Botanical Garden* vol. 6 (1916): 27–32 (with I.W. Bailey).

"Independent Evolution of Vessels in *Gnetales* and Angiosperms." *Botanical Gazette* vol. 65 (January 1918): 83–90.

"The Canons of Comparative Anatomy." *Science* vol. 48 (October 1918): 371–2.

"Additional Notes on Angiosperms in Which Vessels are Absent from the Wood." *Annals of Botany* vol. 32 (October 1918): 503–13 (with I.W. Bailey).

"Companion Cells in the Bast of Gnetum and Angiosperms." *Botanical Gazette* vol. 68 (December 1919): 451–9.

"Development of the Embryo of Gnetum." *Botanical Gazette* vol. 60 (December 1920): 436–45 (with Hulda Haining).

"Marsilia Vestita in Western Canada." *American Fern Journal* vol. 16 (January 1926): 24–5.

"The Relationships of the Different Types of Angiospermic Vessels." *Annals of Botany* vol. 37 no. 2 (April 1923): 183–92.

"Heredity and Education." Eighth Annual Convention of the Saskatchewan Educational Association at Prince Albert, April, 1916.

ON GENETICS

"The Inheritance of the Length of the Flowering and Ripening Periods in Wheat." *Transactions of the Royal Society of Canada* vol. 12 (1918): 69–87.

"Modern Views on the Origin of Species." *Transactions of the Saskatchewan Naturalists Club,* 1919.

"Scientific Research in Relation to Agricultural Problems." *Science* vol. 52 (October 1920): 301–8.

"Earliness in Wheat and its Inheritance." *Scientific Agriculture* 1921.

"Cytological Condition in Wheat in Relation to the Rust Problem." *Scientific Agriculture* vol. 5 (April 1925): 237–9

"The Correlation of Characters in Hybrids of *Triticum durum* and *Triticum vulgare*." *Genetics* vol. 10 (May 1925): 285–304.

"Chromosome Behaviour in Triploid Wheat Hybrids." *Journal of Genetics* vol. 17 (August 1926): 43–9.

"Chromosome Behaviour in a Cross between Wheat and Rye." *Genetics* vol. 11 (July 1926): 317–32.

"Preponderance of Dicoccum-like Characters and Chromosome Numbers in Hybrids Between *Triticum dicoccum* and *Triticum vulgare*." *Journal of Genetics* vol. 17 (January 1927) (with Lillian Hollingshead).

"The Cytology of a Tetraploid Wheat Hybrid (*Triticum spelta* × *T. monoccum*." *American Journal of Botany* vol. 14 (June 1927): 327–33 (with M.C. Melburn).

"The Cytology of Species Hybrids in Wheat." *Scientific Agriculture* vol. 8 (September 1927): 56–62.

"Characters of Common Wheat in Plants with Fourteen Chromosomes." *Transactions of the Royal Society of Canada* (1927): 273–7.

"Chromosome Lumbers in Functioning Germ Cells of Species Hybrids in Wheat." *Genetics* vol. 13 (November 1928): 456–69 (with D.R. Cameron).

"The Genetics and Cytology of a Dwarf Wheat." *Transactions of the Royal Society of Canada* (1928): 335–48.

"Heterotypic Prophases in the Absence of Chromosome Pairing." *Canadian Journal of Research* vol. 1 (1929): 512–27 (with M.C. Melburn).

"Chromosome Homologies in Wheat and Aegilops," *American Journal of Botany* vol. 16 (April 1929): 238–45 (with J.A. Jenkins).

"Shrivelled Endosperm in Species Crosses in Wheat, its Cytological Causes and Genetical Effects." *Genetics* vol. 15 (March 1930): 99–113.

"Chromosome Conditions in the Second and Third Generations of Pentaploid Wheat hybrids." *Canadian Journal of Research* 2nd series, (1930): 162–70 (with J.A. Jenkins).

"Cytological Irregularities in Hybrids between Species of Wheat with the Same Chromosome Number." *Cytologia* 1st series (1930): 252–62 (with H.T. Robertson).

"Chromosomes," in *Book of Popular Science*. The Grolier Society, 1920.

"Causes of Difference in Success of Reciprocal Interspecific Crosses." *American Nature* vol. 54 (1930): 407–19.

"Cytology and Genetics of Crosses between Fourteen- and Seven-Chromosome Species of Wheat." *Genetics* 16th series (July 1931): 309–24.

"Chromosome Homologies in Wheat, Rye and Aegilops." *Canadian Journal of Research* vol. 4 (1931): 624–34.

"Studies on the Failure of Hybrid Germ Cells to Function in Wheat Species Crosses." *Canadian Journal of Research* vol. 6 (1932): 362–73 (with J.M. Armstrong).

"The Causes of the Cytological Results Obtained in Species Crosses in Wheat." *Canadian Journal of Research* vol. 10 (1934): 190–8.

"A Case of Recessive Polydactylism." *Transactions of The Royal Society of Canada* (1933): 169–71 (with W. Shevkenek).

"Some Factors in the Different Chromosome Sets of Common Vulgare Wheat." *Canadian Journal of Research* vol. 12 (1935): 335–45 (with T.J. Arnason and R.M. Love).

"Development of Endosperm and Embryo in Reciprocal Interspecfic Intercrosses." *Journal of Genetics* vol. 34 (1937) (with J.W. Boyes).

"Reciprocal Chromosome Translocations without Semi-Sterility." *Cytologia*. Fujii Jubilee volume (1937): 336–42 (with Mary Thompson).

"The Cytogenetics of Non-Amphidiploid Derivatives of Wheat-Rye Hybrids." *Cytologia* vol. 8 (February 1938): 377–97 (with G.F. Ledingham).

"The Causes of Self-Sterility in Rye." *American Journal of Botany* vol. 20 (October 1939): 567–71 (with Margaret Landis).

"The Causes of Hybrid Sterility and Incompatibility." *Transactions of the Royal Society of Canada* vol. 34 (1940) 1–13.

"The Artificial Synthesis of a 42-chromosome Species Resembling Common Wheat." *Science* vol. 93 (1941): 479–80.

"Chromosome Behaviour and Fertility in Diploid Wheat with Translocation Complexes of Four and Six Chromosomes." *Canadian Journal of Research* vol. 20 (1942): 267–81 (with I. Hutcheson).

"The Artificial Synthesis of a 42-chromosome Species Resembling Common Wheat." *Canadian Journal of Research* vol. 21 (April 1943): 134–44 (with E.J. Britten and J.C. Harding.)

"The Causes of Incompatibility Between Barley and Rye." *Canadian Journal of Research* vol. 23 (February 1945): 1–15 (with D.M. Johnson).

"Mutations." *Transactions of the Royal Society of Canada* vol. 42 (1948): 63–76.

"Some Problems in the Cytogenetics of Cereals: a Historical Review." *Transactions of the Royal Society of Canada* vol. 43 (1949): 35–44.

"The Cause and Mode of Evolution." In *Evolution: Its Science and Doctrine*, symposium presented to the Royal Society of Canada. Toronto (1960): 90–7.

ON EDUCATION

"The Junior College Within the University." *Proceedings of the National Conference of Canadian Universities* (1934): 72–5.

"Education and Moral Values." *Canadian Education* vol. 7 (1951): 30–9.

"Presidential Address." *Proceedings of the National Conference of Canadian Universities* (1954).

"The Job of a University President." *Proceedings of the National Conference of Canadian Universities. Queen's Quarterly* vol. 62 (Winter 1956).

"A University President Looks at Research." *Queen's Quarterly* vol. 64 (Summer 1957).

"The Faculty Association and the Administration." CAUT *Bulletin* 7 (October 1958): 6–9.

"Annual Reports of President," University of Saskatchewan 1949–50 to 1958–59.

"Canadian Botany: An Appraisal." *Proceedings of the IX International Botanical Congress* III (1959): 8–12 (presidential address).

"University Government." CAUT *Bulletin* 9 (1960): 4–9.

"The Number of University Teachers: Needs and Prospects." CAUT *Bulletin* 12 (1963): 16–23.

"A University in Trouble." *Saskatchewan History* 17 (1964): 81–104.

"Saskatchewan Doctors' Opinions of Medicare: A Questionnaire Survey." *Canadian Medical Association Journal* vol. 93 (1965): 971–6.

"The Saskatchewan Medicare Survey: A Follow-Up Study." *Canadian Doctor* (December 1965).

BOOKS

Report of the Advisory Planning Committee on Medical Care to the Government of Saskatchewan. Regina: Queen's Printer, 1962 (with committee).

Documents on Health Care – submitted to the Advisory Planning Committee on Medical Care. Vol. 1. Selected Briefs. Regina: Saskatchewan Department of Public Health, 1963 (with committee).

Graduate Education in the Sciences in Canadian Universities. Toronto: University of Toronto Press, 1963.

Medical Care: Programs and Issues. Toronto: Clarke, Irwin, 1964.

The University of Saskatchewan: A Personal History. Toronto, University of Toronto Press, 1970.

UNPUBLISHED WORKS

An Academic's Progress, 1970.

Notes

PREFACE

1 Thompson fonds, IX. a). viii), Regina Alumni, handwritten manuscript undated; probably given as a speech in the spring of 1943.

CHAPTER ONE

1 Thompson fonds, VI, *An Academic's Progress*, 13–14.
2 Richard Rempel fonds, Margaret Thompson, Memories of the Thompson family.
3 Palmer, *Canada's 1960s*, 416.
4 Thompson to Mary Smith, Mary Thompson Smith Papers, 14 October 1951.
5 Thompson to Mary Smith, Mary Thompson Smith Papers, 21 July 1954.
6 Garvin, *Joseph Chamberlain*, Volume 1, 392.
7 Thompson fonds, IX. a). i) General.
8 Thompson, *An Academic's Progress*, 28.
9 Thompson fonds, IX. a). viii) Alumni.
10 Thompson, *An Academic's Progress*, 27.
11 Faculty Biographies file – Thompson fonds.
12 From 1910 to 1920 John Bracken was professor of field husbandry; later he became head of the Progressive Conservative party, first in Manitoba and then in Canada.
13 Thompson family photograph album; digital copy with University of Saskatchewan Archives.
14 Bruneau, William. "A Rural Secondary Education: Saskatchewan, 1958–61." Draft copy with author.

15 Wise, "God's Peculiar Peoples," *The Shield of Achilles*, 36–61.
16 Thompson, *An Academic's Progress*, 26.
17 Ibid., 17.
18 Ibid., 26.
19 Ibid., 22.
20 Thompson fonds, IX. a). ix). University.
21 Neville Thompson cites this view of Toronto in his 2009 unpublished paper "Winston Churchill in the Second World War: A Canadian Perspective," taken from Armstrong and Nelles, *Methodist Bicycle Company*, 6.
22 Author conversation with Margaret Thompson, 12 September 2008.
23 Thompson, *An Academic's Progress*, 29.
24 Ibid., 26.
25 Harvard University Archives, UAV 161, 201–10. Thompson's academic records as a PhD candidate.
26 Neatby, *Queen's University*, 256. Neatby notes that the University of Toronto's endowment in 1904 was "less than $800,000," while senior universities in the United States, notably Harvard, had an endowment of $22,000,000 in 1909, when President Eliot retired.
27 Greenlee, *Falconer*, 107.
28 Humphries, "*Honest Enough*," 128.
29 In fact, the wealthy meatpacking businessman, Sir Joseph Flavelle (1858–1939), had been the chairman, not Goldwin Smith.
30 Thompson, *An Academic's Progress*, 57.
31 Thompson fonds, IV. b) Faculty Association, 1955–59. Verso of page 2. Thompson's marginal criticisms of a November 1959 *Report of Saskatchewan Faculty Association Committee on Faculty Participation in University Governance*. Thompson never lost his critical assessments of Oxford and Cambridge, commenting in his marginalia that Oxford and Cambridge "gradually evolved techniques of democratic self-government." However, "academic self-government at Oxford and Cambridge (so often quoted) led to stagnation and decay and that parliamentary intervention was necessary and led to admirable reforms."
32 Thompson, *An Academic's Progress*, 92–3.
33 Thompson, "Ray Tracheids in the Coniferae," 101–16.
34 Gingras, "Financial Support for Post-graduate Students and the Development of Scientific Research in Canada," 308–9. Roy M. MacLeod and E. Kay Andrews published a useful history of the Exhibition scholars, "Scientific careers of Exhibition Scholars," 1011–16.
35 Brebner, *Scholarship for Canada*, 427.

36 Thompson, *An Academic's Progress*, 95.
37 Ibid., 95.
38 Thompson had cited Jeffery twice in his first article, so was acquainted with some of Jeffery's work.
39 Thompson, *An Academic's Progress*, 106.
40 The same sum in 2013 would have had the purchasing power of approximately $59,000.
41 President's Office fonds, Series I, file B.8, Jeffrey to Murray, 13 January 1913. The sum of $2,000 in 1912 would have the purchasing power of $48,000 in 2013.
42 Richard Rempel fonds, from Margaret Thompson, notes of a talk W.P. Thompson gave when reviewing his career at a biology department function in Saskatoon circa late 1967.
43 Thompson, "Morphology and Affinities of *Gnetum*" vol. 4, 135–84. Paleobotanist Dr Margaret Steeves helpfully drew my attention to this article and composed significant parts of this section on the nature and importance of Dr Thompson's research on the *Gnetales*. (Genus = a classification term in biology designating plants above species and below families.)
44 "Biology and Evolution of the *Gnetales*."
45 Thompson, "A Botanical Trip."
46 The Polish scholar Raphael Lemkin first coined the term "genocide" to describe the Nazi program of exterminating the Jews in 1944. The term was then used at the Nuremberg Trials in 1946. In 1985, the United Nations recognized and condemned the German attempt to exterminate the Herero and Nama peoples as one of the earliest twentieth-century forms of genocide. Thompson published recollections of his time in South West Africa in *The Sheaf* in 1916, and mentioned the capture of the former German colony by Smuts and Botha, but said nothing about – or still knew nothing about – the earlier German massacre. See Thompson fonds, IX. a) ix) Botanical Addresses.
47 Thompson, *An Academic's Progress*, 29.
48 Ibid., 92–3.
49 Wallace, it will be recalled, developed his theory of evolution based on natural selection independently of Darwin. In early 1859 Wallace sent the paper outlining his hypothesis to Darwin, who was prompted to publish later in 1859 his *Origin of Species* so as not to be denied the honour of being the originator of the theory.
50 Richard Rempel fonds, Dr Margaret Steeves, *The Gnetales*.
51 President's Office fonds, Series I, B38/13 Departmental Reports Biology (1917–37). *The American Journal of Botany* was the official publication of

the Botanical Society of America. Thompson was also collaborating with Professor I.W. Bailey of Harvard on a series of articles on the anatomy of flowering plants.

52 Thompson, *An Academic's Progress*, 125.

53 Mary Thompson Smith Papers, *The Fortunate Man*, 5.

54 Thompson, *An Academic's Progress*, 112–13. The other two scientists who rediscovered Mendel were the German, Carl Erich Correns (1864–1935) and the Austrian, Erich von Tschermak-Seysenegg (1871–1962).

55 Thompson, *An Academic's Progress*, 112.

56 Kandel, Eric, Thomas Hunt Morgan, 8.

57 Thompson fonds, misc. Thompson to Murray, 15 August 1912.

58 President's Office fonds, Series I, B.8 Appointments, 1907–1937 – Te-Th.

59 Thompson fonds, IX. a). viii) "Alumni Dinner ... to Celebrate 50th Anniversary of Arrival at University," 14 September 1963, 5.

60 Ibid., 5.

61 President's Office fonds, Series I, Appointments, E.C. Jeffrey to Murray, 26 January 1913 and R.B. Thomson to Murray, 29 March 1913.

62 Kerr, Don "The College Building," 3.

63 Thompson fonds, IX. a). ix) Botanical Addresses. "Dinner in Connection with Opening of Biology Building," September 1960. Thompson acknowledged that Murray later "completely changed his opinion of biology and biologists." 2.

64 Murray and Murray, *Prairie Builder*, 61.

65 Hayden, *Balance*, 43.

66 Murray and Murray, *Prairie Builder*, 62–5.

67 Emmanuel was built between the years 1914 to 1929. Qu'Appelle Hall was built in 1914–16; Physics in 1919–21; Chemistry 1922–24; St. Andrews, 1922–25; Memorial Gates, 1927–28; the Observatory, 1928–29; Crop Science and Field Husbandry, 1929, and Rutherford Rink, 1929.

68 Thompson fonds, IX. a). viii) Alumni. "Welcome to Agricultural Graduates" 10 January 1955.

69 Mary Thompson Smith Papers, *The Fortunate Man*, 5.

70 Ibid., 4.

71 Wingham is noted for being the birthplace and home during her early years of the writer Alice Munro, nee Laidlaw, in 1931.

72 Just before the collapse of the "boom," President Murray had epitomized the optimism claiming: "the population of Saskatchewan would reach two million by 1931, at which time the University of Saskatchewan would rival the University of Toronto. Vaughan, *Aggressive in Pursuit*, 18.

73 Waiser, *Saskatchewan*, 162.
74 Kerr and Hanson, *Saskatoon*, 105.
75 Waiser, *Saskatchewan*, 156.
76 Kerr and Hanson, 105–13 and *passim*.
77 Murray and Murray, *Prairie Builder*, 69.
78 Hayden, *Balance*, 20.
79 Thompson and Jenkins, "Chromosome Homologies" and "Chromosome Conditions."
80 Cameron and Thompson, "Chromosome Numbers."
81 Thompson, Arnason, and Love, "Factors in the Different Chromosome."
82 Thompson fonds IX, a), vi), Biology Dinner speech. 14 September 1963.
83 Thompson fonds, Thompson to Murray, 9 December 1929, from Berkeley where Thompson was on sabbatical.
84 Thompson fonds, Murray to Thompson, 17 March 1930.
85 Dr Margaret Thompson's conversation with Richard Rempel in Toronto, 14 June 2007.
86 Thompson fonds, IX. a). vi), Biology Dinner speech, 14 September 1963.
87 Hayden, *Balance*, 97–8.
88 Horn, *Academic Freedom*, 53.
89 Address to the biology department, 1963, 7.
90 Thompson, "A University in Trouble," 81–104.
91 Thompson, *A Personal History*, 106–18, particularly 109–11.
92 Hayden, *Balance*, 78–116.
93 Hayden, "The Fight," 53–6.
94 Murray and Murray, *Prairie Builder*, 127.
95 Spafford, *No Ordinary Academics*, 85. MacKay had been a popular speaker during the war as well as a former student of Murray's at Dalhousie and had been considered a friend of the president. After his dismissal, MacKay went on to have a good career at McGill where he became professor of logic and metaphysics and, eventually, dean of arts.
96 Ibid., 94. Greenway was not a member of Council.
97 Hayden, *Balance*, 99.
98 Murray placed his own letter of resignation before the Board of Governors. The board refused to accept Murray's offer.
99 Kerr and Hanson, *Saskatoon*, 220.
100 Horn, *Academic Freedom*, 58.
101 Spafford, *No Ordinary Academics*, 89.
102 Thompson, "A University in Trouble," 83.
103 Thompson, *A Personal History*, 106–17.
104 Thompson, "A University in Trouble," 99.

105 See Section 661 of the University Act, which provided that no member of the teaching staff could be removed without the recommendation of the president.
106 Thompson, "A University in Trouble," 104.
107 Thompson fonds, IX. a). viii), Alumni. "To the Reunion of Class of 1923," 11 May 1963.
108 Daniel Soberman, quoted in Horn, 286.
109 All of these verdicts are taken from his biography. Murray and Murray, *Prairie Builder*, 234.

CHAPTER TWO

1 Zhong, "The Position of Gnetales."
2 Thompson fonds, Faculty Publications file.
3 Thompson and Haining, "Development of the Embryo," 436–45.
4 Richard Rempel fonds, "Notes taken by Margaret Thompson in 1959 of W.P. Thompson's oral account of his scientific career." Unpublished.
5 Ibid., 2.
6 President's Office fonds, Series I. B 38/13. Departmental Reports – Biology Department 1914–37.
7 Kandel, Morgan, 8.
8 Richard Rempel fonds, notes given to Richard Rempel by Dr Margaret Thompson, summer of 2006, 10.
9 Thompson, "Mutations," 63. Morgan was awarded a Nobel Prize in 1933.
10 Fowke, *Wheat Economy*, 78 and *passim*.
11 Ibid., 78; and Estey, *History of Plant Pathology*, 87.
12 Thompson fonds, VIII. a) Honorary Degrees, 1913–1968 and *An Academic's Progress*, 151.
13 Waiser, *Saskatchewan*, 220–21.
14 Martens and Dyck, "Genetics of Resistance," 82.
15 Fowke, *Wheat Economy*, 78 and Waiser, *Saskatchewan*, 218.
16 Appendix 2, "The Nature of Rust Fungi."
17 "The Solving of the Wheat Rust Problem," paper delivered to the Royal Society of Canada, 1949. Thompson fonds, IX, a).
18 Thompson fonds, IX a) ix) Botanical addresses. "Heredity And Education," delivered at the Eighth Annual Convention of the Saskatchewan Educational Association, April 1916; Biffen, 12.
19 Buller, (1874–1944) established the Department of Botany at the University of Manitoba, and was elected to the Royal Society of Canada and the Royal Society of London in 1937, the year he won the Flavelle

Medal, the greatest honour that the Royal Society of Canada can bestow upon a botanist.

20 Thompson fonds MG 17, IX; ix. Presidential Office, U. of S. a) Addresses vii) Tributes, Honorary Degrees, speech to the Kiwanis Club on 14 May 1957.The Murray Memorial Day Annual Luncheon.

21 Thompson, "Young Professor: Research." Xeroxed copy of statement prepared for the staff of the Dept. of Biology by Dr Thompson, 9 Oct. 1968 [signed L. C. Paul].

22 Richard Rempel fonds, unpublished notes taken by Dr Margaret Thompson of a talk the recently retired president gave on his career as a geneticist, late 1959.

23 Because of his support of Thompson's idea and because of his extraordinary knowledge of plants, W.P. Fraser was hired at the University of Saskatchewan in 1923.

24 Richard Rempel fonds, unpublished notes taken by Dr Margaret Thompson of a talk the President gave on his career as a geneticist, late 1959.

25 President's Office fonds, Series I, B.78. National Research Council, folder. 1. Report of the Administrative Chairman of the Canada Honorary Advisory Council for Scientific and Industrial Research, 1918.

26 Gridgeman, *Biological Sciences*, 7.

27 Thompson fonds, IX a) viii) Alumni. "Dinner ... to Celebrate 50th Anniversary of Arrival at University," 14 September 1963. In 1917 Fraser was appointed to the Federal Department of Agriculture. In 1925, Fraser became a full professor at the University of Saskatchewan. Earlier, in 1918, Murray and Thompson persuaded the Federal Department of Agriculture to establish a laboratory at the University of Saskatchewan under Fraser's authority.

28 Board of Governors minutes, 8 May 1920.

29 Kimber, "Polyploid Wheats," 487–92.

30 Thompson fonds, IX a) ix) Botanical, "Genomic Constitution of Wheat and Some Consequences," March 1960, unpublished.

31 Thompson, *An Academic's Progress*, 138–9.

32 Ibid., 140.

33 Ibid.

34 Ibid., 156.

35 Thompson fonds, Flavelle lecture, presented to the Royal Society of Canada in 1949, IX a). "The Solving of the Wheat Rust Problem," 7.

36 Ibid., 7.

37 Thompson, "Chromosome Behaviour," 317–31.

38 Thompson, *An Academic's Progress*, 120.
39 Thompson and Hollingshead, "The Preponderance of *dicoccum*-like Characters and Chromosome Numbers," 283–307.
40 Martin, et al, "Retention of D Genome, 315–19.
41 Appendix 2, Thompson's Work on Endosperm.
42 Appendix 4, for a list of Thompson's published articles.
43 Thompson fonds, VIII a) Honorary Degrees, 1915–68, 9.
44 Based on the analysis of the geneticist Dr Maureen Rever-DuWors, interview 22 August 2008.
45 President's Office fonds, Series I B. 38/13. Departmental Reports – Biology (1914–37).
46 Thompson fonds, IX a) viii) Alumni. Speech ca. 1952.
47 Thompson fonds, IX e) Congratulations, 1948–50. Newton to Thompson, 2 June 1949.
48 Ibid., 7.
49 Saskatchewan Agricultural Hall of Fame, 5.
50 Arnason fonds, T.C. Vanterpool, talk at retirement banquet, April 1965, 3.
51 Thompson, Flavelle lecture, 40. Thompson emphasized the impact of rust resistant wheat, referring to the years from 1940 to 1944 as producing 403 million bushels with an annual value of $334 million dollars. In the single year 1946 the value of the wheat crop was $460 dollars.
52 President's Office fonds, Series: 1 A. 93. Thompson to Murray, 7 December 1927.
53 Dr Lawrence E. Kirk (1886–1969) took his PhD at Minnesota in 1927 and taught at the University of Saskatchewan until 1931 when he became Dominion Agrologist and returned to the University as dean of agriculture 1937–47. Dr J.B. Harrington (1894–1979) received his PhD from Minnesota in 1924 and immediately became an assistant professor in field husbandry, becoming head from 1950–56. He developed ten varieties of grain crops, with the best known being Apex wheat, which produced a greater yield than Marquis.
54 President's Office fonds, Series: 1. B.38/13. Departmental Reports – Biology (1914–37), 1927.
55 Preston and Howard-Lock, "Emergence of Physics Graduate," 155.
56 Thompson fonds, IX. a). ii Arts and Science. Arts Dinner, "Work of Survey Committee," February 1946, 2.
57 Thompson fonds, IX. a). viii) Alumni. "To Reunion of Class of 1923," 11 May, 1963.
58 Thompson, *Graduate Education*, 25.

59 Thompson fonds, IX. A). vii) Tributes, Hon. Degree, 1949.
60 King, *First Fifty*, 91.
61 Thompson and Hollingshead, "Preponderance of *dicoccum*," 283–307.
62 Thompson and Melburn, "Heterotypic Prophases," 512–27.
63 Avis Williamson telephone conversation with Richard Rempel, 1 May 2008.
64 Richard Rempel fonds, Isabel Auld email to Richard Rempel, 15 November 2009.
65 Thompson fonds, speech given to the Agricultural Societies Convention, January 1954.
66 Mary Thompson Smith, *The Fortunate Man*, 4.
67 Thompson fonds, II. a) Staff Recommendations, 1947–56, Thompson to Robertson, 23 May 1956. Robertson later became Under-Secretary of State for External Affairs, Clerk of the Privy Council and Cabinet Secretary, 1963–75. Earlier, Thompson commented to President Norman MacKenzie of the University of British Columbia that Neatby was "the best man in Canada" as a possible Dean of Agriculture … but that Saskatchewan was "not able to attract him"; Ibid., Thompson to MacKenzie, 26 January 1949.
68 Hugh McKenzie Dundas. Dundas died at ninety-eight in 2008. Born on a homestead near Pelly, Saskatchewan on 3 June 1910, he was a descendant of the famous Scottish cabinet minister, Henry Dundas, later Viscount Melville, who, along with the Younger Pitt, was the architect of the Second British Empire anchored in India, after the collapse of the first Empire in the American Revolution.
69 Lorne Paul, quoted in Taft, *Inside These Greystone Walls*, 161.
70 Thompson fonds, speech to Canadian Economics Association, June 1952, 4.
71 Richard Rempel fonds, Isabel Auld email to Richard Rempel, 2 September 2008.
72 Hayden, *Balance*, 186–7.
73 President's Office fonds Series I. B. 85, Thompson to Murray, and, but probably sometime in August 1930.
74 Thompson, *An Academic's Progress*, 143.
75 Mary Thompson Smith Papers, Thompson to Mary Smith and her family, 29 September 1968. Hollingshead published two papers as first author with Babcock, while Cameron published four, and Jenkins published three, one as first author. See Stebbins, 50–66.
76 President's Office fonds, Series I, A.93. Thompson to Murray, 8 March 1929.
77 Jenkins died suddenly and at a relatively young age in 1965. His obituary in "University of California In Memoriam, June 1967" stated, "among

other notable events in his life" that he had "earned a degree with high honors in biology in 1927 and a master's degree two years later. It was during this period the he came under the influence of Professor W.P. Thompson, the dean of Canadian cytologists. The association undoubtedly played a large part in deciding the course of his future role in science. Jim came to Berkeley in 1929 as a graduate student and remained to serve the University of California until his death." http://texts.cdlib.org/view?docId=hb629006vt&doc.view=frames&chunk.id=div00014&toc.depth=1&toc.id=.

78 Thompson, *An Academic's Progress*, 156.

79 Appendix 4.

80 Thompson fonds, VIII. a) Honorary Degrees, 1913–68, 9. Note written by Professor L.C. Paul, 9 October 1968, "Xeroxed copy of statement prepared for the staff of Department of Biology," by Thompson.

81 Thompson, *An Academic's Progress*, 218. Thompson ranked a number of individuals he worked with on a variety of issues as superior in intellectual ability, notably Sir Julian Huxley, T.C. Douglas, Charles Dunning, Walter Murray, and the Saskatchewan and, later, Ottawa civil servant Al Johnson.

82 Richard Rempel fonds, email assessment by Dr Doug Knott to Richard Rempel, 15 March 2008. Appendix 4.

83 Murray fonds, University of Saskatchewan Archives, Murray to Mr McAfee, 18 October 1924, and McAfee to Murray, 28 October 1924.

84 Thompson, *An Academic's Progress*, 219.

85 "The Assiniboia Club." News of the formation and aims of this club was published in *The Sheaf*, 1 December 1915, 110.

86 Thompson fonds, IX a) ix) Botanical Addresses. "The Origin of Life," 29–30.

87 Beckwith, Jon "A Historical View," 327.

88 Thompson fonds, Canadian Education file, "Heredity and Education." Paper delivered at the Eighth Annual Convention of the Saskatchewan Educational Association at Prince Albert, April 1916, 1–19.

89 "Heredity and Education," 17. Thompson's arguments reflected the still-developing study of genetics in 1916. Although the unit of inheritance, the gene, had first been defined in 1909 by the Danish scientist Johannsen, Thompson must have been unaware of this new definition, for he still used the term Mendel had employed, "factor," as the unit of inheritance. Thompson believed that each cell of a woman "has 48 rod-like chromosomes" while "every cell of the body of a man 47 rods." However, Thompson said that "there cannot be one-half chromosome ... The numbers of chromosomes must be equal."

90 Ibid., 18. He attempted to explain the discrepancy in this manner: If an egg is fertilized by a sperm with 24 rods the resulting cell will have 24 + 24, equal to 48 chromosomes which is the number in the female body. If, on the other hand, an egg is fertilized by a sperm with 23 the resulting number is 24 and 23 equal to 47 and the offspring will be male. But since the two kinds of sperm are produced in equal numbers, in the long run the numbers of the two sexes must be equal. The dogma of humans having 48 chromosomes was not corrected until 1956 when Tijo and Levan showed that the diploid chromosome number for humans is 46.
91 McLaren, *Our Own Master Race*, 113.
92 Thompson fonds, IX. a) ix), Botanical Addresses. "The Biological Conception of Progress," and "The Biological Effects of Race Mixture."
93 Inge, *Idea of Progress*, address delivered in the Sheldonian Theatre, Oxford, England.
94 Thompson, "The Biological Effects of Race Mixture," 11.
95 Ibid., 5.
96 Ibid., 15.
97 Thompson, "The Biological Conception of Progress."
98 Thompson, "Mode of Evolution," 90–7.
99 Thompson, *A Personal History*, 122. Hayden notes, however, that the University of Saskatchewan's provincial grant was at least as large, and probably slightly better than the other western provincial universities. Hayden, *Balance*, 164.
100 Petry, "Walter Murray and the State University," 12–18. Petry disputes Thompson's praise of Murray's policies for the University during the Depression, arguing that Murray's insistence on making the University of Saskatchewan an "apolitical" institution was detrimental. By so doing, Murray "constrained" the University, preventing it from interacting "with the wider public to address social and economic issues facing the province."
101 Publications Collection, President's Annual Report, 1933–34, 3.
102 *Canadian Encyclopedia*, http://www.thecanadianencyclopedia.com/articles/saskatoon.
103 Thomson, *Louis St. Laurent*, 97.
104 Thompson, *A Personal History*, 122, and cited in Harris, *Higher Education*, 365.
105 President's Annual Report, 1933–34, 8.
106 President's Office fonds, Series I, B, 38/13, Departmental Reports – Biology. Thompson to Murray from WPT, 16 April 1934.
107 Axelrod and Reid, *Youth, University, and Canadian Society*, xix.

108 Allemang, "Facts and Arguments."
109 Axelrod and Reid, xix; Thompson, *Personal History*, 125.
110 Johns, *University of Alberta*, 160.
111 Axelrod, *Making a Middle Class*, 17.
112 Arnason fonds, V. Faculty Association. T.C. Vanterpool talk at retirement banquet, April 1965, 3.
113 Harris, *A History*, Toronto, 1976, 365. And see Thompson, *Personal History*, 122. Hayden argues that on the matter of maintaining modest salaries Murray was effective during his presidency up to his retirement in 1937; *Balance*, 190–1. Hayden's account of the coming of Herzberg to the university is explained on page 190. Hayden further argues that "in absolute terms, the University of Saskatchewan seems to have done better than the Universities of Manitoba and British Columbia and as well as the University of Alberta. In relative terms, it did much better"; Ibid., 164.
114 Thompson fonds, Address to Association of Universities of the British Commonwealth, 9 September 1958.
115 Thompson fonds, President Murray to Dean Thompson, 15 December 1936. The money was to be used for Thompson to read a paper at the Congress that was to be held in Moscow in 1937. For reasons explained in the text, the Congress did not meet until 1939 and then in Edinburgh, not Moscow. Thompson left a list of important notes about the Congress, "Seventh International Congress of Genetics," Thompson fonds, Personal Papers, IX, a) Address, ix) Botanical Addresses.
116 Thompson fonds, Thompson to Dr Murray, 17 December 1938. Thompson's paper was entitled "The Frequency of Fertilization and the Nature of Embryo Development in Intergeneric Crosses in Cereals." Minutes of the Executive of the Board of Governors, 24 March 1939.
117 Mary Thompson Smith Papers, Thompson to Mary Smith, 11 August 1939.
118 Ibid.
119 Comments made by Margaret Thompson to Richard Rempel concerning her future mother-in-law's state of mind on the eve of war, 10 January 2008.
120 Margaret Thompson's "Notes" of Thompson's 1968 speech.
121 *The Sheaf*, 29 September 1939, 1.
122 *The Sheaf*, 20 October 1939, 2.

CHAPTER THREE

1 Mary Thompson Smith, *The Fortunate Man*, 7.
2 Thompson fonds, IX. a) vii), speech to the Kiwanis Club, 14 May 1957.

3 Thompson fonds, IX. a). viii) Alumni, Speech at the University of Saskatchewan, October 1949.
4 President's Office fonds, Series I, Name and Subject Files, Ling to Murray, 1 August 1936.
5 Murray and Murray, *Prairie Builder*, 219.
6 Mary Thompson Smith, *The Fortunate Man*, 6.
7 Ibid.
8 Thompson, *A Personal History*, 156.
9 Ibid., 155.
10 President's Office fonds, Series III, B 22/1, Annual Reports, 1943–44, 7.
11 Thompson, *A Personal* History, 156.
12 *The Sheaf*, 5 January 1939, 1.
13 *The Sheaf*, 9 February 1940, 1.
14 Thompson, *A Personal History*, 154–5.
15 Ibid., 157-9; and Thompson fonds, IX. a). ii) Arts and Science.
16 Joint Committee on Art, Drama and Music, 22 November 1946, University of Regina Archives, 75.2 File 78.
17 "New Arts Curriculum Introduced this term," *The Sheaf*, 19 September 1941, 1.
18 Thomson, *Yesteryears*. This was not an entirely new innovation: Walter Murray taught during his tenure as president.
19 Harris, *A History*, 504.
20 Mary Thompson Smith Papers, Thompson to Mary Smith, 4 April 1943. Dean Ling would have liked to have had Steinhauer teach advanced French in 1938, but the latter did not wish to "supplant" a junior faculty member.
21 Thompson fonds, IX. a). viii) Alumni, 14 May 1943.
22 Board of Governors Minutes, 15 October 1942. The Dean asked Avis Williamson to help Dr Simpson with administrative issues when Thompson was acting president. Thompson reassured her by remarking that if there were any complex difficulties "he was just down the hall."
23 Citation by Jean Murray for honorary degree award to GW Simpson, 29 September 1959; see http://www.usask.ca/archives/history/hondegrees.php?id=121&view=detail&keyword=&campuses=.
24 Thompson, *A Personal History*, 162.
25 Thompson fonds, IX. a). viii) Alumni.
26 President's Office fonds, Series III, B 22/1, Annual Report 1944–45, 6.
27 Richard Rempel fonds, letter from Avis [Kirkpatrick] Williamson, 8 December 2007.
28 Richard Rempel fonds, see especially the story, "How I got to University 1935." Avis Williamson wrote this account to her great niece, Marcia,

29 July 1998. Document sent by Avis, 10 May 2008. She writes that she "was thoroughly spoiled by the Faculty and many of them included me in parties and dinners. I knew Dean Thompson's son and daughter and I became almost a member of the family. When son, Jim, was married, I helped with the wedding, even made the bride's [Dr Margaret Thompson] bouquet...with flowers from the garden." 17–18. Avis's title when she worked for Thompson was private secretary and administrative assistant.

29 Avis Williamson phone conversation with Richard Rempel, 11 May 2009.

30 King, *First Fifty*, 64–5.

31 Thompson, *A Personal History*, 171.

32 President's Office fonds, Series III, B 22/1, Annual Reports, 1943–44, 5.

33 Francis Leddy to Michael Hayden, 13 October 1981, Leddy Papers, University of Windsor, files still to be catalogued.

34 Mary Thompson Smith Papers, copy of Thompson's speech at a Board of Governors dinner in his honour, spring 1959.

35 Thompson fonds, IX. a) xii, 1943 Convocation address, 7.

36 Currie, *Physics Department*, 65.

37 Thompson, *A Personal History*, 137. Ferns was a distinguished professor of mathematics.

38 Thompson fonds, IX. b) Correspondence , 1948–64, Charles Waywell to Thompson, 27 December 1959. Waywell earned his BSA in 1946 and MSA in 1949. He later received a PhD.

39 Thompson fonds, IX. a) xii, 1943 Convocation address, 9–10.

40 Ibid., 11–12.

41 Thompson fonds, VII Notes and Comments, 1968–70. Thomson also refused to talk to the deputy provincial treasurer, who was in charge of university grants. Thomson claimed that, since the deputy minister had never attended university, he should keep silent on any financial matter.

42 Thompson, *A Personal History*, 24.

43 Hayden, *Balance*, 196–7.

44 McLeod and McLeod, *Douglas*, 207.

45 Johnson, *Dream No Little Dreams*, 52.

46 Hayden, *Balance*, 196.

47 Board of Governors Minutes, 16 September 1944.

48 James Gardiner speech at Wolseley, 9 August 1933, cited in the Saskatoon *Star Phoenix*.

49 Hayden fonds, G. University History, 1. Correspondence 1979–83. Correspondence from Francis Leddy, 5.

50 Warnock, *Saskatchewan*, 5.

51 Ibid.

52 Thomson, *Yesteryears*, 57–60.
53 Board of Governors Minutes, 29 January 1945, 7.
54 Thompson fonds, IX a) viii) Alumni Dinner ... To Celebrate 50th Anniversary of Arrival at University, 14 September 1963.
55 Thompson fonds, IX. a) viii.
56 College of Law fonds, II.A (3) University Committees, b. Survey Committee, 1945.
57 Thompson fonds, General Summary of University Statutes, 1.
58 President's Office fonds, Series II, B.181, Survey Committee, 1945–46. Leddy to President Thomson, 25 October 1945.
59 President's Office fonds, Series III, B.181 Survey Committee 1945–46, 1.
60 Thompson, *An Academic's Progress*, 195.
61 Thompson, *A Personal History*, 197.
62 Cronkite fonds, "The Report of ... Survey Committee," 14 December 1945, 3.
63 Thompson, *A Personal History*, 19–20.
64 Leddy fonds, Leddy to Hayden, critique of appendix no. 2, 21 September 1981.
65 Thompson fonds, IX. a). xi) University, no date, but probably 30 November 1956 when the new library was opened and the cornerstone laid.
66 Thompson, Presidential Address, "Extract from Proceedings of the National Conference of Canadian Universities," 1954, 17.
67 Thompson fonds, IX. a) Address to Union Institute, February 1953.
68 Thompson fonds, IX. e) Congratulations, 1948–50, Gerhard Herzberg to Thompson, 5 December 1948.
69 Ibid., Lloyd to Thompson, 7 December 1948.
70 Ibid., Thompson to Lloyd, 9 December 1948.
71 Thompson fonds, IX. a). viii) Alumni, 4 May 1959. When Arthur Moxon received an honorary degree in 1953, Thompson wrote and read the citation, and claimed: "No living man has had a greater influence in University affairs." University of Saskatchewan Archives, Honorary degree recipients, http://www.usask.ca/archives/history/hondegrees.
72 Thompson fonds, speech at alumni dinner, May 8 1959.
73 Richard Rempel fonds, email from T.H. McLeod, 9 January 2007, dictated by McLeod to his wife, Beryl McLeod, who typed the document.
74 Thompson fonds, IX. a). v) Welcomes.
75 Thompson fonds, Addresses and Papers. "The Job of a President," address to NCCU, 1955, 16.
76 Thompson fonds, IX. a) viii) Alumni, October 1949, 3.

77 Mary Thompson Smith Papers, Thompson to Mary Smith, 10 April 1949. Muriel Stein remained Thompson's secretary through his entire presidency and wrote a thoughtful letter of condolence to his daughter when he died. She was paid $175 a month with a cost of living bonus.
78 Mary Thompson Smith Papers, Thompson to Mary Smith, 17 June 1949.
79 Spinks fonds, Staffing, NRC, Trips, Media, 1949–59. Thompson to Spinks, undated, but probably late 1958.
80 Spinks, *Two Blades*, preface, and Spinks fonds, tribute to Miss Stein by Spinks, 23 June 1975.
81 Spinks fonds, 14.A. file Leddy, Leddy to Spinks, 7 November 1980.
82 Riddell fonds, "How Well I Remember," unpublished recollections.
83 Thompson fonds, II. b Staff Recommendations, Rawson to Thompson, 5 November 1949.
84 Rawson fonds, Thompson to Rawson, 22 January 1950.
85 Mary Thompson Smith Papers, Thompson to Mary Smith, 5 April 1948.
86 Richard Rempel fonds, Interview with Mrs Morrison, 18 July 2006. She remembers Marjorie Thompson as "a gracious, kind and caring person" who "never said anything cruel about anyone."
87 Taft, *Inside These Greystone Walls*, 214.
88 Richard Rempel fonds, email from Herb Pinder, 4 Aug 2008.
89 Thompson's talk to the biology dinner, unpublished, 14 September 1963.
90 Information provided by his daughter-in-law, Dr Margaret Thompson, and his granddaughter, Lucy Smith. See Jean E. Murray fonds, VIII. Faculty clippings. The undated *Star Phoenix* article also contains a list of past and present members of the Saturday luncheon club, including Father Carr.
91 Mary Thompson Smith Papers, Thompson to Mary Smith, 21 July 1954.
92 Mary Thompson Smith Papers, Thompson to Mary Smith, 20 May 1950. Thompson clearly was not interested in going as far into the wild as Dr and Mrs Murray who tended to take their annual vacation near Big River in northern Saskatchewan.
93 Thompson's account of this Congress, written sometime between late 1959 and 1963, 3. Memorandum found in Dr Margaret Thompson's home. The document had eight pages, but page one is now missing.
94 *Saskatoon Daily Star*, 23 March 1920, 3–9.
95 Hewitt, "The RCMP's Secret Activities," 22–30. The RCMP also investigated *The Sheaf*, notably in November 1935, because of an article critical of the British Empire. President Murray dismissed the RCMP inquiry, stating that students were "free to publish such articles." Hewitt, "RCMP," 23.

96 Djwa, *Politics of Imagination*, 225.
97 President's Office fonds, Series III, A. 27, A. General Correspondence, (Sc–Sy), Thompson to Scott, 3 March 1959.
98 Thompson fonds, IX a) viii) Alumni, Government Dinner, Regina, 25 February 1959. He was not, however, opposed to faculty members entering politics. "Nevertheless, I am just as strongly of the opinion that any faculty member who wishes to take an active part in politics should be entirely free to do so ... And he should not suffer in any way if he does take part."
99 Thompson fonds, IX. d), Retirement, 1957–60.
100 Mary Thompson Smith Papers, Thompson to Mary Smith, 14 October 1951.
101 Mary Thompson Smith Papers, Thompson to Mary Thompson Smith, 6 June 1952.
102 Richard Rempel fonds, letter sent by Ruth Miller, 18 December 2008. In Wright's unpublished autobiography, he remarked that as a writer with the *Star Phoenix* in the 1950s, because of his fine record as a student in Thompson's classes during the 1930s, later, when Thompson was university president, Wright "always got a hearing when I wanted it and a favourable one at that."
103 Margaret Thompson, telephone conversation with Richard Rempel, 9 December 2007. Thompson mentioned his new assistant for the first time to Mary on 12 August 1949, noting that "Ordinarily the load is not heavy because McEown (executive assistant – a new job) can be given all the details to look after, but these [Board] meetings were policy-making." Mary Thompson Smith Papers, Thompson to Mary Smith, 12 August 1949.
104 Mary Thompson Smith Papers, Thompson to Mary Thompson Smith, 7 August 1952.
105 Mary Thompson Smith Papers, *The Fortunate Man*, 3.
106 Thompson fonds, "Education Dinner," February 1953.
107 T.C. Douglas fonds, Douglas to Dr Harry M. Cassidy, University of Toronto, 8 December 1948.
108 Mary Thompson Smith Papers, Thompson to Mary Smith, 1 August 1949.

CHAPTER FOUR

1 Mary Thompson Smith Papers, Thompson to Mary Smith, 20 May 1951.
2 Thompson, *A Personal History*, 200.
3 Board of Governors Minutes, Exhibit L, Report for Board of Governors, "Re-consideration of Promotions to rank of Professor," 29 April 1949.
4 Woodside, *The University Question*, 135.

5 Fowke, *Salaries and Related Conditions*, paper presented to the National Conference of Canadian Universities, November 1956. Thompson admired Fowke. When Dr Britnell informed Fowke that the Board in 1947 had refused to consider any promotions to Full Professor that year. "W.P., busy as now as he was, took time to stop into my office the day before convocation to express regrets about the failure to get your particular adjustment through." Britnell to Fowke, 18 May 1947, Fowke fonds, 95/5, XVII (a) (5) Department of Political Science (4).
6 Horlick, *Red Dean*, 55.
7 President's Office fonds, Series III, B.113. Dean Cronkite to Thompson, 2 September 1955.
8 Thompson fonds, IX. a). x), Outside Bodies [not used].
9 Thompson fonds, IX. a). i) General, "Color Night," ca. early May 1959. Thompson appended a note at the top of page 1, indicating that the speech was "not given." Color Night was a traditional university annual event that was the climax to each social year when awards were given to outstanding students and to winning colleges of interfaculty competition.
10 Thompson, *A Personal History*, 201.
11 Vice-President (Administration) – McEown. I.4 b) General, 1958–59, University of Saskatchewan Institutional Questionnaire, 26. The Questionnaire also stated that "In general salaries are as high as most American universities with the exception of salaries paid to professors of outstanding distinction at some of the big private institutions."
12 Thompson fonds, "The Job of a University President," 19. This judgment is quoted in bold in Cameron, 319.
13 Thompson fonds, IX. a). ii) Arts and Science, Address [to Phytopathic Society], June 1953.
14 Thompson, *An Academic's Progress*, 104.
15 King, *Extending the Boundaries*, 42.
16 Thompson fonds, IX. a). vii) [1965].
17 Vice-President (Administration) – McEown, I.4.a) Brakeley 1958–59.
18 King, *First Fifty*, 73-4.
19 Quoted in Pilkington, *Speaking With One Voice*, 28–9.
20 Thompson fonds, Speech to Winnipeg Alumni, January 1943.
21 Horn, *Academic Freedom*, 246.
22 Axelrod, *Scholars and Dollars*, 25.
23 Thompson fonds, Speech to "Cooperative School," 9 July 1956.
24 Richard Rempel fonds. Interview with the Hon. Allan Blakeney, 8 December, 2006, 4.
25 Thompson fonds, Arts Dinner, Spring 1948.

26 Thompson, *A Personal History*, 126.
27 Hayden, *Balance*, 160.
28 Thompson, *A Personal History*, 126.
29 Hayden, *Balance*, 227.
30 President's Office fonds, Series III, B.22/1 – 1946–47. Thompson made the same arguments in his 1945–46 Report of the College of Arts and Science.
31 Bothwell, Drummond, and English, *Canada Since 1945*, 127.
32 Thompson fonds, MG 17, IX, a) ii, Arts and Science, March 1945.
33 The Fellows of the Royal Society of Canada in 1946 were, in science, W.P. Thompson (biology); T. Thorvaldson (chemistry); J.W.T. Spinks (chemistry); E. Kirk (agriculture); J.B. Mawdsley (geology); E.L. Harrington (physics); W.H. Watson (physics). But in the humanities and social sciences only J.S. Thomson (theology), was a member.
34 Thompson fonds, President's Office, President J.S. Thomson to Dean W.P. Thompson, 18 October 1947.
35 Thompson, *A Personal History*, 21.
36 See Harris, *Higher Education*, 566–71, for an excellent account of the creation and purposes of these councils.
37 Ibid., 566–71.
38 Kuffert, "Reconstructing Canadian Culture," 27, 29, 45–50.
39 Hilda Neatby, Talk at Memorial Service for W.P. Thompson, Saskatoon, 3 April 1970.
40 Board of Governors Minutes, 23 May 1950.
41 Board of Governors Minutes, 13 February 1951 and 27 March 1951.
42 Royal Commission fonds, Thompson to Dr A.A. Day, secretary to the Commission, 15 September 1949, 3.
43 *Proceedings of The Royal Commission*, 131–49.
44 Woodside, *University Question*, 38.
45 *Report: Royal Commission ...* (Massey Commission), 377.
46 Massey Commission, 161, quoted in Harris, *Higher Education*, 563.
47 Massey Commission, 136–8.
48 Thompson fonds, Presidential Address, from the *Proceedings of the National Conference of Canadian Universities*, 1954, 12. Conant (1893–1978) studied Chemistry at Harvard at the same time as Thompson worked on Botany. As president, Conant, moved the curriculum away from the traditional emphasis on the Classics and developed the Natural Sciences, as well as stressing the "History of Science." Thompson may have been influenced in developing his program at the University of Saskatchewan for introductory classes for all students in the humanities, social sciences, and natural sciences by Conant's innovation.

49 Thompson fonds, Presidential Address, extract from the *Proceedings of the National Conference of Canadian Universities* 1954, 11–18.
50 Thompson, "Education and Moral Values," *Canadian Education* vol. VII, no. I, 30–8. The CEA was organized first in July 1891.
51 Pilkington, *Speaking with One Voice*, vi–vii.
52 Harris, *Higher Education*, 457–8.
53 Ibid., 465.
54 Thompson fonds, IX. a).i) General, St. Andrews College, February 1952.
55 President's Office fonds, Series III, A.17. Thompson to Lloyd, 22 June 1950.
56 Ibid., Lloyd to Thompson, 26 June 1950.
57 Board of Governors Minutes, 15 June 1951, 8.
58 Mary Thompson Smith Papers, Thompson to Mary Smith, 26 September 1950.
59 Richard Rempel fonds, copy of Hall to Thompson, 10 October 1956. G.E. Hall was the president of the University of Western Ontario.
60 Richard Rempel fonds, Copy of Thompson Letter to Edward Hall, 15 October 1956.
61 Thompson fonds, IX. a). v) Welcome.
62 Mary Thompson Smith Papers, Thompson to Mary Smith, 24 June 1954.
63 President's Office fonds, Series III, A.17, Thompson to R.R. Knight, 21 January 1957. Thompson was by no means hostile to the creation of the Canada Council. He just hoped that some of the money allocated to it would go to the sciences.
64 Mary Thompson Smith, *The Fortunate Man*, 11.
65 Thompson fonds, speech to alumni reunion, Oct. 18 [1952]. Thompson also noted that Adaskin had accepted "a substantial financial sacrifice in coming to our University."
66 Lazarevich, *Francis James and Murray Adaskin*, 179.
67 Eli Bornstein to Richard Rempel, phone conversation on 25 September 2007.
68 Bornstein, "The Vision of Murray Adaskin (1906–2002)": *His Contributions to the Musical Scene of Canada.*" http://goldenpages.jpehs.co.uk/static/conferencearchive/07-c-vma.html.
69 Thompson fonds, 1 February 1954, IX a) vi) *Recital and Exhibition by Professors Adaskin and Bornstein* Introductions. Mrs Thompson mentioned in a letter to her son, Jimmy, and to Margaret, they had just "had the most heart-warming letter from the Adaskins this last week, telling us of their happiness in belonging to the University;" May 1954; from Marjorie Thompson.

70 Shirley Spafford to Richard Rempel, email, 24 May 2009, and Spafford, *No Ordinary Academics*, 156.
71 President's Office fonds, Series III B.12/2, Drama, 1951–52.
72 President's Office fonds, Series III B.12/11, Art Department.
73 Mary Thompson Smith Papers, Thompson to Mary Smith, 12 June 1957. Names of the various recipients, eight each year with every one of them receiving $800, are recorded in the Board of Governor's Agendas and in the annual Reports of the Department Heads to the President. For example, 2 April 1958.
74 President's Office fonds, Series III, B, Name and Subject Files, Annual reports – Slavic Studies.
75 Thompson fonds, IX. d) 1957–60, Thompson to Frank Stilling, 5 September 1958.

CHAPTER FIVE

1 Thompson fonds, Fowke to Thompson, 18 January 1952. Fowke, Secretary Faculty Negotiating Committee. Fowke was president of CAUT for two years, 1954–55 and 1955–56. See also *An Academic's Progress*, 193.
2 Thompson, *A Personal History*, 142. Thompson states that the Board "welcomed the establishment of the association," but he had to convince some board members.
3 Thompson, *Annual Report*, 1952–53, 15–16.
4 Mary Thompson Smith fonds. Colb McEown forwarded to Thompson this section of Dr Britnell's report to the Faculty Association on 27 November 1952.
5 Richard Rempel fonds, "Welcome: Labour Union Institute February 1953". Smishek had already developed a cordial working relationship with Thompson in 1948 when he was dean of arts and science. Smishek interview transcription, 3–4.
6 Board of Governors Minutes, 2 February 1954. Moved by Thompson and seconded by Hedley Auld.
7 President's Office fonds, Series III. B. 75. Faculty Association, Thompson to Britnell, 3 March 1954.
8 Thompson fonds, IX. a). xiii) Government Dinner, Regina, February 1959.
9 Thompson, *An Academic's Progress*, 191.
10 Hayden, *Balance*, 199.
11 Thompson fonds, IV. b) Faculty Association, 1955–1959, *Report of the University of Saskatchewan Faculty Association Committee on Faculty*

Participation in University Governance, signed by Professor R.N.H. Haslam, chairman, 16 March 1960.

12 Horn, *Academic Freedom*, 220.

13 *Faculty Participation Report*, 3.

14 Ibid., 7.

15 Ibid., 7.

16 Ibid., back of 9, where Thompson wrote his views at length.

17 Cameron, *Academic Question*, 300–2.

18 Thompson, "University Government," CAUT *Bulletin*, vol. 9, no. 2 (December 1960), 6, also quoted in Cameron, 335.

19 Cameron, *Academic Question*, 302.

20 Thompson fonds, IX. a). i) General, 1955.

21 Thompson fonds, IX. a). i) General, 1955, Color Night Speech.

22 Thompson fonds, IX. a). viii) Law Students and Alumni, 25 September 1959.

23 Thompson, *An Academic's Progress*, 222–3.

24 President's Office fonds, Series III, A.6, Correspondence, (Can. S – Ch), Thompson to Mr R. W. Cantelon, Principal, Unity High School, 14 December 1956 and Cantelon to Thompson, 18 December 1956.

25 President's Office fonds, Series III, B.57. Counselling.

26 Thompson fonds, IX Presidential Office, a) Address, f) General. "Foreign Students October 1950."

27 *Jugoslav Encounter*, Ottawa Ninth International Seminar, World University Service of Canada, Jugoslavia Seminar – 1958, iv.

28 President's Office fonds, Series III, B.102, Hungarian Students. Most other university presidents in Canada had also helped in finding places for Hungarian students. Many agencies assisted in finding university places or jobs. 958 students were registered and 456 received some financial help.

29 Mary Thompson Smith fonds, Lewis Perinbam to Thompson, 22 September 1959.

30 Dr John King, telephone conversation with Richard Rempel, 15 August 2007.

31 McEown, Memorandum, 2.

32 Mary Thompson Smith, *The Fortunate Man*, 9, and Pitsula, "Higher Education Policy," 17.

33 Stager, "Grants to Canadian Universities," 287–8.

34 Thompson fonds, IX. a). v) Welcome, *Homemakers*, June 1949.

35 Bothwell, Drummond, English, *Power, Politics*, 126–7.

36 Axelrod, *Scholars and Dollars*, 52. By contrast, the American president of the Council for Aid to Education, Dr Compton, predicted that "by 1970

the annual donations of American industry to colleges and universities will exceed $500 million." Published speech by President H.J. Somers of St Francis Xavier University, "Private and Corporate Support of Canadian Universities," 207, delivered at the NCCU special conference in Ottawa, 12–14 November 1956 and published in Bissell, *Crisis in Higher Education.*

37 Thompson fonds, IX. a). viii) Alumni.

38 Richard Rempel fonds, Memorandum from Donald McEown to author, 20 October 2007. This constructive, efficient process broke down when Ross Thatcher became premier in 1964.

39 McEown Vice President (Administration). I. 4. Fund Raising, a) Brakeley 1958–59, "Institutional Questionnaire" from the University to the Brakeley firm, 16.

40 Thompson fonds, IX., a). viii), Winnipeg Alumni, December 1951.

41 Houston, *Steps On the Road*, 89.

42 Lloyd, *Woodrow*, 116.

43 Hayden fonds, Research and Writing – History, file "Medical College in Perspective," C.S. Houston, 1.

44 Houston, *Steps on the Road*, 125–6.

45 The other two were Dr Maurice Seymour and Dr Robert Ferguson in treating tuberculosis. Houston, *Steps on the Road*, 126.

46 King, *First Fifty*, 53.

47 Thompson, *A Personal History*, 177.

48 Horlick, *Medical College*, 28, 64.

49 Buchan, *Greenhouse to Medical Centre*, 35.

50 Ibid., 36.

51 Ibid., 150–1.

52 Board of Governors Minutes, November 1944. Mr Justice H. Y. Macdonald moved the motion that was then seconded by Arthur Moxon.

53 Thompson fonds, MG 17 IX. a). i. notes, medical school talk, 14 November 1945.

54 Horlick, *Red Dean*, 40.

55 Ibid., 10.

56 Thompson fonds," Speech at Farewell Party for Dean Wendell Macleod," 3 January 1963.

57 Thompson fonds, WPT and the Massey Commission, speech given at St Andrews College, February 1952.

58 Saskatchewan Archives Board, Saskatoon, transcript of an interview Professor Ed Tollefson conducted with Thompson, 12 May 1966, 6.

59 Thompson, *An Academic's Progress*, 201.

60 Ibid.
61 For the voluminous correspondence between Thompson and Macleod see College of Medicine. U.2, 1c "President W.P. Thompson, 1949–59," and within that correspondence see Thompson to Macleod, 15 April 1955.
62 Richard Rempel fonds, information given to author by Dr Louis Horlick, 22 March 2008.
63 Horlick, *Medical College*, 278.
64 Thompson fonds, Speech at Farewell Party for Dean Wendell Macleod, 3 January 1962.
65 Buchan, *Greenhouse*, 68.
66 Richard Rempel fonds, Horlick to author, email, 3 August 2008.
67 Horlick, *Red Dean*, 60-2. Dr Douglas Buchan, when writing his book on the origins and development of the Medical College, contacted Dr Jimmy Thompson asking for some pages of *An Academic's Progress*. Buchan remarked: "It is of some interest that Wendell Macleod insists to this day (I talked to him in Sept.) that he left, not because of Medicare, but due to his difficulty in getting along with John Spinks after his fruitful relationships with your father." Margaret Thompson fonds, Dr James Thompson to Dr Horlick, written on 7 November 1981.
68 Thompson, *An Academic's Progress*, 198.
69 Buchan, *Greenhouse*, 68.

CHAPTER SIX

1 Paul, "Extension at the University," 17 and *passim*.
2 Thompson fonds, Report of Work of Extension, 1 May 1953 to 30 April 1954, 10–11.
3 President's Office fonds, Series III, Rupert Ramsay Annual Report, 1953–54.
4 Thompson fonds IX. a). viii) Address of Welcome to 4-H Leaders, 18 June 1957.
5 President's Office fonds, Series III, B12/32. Annual Reports, Extension Department, 1957–58, 3.
6 Richard Rempel fonds, Donald McEown's email to author, recalling his memories of that occasion, 5 January 2008.
7 Thompson fonds, Speech to Associated Country Women of the World, Saskatoon. 10 September 1953.
8 Ibid., 3, 20.
9 Telephone conversation between Lucy Thompson Smith and Richard Rempel, 11 May 2008.

10 Paul, "Extension," 82.
11 Saskatchewan Homemakers' Clubs and Saskatchewan Institutes fonds.
12 Senate Minutes, 7 May 1959, 3.
13 Paul, "Extension," 110.
14 Arnason fonds, V, April 1965.
15 President's Office fonds, Series III, B.12/32, Annual Reports Extension Department, 1957–58, 1.
16 Johnson, *Dream No Little Dreams*, 159.
17 Rein, "Changing Conditions," Abstract, 9.
18 Fowke fonds, XI– Royal Commission on Agriculture and Rural Life.
19 Gruending, *Promises to Keep*, 105.
20 Houston and Waiser, *Tommy's Team*, 1.
21 Bill Baker to Douglas, 20 March 1953, Saskatchewan Archives Board, Saskatoon.
22 Johnson, *Dream No Little Dream*, 225.
23 Fowke fonds, XI – Royal Commission on Agriculture and Rural Life. Memorandum "B" by W.B. Baker, submitted to the Board of Governors by President Thompson ca. early March 1955.
24 "Proposal for 'Community Services Institute,' University of Saskatchewan," Lloyd to Douglas, 11 October 1955, Saskatchewan Archives Board, Saskatoon. Shoyama was the Director of the Economic Advisory Planning Board (EAPB) and was described as "a new kind of 'personal' authority as [he] "increasingly became the premier's personal confidante." Johnson, *Dream No Little Dreams*, 195.
25 Board of Governors Minutes, Douglas to Thompson, 20 December 1956, Exhibit H.
26 King, *First Fifty*, 142. King dedicated this history to: "W.P. Thompson, who as teacher, dean and president has been with the University ... for forty-six years of the First Fifty."
27 Conversation in Saskatoon between Harold Baker and author, 9 September 2008.
28 President's Office fonds Series III, B-172, Thompson to T.H. McLeod, 9 March 1955.
29 Board of Governors Minutes, January to May 1955, 5 and Memorandum "B," 5.
30 Board of Governors Minutes, Exhibit H, Douglas to Thompson, 20 December 1956.
31 Harold R. Baker's article from "The University of Regina and Canadian Plains Research Centre," 2007.
32 Thompson fonds, IX. a) i) General, Spring 1955.

33 Thompson fonds, B. 64. Royal Commission on Agriculture and Rural Life.
34 Ibid., handwritten note at top of first page, Board file. Thompson to Bill Baker, 29 April 1957. Thompson mentioned by name and high reputation a number of academics. From Political Science and Economics, Thompson designated George Britnell, Vernon Fowke, Mabel Timlin, Kenneth Buckley and Norman Ward. From History he drew attention to Hilda Neatby and George Simpson. Thompson sent an annotated copy of his Memorandum to the Board of Governors for their meeting on 15 January 1958, (Exhibit A, Board of Governors Agendas). In an annotation, Thompson wrote that on 21 December 1957, "by action of the Senate and Board of Governors that department [Sociology, with two members] was established in June last, before the printed report of the Commission was published." Since Baker was a member of Council, he would have known of that 1957 decision.
35 Fowke fonds, 95/5 XVII. (a) (4) University Planning Committee. Submission to the Forward Planning Committee, November 1954.
36 President's Office fonds, Series III, B. 176, Bill Baker to Thompson, 24 May 1957.
37 Thompson fonds, B.64. Royal Commission on Agriculture and Rural Life.
38 *Star Phoenix*, 20 December 1957, 3.
39 Ibid.
40 Thompson fonds, "Memorandum Regarding Report of Royal Commission on Agriculture and Rural Life," President's Office, 10 January 1958.
41 Thompson fonds, Douglas to Thompson, 2 May 1958.
42 Spafford, *No Ordinary Academics*, 175.
43 Harris, *Higher Education*, 519.
44 University of Saskatchewan Calendar for 1952–53, 147.
45 Board of Governors Minutes, Britnell to Thompson, 28 February 1950.
46 McEown, VP (Admin), F. Misc. 10. Regina College, 1934–54.
47 Thompson fonds, Memorandum, Kirkpatrick to Thompson, 16 December 1957 and Thompson to Kirkpatrick, 17 December 1957.
48 Board of Governors Minutes, 19 June 1957, 3.
49 James N. McCrorie, cited in David Nock, *Society*.
50 Phone conversation between author and Professor Emeritus G. Basran, who was a member of the Sociology department from 1965 to 2002, 31 January 2008.
51 Professor Don Kerr recalls Abramson telling him that he decided to stay at the University of Saskatchewan when he attended a council meeting and heard Hilda Neatby contradict Dean Spinks.
52 Hayden, *Balance*, 231–2.

53 Thompson fonds, Bill Baker to Thompson, 24 May 1957.
54 Richard Rempel fonds, McCrorie email to author, 15 February 2008. McCrorie admired the scholarship and sense of "service" throughout the university and the centre. "If a social scientist from abroad sought but one book" to gain a "preliminary grounding in what Canada is like as a society, I would recommend Vernon Fowke's *The National Policy and the Wheat Economy*."
55 Harold Baker's conversation with author in Saskatoon, 9 September 2008.
56 Waiser, *Saskatchewan*, 369.
57 Eisler, *False Expectations*, 149.
58 McCrorie, "A.K. Davis," 8.
59 Ibid., 8–9.
60 Harold R. Baker, Canadian Plains Research, 198–9.
61 Thompson, *A Personal History*, 224.
62 Horlick, *Red Dean*, 62–3.

CHAPTER SEVEN

1 Bigland, *Western College of Veterinary Medicine*, 42.
2 President's Office fonds, Series III, B. 209, Veterinary College, Thompson to T.H. McLeod, also to Secretary-Treasurer, Saskatchewan Cattle Breeders' Association, 14 February 1951, and Hayden, *Balance*, 250.
3 President's Office fonds, Series III, B. 209, Veterinary College, 20 December 1957.
4 Ibid.
5 Currie stated in his report to Council on the Council Committee on Veterinary Medicine's meetings of 31 December 1957 and 31 January 1958 that Thompson had informed the Committee of his telephone discussions and exchange of letters with Stewart at a 31 January 1958 meeting.
6 President's Office fonds, Series III, B. 209, B.W. Currie, early February 1959, "Western Canadian Veterinary Study Committee: Report of January 30 Meeting."
7 "1963: Western College of Veterinary Medicine," *Deo et Patria*, http://scaa.sk.ca/gallery/uofs_events/.
8 President's Office fonds, Series III, B. 209, Thompson to B.W. Currie, 12 December 1958.
9 Ibid., "Notes handwritten by Thompson," undated but probably early 1959.
10 University Council Minutes, 12 March 1959, 6.
11 Publications Collection, President's Annual Report, 1958–59.

12 T.C. Douglas fonds, Douglas to Thompson, 27 July 1959.

13 President's Office fonds, Series IV, B. 299, Veterinary College (1957–62), Spinks to McEown, 8 February 1962.

14 Bigland, *Veterinary Medicine*, 61–2.

15 Spinks, *Two Blades of Grass*, 96–7.

16 Ibid., 15.

17 Hallman, Dianne, "Traditions and Transitions," 3.

18 Thompson, *A Personal History*, 164.

19 Thompson, "Address to Convocation," 8 May 1959, 15.

20 Thompson fonds, "Education Dinner," February 1953. Thompson crossed out the last lines from "one" to "content," perhaps because, upon reflection, he found them too harsh for his audience of Education students and faculty.

21 Thompson fonds, "Criticisms of Education," Education Dinner, February 1953, 1–2, 9–10.

22 Spinks fonds, Thompson to Spinks, late July 1959, Canadian Educational Conference, 1959.

23 Thompson, *University of Saskatchewan*, 165–6.

24 Gauvreau, Michael, "Recasting Canada's Post-war Decade," Christie and Gauvreau, *Cultures of Citizenship*, 4–17.

25 Owram, 178 and 179.

26 Woodside, 17–24 provides a clear survey. E.F. Sheffield undertook his analysis at the request of the National Conference of Canadian Universities (NCCU). *Canadian University and College Enrolment Projected to 1965: Prepared for a symposium on "The Expansion of Enrolment, 1955–1965,"* 1–10 *and University and College Enrolment in the Province of Saskatchewan – Projected to 1961–62*, 1–6.

27 Sheffield, *University ... Enrolment ... Saskatchewan*, 4. Thompson was not alone among university presidents in consulting Sheffield individually, for records of both the University of Toronto and Western Ontario contain references to Sheffield's projections. Garron Wells (University Archivist, University of Toronto) to Cheryl Avery, 5 December 2007, Avery to Tom Belton, Archivist, University of Western Ontario, email 4 December 2007, and Brett Lougheed, Archivist, University of Manitoba, to Cheryl Avery, 10 December 2007.

28 Massoling, "Modernization and Reaction, 1–18.

29 Thompson, "Annual Address to Convocation," published in *The Sheaf*, Friday, 18 September 1953.

30 Pilkington, *Speaking With One Voice*, 69. Sheffield launched the periodical *University Affairs* in 1959.

31 Ibid., 85.

32 Thompson, Annual Report: 1958–59, 12 and 13.
33 Vice-President (Administration) – McEown, I. 4. a) Brakeley 1958–59, 14 and V. Public Relations and Fund Raising, 5.
34 Other junior colleges that developed in the province were three in Regina: Campion College (Catholic), Sacred Heart College (Catholic), Luther College (Lutheran); one in Outlook, Outlook College (Lutheran); one in Muenster, St. Peter's College (Catholic), and Moose Jaw Central Collegiate. Luther and Campion are now affiliated with the University of Regina.
35 Vice-President (Administration) – McEown, F. Misc. 10, Regina College, 1934–54.
36 Pitsula, *As One Who Serves*, 118.
37 President's Office fonds, Series 3, B.163, Regina College. Thompson to Lloyd, 25 May 1954.
38 Ibid. Article sent to Thompson from the *Regina Leader Post*, 10 February 1956, article sent to Thompson a few days later.
39 Leddy fonds, Leddy to Hayden, 9 November 1982.
40 Pitsula, *As One Who Serves*, 123. Much of this section on the development of Regina College is dependent on the narrative and analysis of Professor Pitsula.
41 Woodside, *University Question*, 105.
42 Thompson fonds, IX. a) viii), Regina Alumni 4 December 1956. Only one (unnamed) Canadian university stood higher.
43 President's Office fonds, Series III, B.163 Regina College (1956–57). *Leader Post* article of 3 February 1957, sent to Thompson a few days later.
44 Vice-President (Administration) – McEown, Minutes of the Forward Planning Committee, 47.
45 Senate Minutes, Report of the Forward Planning Committee, 20 November 1959, 47 and 48; and particularly 49.
46 Board of Governors Minutes, 9 January 1957, 2.
47 Information from President Emeritus (University of Regina), Dr Lloyd Barber, given to Richard Rempel by phone on 19 December 2008. Barber, as a faculty member in Commerce, was at the Council Meeting of 6 July 1959.
48 Vice-President (Administration) – McEown, 4. Fund Raising, b) General, 1958–59, Lovell's memorandum of 5 January 1959.
49 Ibid., *Report of the Fund Solicitation Committee*, 9 January 1959.
50 50 Herb Pinder, conversation with author, 20 July, 2010.
51 Vice-President (Administration) – McEown. I.b). McEown to Donald J. Duff, 20 January 1959.

52 Pitsula,.*As One Who Serves*, 126–7. And the Saskatchewan Archives Board, Regina, Lloyd to Douglas, 30 December 1958.
53 Thompson's speech to Alumni, "University Still Has Many Needs, Retiring President's Warning, 9 May 1959." As late as 1958, Canada had only "about forty universities and most of them were small ... As late as 1961, "only about half of Canadians finished high school and less than 10% attended university." Helmes-Hayes, 109.
54 Board of Governors Minutes relating to material forwarded to the Senate for its special meeting scheduled for 8 July 1959.
55 Ibid.
56 "University of Saskatchewan Survey Analysis and Plan," 10–11. Regina College possessed 25 acres in 1959.
57 President's Office fonds, Series III, B.85, Forward Planning Committee. *Report of the Forward Planning Committee.* The words "adopted in principle" have been written in ink at the top left hand corner.
58 Vice President Administration (McEown), V. Public Relations and Fund Raising, 8.
59 Board of Governors Minutes, 17 June 1959, 1, 2.
60 Riddell, William A. *How Well I Remember*, n.d., 55 and 56. At that time, Riddell was the dean of Regina College and later the principal of the University of Saskatchewan, Regina Campus.
61 Recollection of Professor Edward Safarian in an email to Richard Rempel, 17 November 2008.
62 Riddell, "How Well I Remember," 56, quoted in Pitsula, *Serves*, 128.
63 Ibid., 56.
64 Ibid., 57.
65 Senate Minutes, 8 July 1959 6.
66 Publications Collection, Annual Report, 1958–59, 13.
67 Brakeley "Report," 48.
68 Thompson fonds, V.P. (A.C. McEown) I, General Files, fundraising, b) General
69 Hayden, *Balance*, 236.
70 Controller's Office fonds, Series 3, file 67-11, "Survey, Analysis and Plan," 64.
71 J.F. Leddy fonds (unprocessed collection). Leddy to Hayden, 9 November 1982, "Further comments on Chapter VI (text and notes)."
72 President's Office fonds Series IV, B/22 Arts and Science (1959–68). Leddy to Thompson, 2 July 1959.
73 J.F. Leddy fonds. Leddy to Michael Hayden, "Further comments on Chapter VI (text and notes)," 2.

74 Thompson fonds, IV. b) 1955–59, 23.
75 Ibid.
76 Thompson, *A Personal History*, 174.
77 Pitsula to Richard Rempel, email exchange, 20 December 2008.
78 Spinks, *Two Blades of Grass*, 93. Spinks commented that these were "Wise words indeed!"
79 Thompson, *A Personal History*, 220.
80 Hayden, *Balance*, 240.
81 Axelrod, *Scholars and Dollars*, 96–8.
82 Leddy fonds, Leddy to Hayden, 9 November 1982. All the regret expressed by Hayden and some Saskatchewan faculty over the creation of what was to become the University of Regina ignores the fact that by 1960 both Saskatchewan and Alberta had instituted second campuses, while in Ontario, York University was only one of the several "new" universities created after 1959 to cope with "the phenomenal growth in student numbers ...." Harris *Higher Education*, 468–9.

CHAPTER EIGHT

1 Mary Thompson Smith Papers, Thompson to Mary Smith, 20 November 1958.
2 Mary Thompson Smith Papers, Thompson to Mary Smith, "Early" 1958.
3 Mary Thompson Smith Papers, Thompson to Mary Smith, 20 May 1951, 2.
4 Queen's University Archives, W.P. Francis' letters to Corry of 18 and 26 June 1958, and Neatby, *History of Queen's*, vol. 2, 417–20. Francis and Corry would have known each other well from the latter's years in the Faculty of Law at the University of Saskatchewan.
5 Board of Governors Minutes, 10 May 1958 and 12 November 1958.
6 Thompson fonds, "Departmental Celebratory Dinner, 14 September 1963."
7 Thompson fonds, IX. a). i) General, and Thompson fonds – misc, 1912–68. In fact, Leddy, while an enormously talented academic, highly educated, indeed erudite, was not a publishing scholar. He delivered many thoughtful speeches in diverse venues that were deeply appreciated by university and civic audiences. Nevertheless, despite his aspirations to be elected to the Royal Society of Canada, he was never selected.
8 Mary Thompson Smith Papers, Thompson to Mary Smith, 24 June 1954.
9 Richard Rempel fonds, interview with Professor Safarian, 26 February 2007, in Toronto at the Rotman School of Business.

10 President's Office fonds, Series III, B. 209.
11 Leddy fonds, Leddy to Hayden, 9 November 1982, no evidence exists from his family and other sources close to President Thompson that adds any validity to this speculation.
12 Ibid., Leddy to Hayden, 25 April 1983, "Some Further Reflections," on Hayden's draft of *Balance*, Chapter VII, 7.
13 Ibid., 3.
14 Mary Thompson Smith Papers, Thompson to Mary Smith, 30 November 1958.
15 Spinks fonds, 14.A file Thompson, W.P. Thompson to Spinks, 10 April 1957.
16 Mary Thompson Smith Papers, Thompson to Mary Smith, 30 November 1958.
17 Spinks fonds, 14.A. Thompson, W.P., 10 January 1959.
18 Richard Rempel fonds, Thompson to Jimmy and Peggy Thompson from 403 Copland Crescent, Sunday [ca. 1960].
19 Lyons's record of his interview with Dr E.W. Barootes, who led the "gruelling battle" on behalf of the doctors who opposed Medicare, "The 1962 Battle over Canadian Health Care: Labor Pains," *Whole Earth Review*, 7.
20 Horlick, *Medical College*, 146–7.
21 Houston, *Road to Medicare*, 96–7.
22 Mason, http://www.dufourlaw.com/ndp/tommy.htm. McLeod and McLeod also note that Saskatchewan Government revenues, especially from oil and mineral resources, rose rapidly in the late 1950s.
23 Ibid.
24 Thompson fonds, C. 80, file 93, Douglas to Thompson, 23 November 1959.
25 Ibid., Douglas to Thompson, 23 November 1959.
26 Richard Rempel fonds, Thompson to Jimmy and Peggy, Sunday, 29 November 1959. Given to author by Margaret Thompson.
27 Thompson fonds, C. 81, file 109, Walter Erb to Thompson, 30 December 1959.
28 Mary Thompson Smith Papers, Thompson to Mary Smith and family, 18 March 1960. In fact, the CCF won the 1960 election.
29 Archer, *Saskatchewan*, 303.
30 Thompson fonds, C. 81, file 109. Thompson to Roth, 28 December 1959. None of the physicians he spoke with "know that I have any particular interest in it [the medical care program]."
31 Mary Thompson Smith Papers, Thompson to Mary Smith, 18 April 1960. Sparks had been hired by the provincial government from the federal

Department of Health and Welfare where he was a senior research officer where his specialty was medical economics.

32 *Report of the Advisory Planning Committee*, 10.

33 Thompson fonds, C. 80. Thompson to Sparks, 18 July 1960.

34 Ibid., Thompson to Sparks, 26 August 1960.

35 *Advisory Planning ... Medical Care*, to the Government of Saskatchewan, 10.

36 Thompson fonds, C. 80. J.E Sparks, 28 February 1961.

37 Taylor, *Financial Aspects*, 28.

38 McLeod and McLeod, *Douglas*, 250.

39 Tollefson, *Bitter Medicine*, 55-6.

40 Tollefson fonds, typescript of an interview between Tollefson and Thompson, 12 May 1966, 7.

41 Thompson fonds, C. 80. Beatrice Trew to Thompson, 10 November 1960. Mrs Trew had been a CCF MLA and was a leader in the Saskatchewan Farmers Union.

42 McLeod and McLeod, *Douglas*, 250.

43 Thompson fonds, 21 November 1960.

44 Thompson fonds, C. 80. Thompson to A.W. Johnson, 14 June 1963.

45 Thompson fonds, VI. Mss for Autobiography. Biology Dinner, 14 September 1963.

46 Thompson fonds, C. 80. Thompson to A.W. Johnson, 16 May 1963.

47 Meeting in Regina between Walter Smishek and author, 11 December 2006.

48 Second Richard Rempel interview with Walter Smishek in Regina, 11 January 2010. Smishek is the only living member of the Thompson Committee. Dr Barootes died in 2000.

49 Tollefson fonds, transcript of Tollefson's interview with Thompson, 12 May 1966, 13.

50 McLeod and McLeod, *Douglas*, 250.

51 Badgley and Wolfe, *Doctors' Strike*, 38–9 and 49, where Thompson is referred to "as the architect of the plan."

52 Tollefson fonds, interview with Thompson, 12 May 1966, 10

53 McLeod and McLeod, *Douglas*, 252, and Thompson fonds, C.80. Thompson to Erb, 28 September 1961, and page 6 of the first Smishek tape.

54 Thompson fonds, C.80. Douglas to Thompson, 12 October 1961.

55 Tollefson, *Bitter Medicine*, 62–4.

56 Badgley and Wolfe, *Doctors' Strike*, 39–40, and fn. 51, 179.

57 Tollefson, *Bitter Medicine*, 64.

58 Mary Thompson Smith Papers, Thompson to Mary Smith, [5] October 1961.

59 First Smishek interview.

60 Thompson, *Medical Care*, 154.
61 Begg, R.W. "same letter to all Deans of Medicine, except Sherbrooke," 13 July 1962. See http://scaa.usask.ca/gallery/uofs_events/articles/1962.php.
62 Mary Thompson Smith papers, Thompson to Mary Smith and family, 6 August 1962.
63 Richard Rempel fonds. Interview with the Hon. Allan Blakeney, 8 December 2006, 2.
64 Thompson fonds, Address at Saskatchewan Government. Dinner in Honor of Committee. Saskatoon, 28 Jan. 1963.
65 Mary Smith Thompson papers, Thompson to Mary Smith, 5 October 1961.
66 "Handing Care to Commission Serious Issue, Says Lang," *Saskatoon Star Phoenix*, 17 February 1962, 3.
67 Thompson fonds, C. 80. O. Lang, marked Private, since Thompson did not want "to get into a public controversy."
68 Thompson, *Medical Care*, 162–3.
69 Ibid., 4.
70 Ibid., 109.
71 Ibid., 139. By 1971, Medicare had become universally available all across Canada.
72 Swanson, "Books and Authors," *Saskatoon Star Phoenix*, 13 June 1963.
73 Mary Thompson Smith Papers, Thompson to Mary Smith and family, 26 March 1965.
74 Thompson, W.P. Saskatchewan Doctors' Opinions of Medicare. A Questionnaire, 12 February 1965.
75 Thompson fonds, Swanson's review of *Medical Care*.
76 Mary Thompson Smith papers, Thompson to Mary Thompson Smith, early 1965.
77 Mary Thompson Smith Papers, Thompson to Mary Smith, early 1965.
78 Thompson fonds, C.80.
79 "Saskatchewan Doctors' Opinions of 'Medicare,'" *The Canadian Medical Association Journal* vol. 93, 971–6.
80 Tollefson, *Bitter Medicine*, 64.
81 Woodrow Lloyd fonds, Miscellaneous Papers, 61, 7. Thompson to Lloyd, undated but clearly December 1964, folder 5, Congratulatory Letters, etc.
82 Mary Thompson Smith Papers, Thompson to Mary Smith, 24 June 1964.
83 Vaughan, *Aggressive in Pursuit*, 137.

CHAPTER NINE

1 Mary Thompson Smith Papers, Thompson to Mary Smith, 8 April 1962.
2 Mary Thompson Smith Papers, Thompson to Mary Smith and her family, 18 April 1960. Earlier Thompson had served on other boards, especially the Markle Foundation that assessed candidates who earlier had been awarded post-doctoral fellowships and then sought further financial assistance to go into academic medicine. Mary Thompson Smith Papers, Thompson to Mary Smith 25 December 1951. He served on this Foundation's Board again in December 1958.
3 Mary Thompson Smith Papers, Thompson to Mary Thompson Smith, 8 April 1962, 3.
4 Mary Thompson Smith Papers, Thompson to Mary Smith and family, 18 April 1960.
5 Thompson, *Graduate Education*, 41.
6 Ibid., 95.
7 Ibid., 109.
8 Richard Rempel fonds, Lucy Smith email to author, 12 January 2007.
9 Ibid., Marcia Mayo email to author, 1 January 2007.
10 Ibid.
11 Mary Thompson Smith Papers, Thompson to Mary Thompson Smith, 22 December 1961.
12 Ibid., Mary Thompson Smith to Ben Smith, 19 December 1963.
13 Ibid., Mary Thompson Smith to Ben Smith, 26 November 1963.
14 Margaret Thompson fonds, "A Memoir," 27.
15 Mary Thompson Smith Papers, Thompson to Mary Smith, 6 June 1952.
16 Ibid., Thompson to Mary Smith, 7 August 1952. The Democratic Convention was held late in July.
17 Ibid., Thompson to Mary Smith, 12 June 1957.
18 Ibid., Thompson to Mary Smith, 12 August 1957.
19 Ibid., Thompson to Mary Smith and her family, 22 October 1961.
20 Ibid., Thompson to Mary Smith, 13 October 1963.
21 Mary Thompson Smith Papers, Thompson to Mary Smith, 13 October 1963.
22 Ibid., Thompson to Mary and Ben Smith, 23 May 1964.
23 Ibid., Thompson to Mary Smith, 4 June 1964. During these unsettling political times of June 1964 and earlier in November and December 1963, Thompson was in a constant state of anxiety about the health of his wife, who was in hospital with a thrombosis (clot) in a small blood vessel. As he

said to his daughter in a letter set on 16 June 1964: "It has been a terrific strain and I am not thinking very straight."

24 Richard Rempel fonds, letter provided by Margaret Thompson to author. Thompson to Peggy and Jimmy, 4 September 1967.
25 Mary Thompson Smith Papers, Thompson to Mary Smith, 16 April 1963.
26 Thompson fonds, IX. a). viii). Addresses – Alumni. As noted by Thompson, the numbers were "Saskatchewan 46, and the others 35, 25, 22 (BC, Man, Alta). And Saskatchewan is the smallest of the four, BC having more than twice our enrollment."
27 Thompson fonds, IX, a) vii) Speech to Agricultural Banquet, March 1958.
28 Waite, *Point Grey*, 164.
29 Thompson fonds, Personal Papers, XIV, 10th International Congress of Genetics.
30 Richard Rempel fonds, Hugh Brock, email to author, 3 May 2010.
31 Bayley, *Biology At McMaster*, 57–8.
32 Richard Rempel fonds, Isabel Auld to author, email 3 May 2010. "There was no genetics course [at the University of Manitoba] until Len came back from Saskatoon [late 1953] and he introduced one in Agriculture. He purchased the first electron microscope and the microscope was used by a researcher in the Faculty of Medicine when she was studying the extra chromosome which leads to Downs Syndrome. You can see that W.P. Thompson's influence was really extensive."
33 Woodside, *Who Should Pay?*, 43.
34 Harris, *Higher Education*, 434. Thompson was proud that in 1955 he could announce that "every year we receive $250,000 to $300,000 on grants in aid of research from the NRC, the Defence Research Board, The Canadian Cancer Society, the Federal Department of Agriculture, and private firms.
35 Publications Collection, President's Annual Report, 1952–53, 10.
36 Thompson fonds, IX. d) Retirement. Douglas to Thompson, Regina, 14 November 1958.
37 Eli Bornstein fonds, MG 342 (acc. 2011-60), series 3, file "W.P. Thompson," letter to Eli Bornstein, 9 November 1966.
38 Thompson, *A Personal History*, Preface, 1–2.
39 Mary Thompson Smith Papers, Thompson to Mary Smith, 15 November 1967.
40 Thompson, *A Personal History*, 117–18.
41 Richard Rempel fonds, Thompson to Peggy and Jimmy Thompson, 3 October 1968.
42 Mary Thompson Smith Papers, 26 October, 1968. Thompson to Jimmy and Peggy Thompson. In a covering note, James wrote to his sister that he was

"particularly pleased that Dad got through the whole day of the investiture without a twinge of Angina. He must be doing pretty well to do that."

43 Mary Thompson Smith Papers, Thompson to Mary Smith, 2 October 1969, from Sunnybrook Hospital in Toronto.

44 Richard Rempel fonds, provided by Margaret Thompson to author. Thompson to Peggy and Jimmy, 1 January 1970.

45 Mary Thompson Smith Papers, Margaret Newton to Mary Smith, 30 April 1970.

46 Richard Rempel fonds, Lucy Smith email to author, 11 January 2007.

47 Information from archivist Cheryl Avery to author, email 22 November 2008.

48 "Presidency Changes Hands: Dr Spinks Takes Over Reins," *The Sheaf*, 6 November 1959, 1.

49 Rempel, J.G. "Walter Palmer Thompson," 111.

50 Mary Thompson Smith Papers, Hilda Neatby's Memorial Address, 3 April 1970.

APPENDIX ONE

1 Thompson, Flavelle Lecture: "Some Problems in the Cytogenetics of Cereals: A Historical Review." *Transactions of the Royal Society of Canada*, Vol. XLIII: June 1949, Section Five. 38.

2 Richard Rempel fonds, Analysis of Dr Margaret Steeves, email to author, 11 August 2008.

3 Richard Rempel fonds, Dr Margaret Steeves, note to author, 8 August 2008. Dr Steeves and Dr Maureen-DuWors Rever kindly made much of the analysis and explanations.

4 Thompson, IX, President's Office, a) Address, ix Botanical Addresses.

5 Babcock and Clausen, *Genetics*, 432–3, 437.

6 Gill and Gill, "Mapping in the realm ..."

APPENDIX TWO

1 Sokolov, "Imprinting," 1043–52.

2 Ibid.

3 Thompson, "Shrivelled Endosperm in Species Crosses in Wheat, its Cytological Causes and Genetical Effects," *Genetics* 15: 99–113.

4 Ibid.

5 Haig and Westoby, "Genomic Imprinting," 1–113; and Bushell, Spielman, and Scott, "Artificial Postzygotic Hybridization," 1430–42.

6 Sharma, "How Wide Can a Cross Be?," 43–4.

Bibliography

PRIMARY SOURCES

Auld, Isabel and Murray Auld. Interview with author, Winnipeg, 6 July 2008.

Barber, Lloyd. Interview with author, Regina Beach, 20 August 2009.

Blakeney, Hon. Allan. Interview with author, Saskatoon, 8 December 2008.

Bornstein, Eli. Interview with author, Saskatoon, 15 August 2007.

Dundas, Hugh McKenzie. Interview with author, Pembroke, 3 July 2006.

Knott, Douglas. Interview with author, Saskatoon, 15 March 2008; Hayden, Michael. Interview with author, June 2007.

Library and Archives Canada. Royal Commission on National Development in the Arts, Letters, and Sciences fonds.

Mayo, Marcia. Interview with author, New York, 30 June 2008.

McEown, Donald. Interview with author, Ottawa, 5 January 2008.

Morrison, Frances. Interview with author, Saskatoon, 14 September 2005.

Rever-DuWors, Maureen. Interview with author, Saskatoon, 15 July 2007.

Safarian, Edward. Interview with author, Toronto, 12 November 2006.

Saskatchewan Archives Board:

T.C. Douglas fonds, F 117.

W.S. Lloyd fonds, F 131.

Hilda Neatby fonds.

E.A. Tollefson fonds

Smishek, Hon.Walter. Interview with author, Regina, 11 December 2006 and 11 January 2010.

Smith, Lucy. Interview with author, New York, 30 June 2011.

Steeves, Margaret. Interview with author, Saskatoon, 15 July 2007.

Thompson, Margaret. Interview with author, Toronto, 12 September 2008.
University of Regina Archives. William Riddell fonds.
University of Saskatchewan Archives:
T.J. Arnason fonds, MG 31.
Board of Governors minutes.
Eli Bornstein fonds, MG 342.
College of Law fonds, RG 2082.
Controller's Office fonds, RG 2008.
Faculty Biographies collection.
Faculty Publications collection.
Vernon C. Fowke fonds, MG 13.
J.E. Murray fonds, MG 61.
Office of the President fonds, RG 1, Series 1: Walter Murray.
Office of the President fonds, RG 1, Series 2: J.S. Thomson.
Office of the President fonds, RG 1, Series 3: W.P. Thompson.
Office of the President fonds, RG 1, Series 4: J.W.T. Spinks.
Lorne and Mildred Paul fonds, MG 55.
Donald S. Rawson fonds, MG 8.
Richard Rempel fonds, MG 302.
Saskatchewan Homemakers' Clubs fonds.
Senate minutes.
G.W. Simpson fonds, MG 7.
J.W.T. Spinks fonds, MG 74.
W.P. Thompson fonds, MG 17.
T.C. Vanterpool fonds, MG 69.
Vice-President (Administration) – McEown, RG 2003.
University of Toronto Archives. Margaret Thompson fonds.
University of Windsor Archives. Francis Leddy fonds. Unprocessed collection.

SECONDARY SOURCES

Allemang, John. "Facts and Arguments, Lives Lived: Orvald Gratias." *The Globe and Mail.* 1 August 1996.
Armstrong, Christopher and H.V. Nelles. *The Revenge of the Methodist Bicycle Company: Sunday Streetcars and Municipal Reform in Toronto, 1888–1897.* Toronto: P. Martin Associates, 1977.
Archer, John H. *Saskatchewan: A History.* Saskatoon: Western Producer Prairie Books, 1980.

Arnason, T.J. "Walter Palmer Thompson: 1889–1970." *Canadian Journal of Genetics and Cytology* vol. 12 no. 3 (September 1970): i–ii.

Axelrod, Paul. *Scholars and Dollars: Politics, Economics and the Universities of Ontario, 1945–1980*. Toronto: University of Toronto Press, 1982.

Axelrod, Paul and John G. Reid. *Youth, University and Canadian Society: Essays in the Social History of Higher Education*. Montreal and Kingston: McGill-Queen's University Press, 1989.

Babcock, Ernest Brown and Roy Elwood Clausen. *Genetics in Relation to Agriculture*. New York: McGraw-Hill, 1919.

Badgley, Robin F. and Samuel Wolfe. *Doctor's Strike: Medical Care and Conflict in Saskatchewan*. Toronto: Macmillan, 1967.

Bayley, Stanley T. *Biology at McMaster University: 1890–1990*. Hamilton: Department of Biology, McMaster University, 2008.

Beckwith, Jon. "A Historical View of Social Responsibility in Genetics." *American Journal of Biological Science* vol. 43 no. 5 (May 1993): 327–33.

Bigland, Christopher H. *WCVM, the First Decade and More: The History of the Western College of Veterinary Medicine*. Saskatoon: Western College of Veterinary Medicine, (1990).

"Biology and Evolution of the *Gnetales*." Symposium Supplement of the *International Journal of Plant Sciences* vol. 157 no. 6 (November 1996): 1–125.

Bissell, Claude T. (editor). *Canada's Crisis in Higher Education*. Toronto: University of Toronto Press, 1957.

Borlaug, Norman E. "Stem Rust Never Sleeps." *New York Times*, 26 April 2008.

Bothwell, Robert, Ian Drummond, and John English. *Canada Since 1945: Power, Politics and Provincialism*. Toronto: University of Toronto Press, 1982.

Brebner, John Bartlett. *Scholarship for Canada: The Function of Graduate Studies*. Ottawa: Canadian Social Science Research Council, 1945.

Buchan, D.R. *Greenhouse to Medical Centre: Saskatchewan's Medical School 1926–78*.Saskatoon: University of Saskatchewan, 1983.

Bushell, C.M. Spielman and R.J. Scott. "The Basis of Natural and Artificial Postzygotic Hybridization Barriers in Arabidopsis Species." *The Plant Cell* vol. 15 (2003): 1430–42.

Cameron, David M. *More Than an Academic Question: Universities, Government and Public Policy in Canada*. Halifax: The Institute for Research on Public Policy, 1991.

Cameron, D.R. and W.P. Thompson. "Chromosome Numbers in Functioning Germ Cells of Species Hybrids in Wheat." *Genetics* vol. 13 no. 6 (November 1928): 456–69.

Currie, B.W. *The Physics Department 1910–1976, University of Saskatchewan.* Saskatoon: University of Saskatchewan, 1976.

Djwa, Sandra. *The Politics of Imagination: A Life of F.R. Scott.* Toronto: McClelland andStewart, 1987.

Dyck, Betty L. *Running to Beat Hell: A Biography of A.M. (Sandy) Nicholson.* Regina: Canadian Plains Research Center, University of Regina, 1988.

Estey, Ralph H. *Essays on the History of Plant Pathology and Mycology in Canada.* Montreal and Kingston: McGill-Queen's University Press, 1994.

Evans, Ross. Quoted in "Reliving the Legends: The University of Saskatchewan Hangar Stories." *Green & White* (Spring 2003).

Fairbairn, Garry. *From Prairie Roots: The Remarkable Story of the Saskatchewan Wheat Pool.* Saskatoon: Western Producer Prairie Books, 1984.

Fowke, Vernon. *The National Policy and the Wheat Economy.* Toronto: University of Toronto Press, 1957.

– "Salaries and Related Conditions of Employment in Canadian Universities." Presented to the National Conference of Canadian Universities, November 1956.

Garvin, J.L. *The Life of Joseph Chamberlain. Volume One 1836–1885.* London: Macmillan, 1932.

Gauvreau, Michael. "Recasting Canada's Post-war Decade." In *Cultures of Citizenship in Post-war Canada, 1940–1955,* edited by Nancy Christie and Michael Gauvreau. Montreal and Kingston: McGill-Queen's University Press, 2003, 3–26.

Gill, K.S. and B.S. Gill. "Mapping in the Realm of Polyploidy: The Wheat Model." *BioEssays* vol. 16 no. 11 (1994): 841–846.

Gingras, Yves. "Why Canada Never had a National Association for the Advancement of Science." *La Physique au Canada* vol. 62 no. 6 (November/December 2006): 355–9.

– "Financial Support for Post-Graduate Students and the Development of Scientific Research in Canada." In Paul Axelrod and John G. Reid, eds., *Youth, University and Canadian Society Essays in the Social History of Higher Education.* Montreal and Kingston: McGill-Queen's University Press, 1989, 308–9.

Greenlee, James. *Sir Robert Falconer: A Biography.* Toronto: University of Toronto Press, 1988.

Gruending, Dennis. *Promises to Keep: A Political Biography of Allan Blakeney.* Saskatoon: Western Producer Prairie Books, 1990.

Hallman, Diane M. "Traditions and Transitions: The Case of Saskatchewan." *Journal of Teacher Education* vol. 10 (2003): 169–85.

Haig, D. and M. Westoby. "Genomic Imprinting in Endosperm." *Philosophical Transactions of the Royal Society of London: Biological Sciences* vol. 333 no.1266 (1991): 1–13.

"Handing Care to Commission Serious Issue, Says Lang." *Saskatoon Star Phoenix*, 17 February 1962, 3.

Harris, Robin. *A History of Higher Education in Canada: 1663–1960.* Toronto: University of Toronto Press, (1976).

Hayden, Michael. *Seeking a Balance: The University of Saskatchewan 1907–1983.* Vancouver: University of British Columbia Press, 1983.

– "The Fight that Underhill Missed: Government and Academic Freedom at the University of Saskatchewan, 1919–1920," in *Academic Freedom: Harry Crowe Memorial Lectures, 1986*, edited by Michiel Horn, North York: York University, 1987.

Helmes-Hayes, R. *Measuring the Mosaic: An Intellectual Biography of John Porter.* Toronto: University of Toronto Press, 2010.

Hewitt, S.R. "Spying 101: The RCMP's Secret Activities at the University of Saskatchewan, 1920–71." *Saskatchewan History* vol. 47 no. 2. (Fall 1995): 20–31.

Horlick, Louis. *Wendell Macleod: Saskatchewan's Red Dean.* Montreal and Kingston: McGill-Queen's University Press, 2007.

– *Medical College to Community Resource: Saskatchewan's Medical School 1978–1998: Volume Two: History of the College of Medicine, University of Saskatchewan.* Saskatoon: University of Saskatchewan, 1999.

Horn, Michiel. *Academic Freedom in Canada: A History.* Toronto: University of Toronto Press, 1999.

Houston, C. Stuart. *Steps on the Road to Medicare: Why Saskatchewan led the Way.* Montreal and Kingston: McGill-Queen's University Press, 2002.

Houston, Stuart and Bill Waiser. *Tommy's Team: The People Behind the Douglas Years.*Markham, ON: Fifth House, 2010.

Humphries, Charles W. *"Honest Enough to be Bold:" The Life and Times of Sir James Pliny Whitney.* Toronto: University of Toronto Press, 1985.

Inge, Dean W.R. *The Idea of Progress.* Oxford: Clarendon Press, 1920.

Johns, Walter H. *A History of the University of Alberta.* Edmonton: University of Alberta Press, 1981.

Johnson, A.W. *Dream No Little Dreams: A Biography of the Douglas Government of Saskatchewan, 1944–1961*. Toronto: University of Toronto Press, 2004.

Jugoslav Encounter. Ninth International Seminar, World University Service, Jugoslavia, 1958.

Kandel, Eric. "Thomas Hunt Morgan at Columbia University: Genes, Chromosomes and the Origins of Modern Biology." *Columbia Magazine* (2006) www.Columbia. edu/cu/alumni/Magazine/Morgan/morgan.html.

Kerr, Don. "The College Building." *Saskatoon History Review* 20 (2006).

Kerr, Don and Stan Hanson. *Saskatoon: The First Half-Century.* Edmonton: NeWest Press, 1982.

Kimber, Gordon. "A Reassessment of the Origins of the Polyploid Wheats." Symposium on Origin of Cultivated Plants: XIII International Congress of Genetics in *Genetics* vol. 78 (1974): 487–92.

King, Carlyle. *Extending the Boundaries: Scholarship and Research at the University of Saskatchewan 1909–1966*. Saskatoon: University of Saskatchewan, 1967.

– *The First Fifty: Teaching, Research, and Public Service at the University of Saskatchewan, 1909–1959*. Toronto: McClelland and Stewart, 1959.

Kuffert, Leonard. "Reconstructing Canadian Culture," in *Cultures of Citizenship in Post-war Canada, 1940–1955*, edited by Nancy Christie and Michael Gauvreau. Montreal and Kingston: McGill-Queen's University Press, 2003, 190–5.

Lazarevich, Gordana. *The Musical World of Frances James and Murray Adaskin.* Toronto: University of Toronto Press, 1988.

Lloyd, Dianne. *Woodrow: A Biography of W.S. Lloyd.* Woodrow Lloyd Memorial Fund, 1979.

Lyons, Steven. "The 1962 Battle over Canadian Health Care: Labour Pains." *Whole Earth Review* (Winter 1995): 7.

Proceedings of the National Conference of Canadian Universities (NCCU).

Martens, J.W. and P.L. Dyck. "Genetics of Resistance to Rust in Cereals from a CanadianPerspective." *Canadian Journal of Plant Pathology* vol. 11 (1989): 1–6.

Martin, et al. "Retention of D Genome Chromosomes in Pentaploid Wheat Crosses." *Heredity* vol. 107 (2011): 315–19.

Massolin, Philip A. "Modernization and Reaction: Postwar Evolutions and the Critique of Higher Learning in English-Speaking Canada, 1945–1970." *Journal of Canadian Studies* vol. 36 no. 2 (Summer 2001): 130–63.

MacLeod, Roy M. and E. Kay Andrews "Scientific Careers of Exhibition Scholars," *Nature.* vol. 218 (15 June 1968): 1011–16.

Mason, Andrew. "Tommy Douglas: A Brief History of Medicare," in *Saskatchewan New Democrats*, http://www.dufourlaw.com/ndp/tommy.htm.

McCrorie, James Napier. "A.K. Davis – The Saskatchewan Years," in *Critical Sociology: Essays in Honour of Arthur K. Davis.* New Delhi: B.R. Pub Co., 1995.

McLaren, Angus. *Our Own Master Race: Eugenics in Canada, 1885–1945.* Toronto: McClelland and Stewart, 1990.

McLeod, Thomas H. and Ian McLeod. *Tommy Douglas: The Road to Jerusalem.* Edmonton: Hurtig, 2004.

Murray, David R. and Robert A. Murray. *The Prairie Builder: Walter Murray of Saskatchewan.* Edmonton: NeWest Press, 1984.

Neatby, Hilda, Frederick W. Gibson, and Roger Graham. *Queen's University: to Strive, to Seek, to Find, and Not to Yield.* (1 volume). Montreal: McGill-Queen's University Press, 1978.

Nock, David. "The Sociological Legacy of Arthur K. Davis." *Society* vol. 26 no.1 (April 2002).

Owram, Doug. *Born at the Right Time: A History of the Baby-Boom Generation.* Toronto: University of Toronto Press, 1996.

Palmer, Bryan D. *Canada's 1960s: The Ironies of Identity in a Rebellious Era.* Toronto: University of Toronto Press, 2009.

Petry, Roger. "Walter Murray and the State University: The Response of the University of Saskatchewan to the Great Depression, 1930–1937." *Saskatchewan History* vol. 56 no. 2 (Fall 2004): 5–23.

Pilkington, Gwendoline Evans. *Speaking with One Voice: Universities in Dialogue with Government.* Montreal: McGill University, 1983.

Pitsula, James. *Higher Education Policy in Saskatchewan and the Legacy of Myth.* Public Policy Paper 12 (February 2003): 1–24.

Pitsula, James. *As One Who Serves: The Making of the University of Regina.* Montreal and Kingston: McGill-Queen's University Press, 2006.

"Presidency Changes Hands: Dr. Spinks Takes Over Reins." *The Sheaf*, 6 November 1959, 1.

Preston, Mel A. and Helen E. Howard-Lock. "Emergence of Physics Graduate Work in Canadian Universities, 1945–1960," *La Physique Au Canada* vol. 56 (mars/avril 2000): 153–62.

Priestly, F.E.L. *The Humanities in Canada: A Report for the Humanities Research Council of Canada.* Toronto: University of Toronto Press, 1964.

Raven, P.H. and Evert, R.F. and Curtis, H. *Biology of Plants*. New York: Worth Publications, 1986.

Rein, Paula Fay. "The Changing Conditions: A Study of the Saskatchewan Royal Commission on Agriculture and Rural Life." M.A. thesis, University of Regina, 1994.

Rempel, J.G. "Walter Palmer Thompson, 1889–1970." *Transactions of the Royal Society of Canada* vol. 9 (1971): 111.

Riddell, William, A. "How Well I Remember." University of Regina Archives, [Publications] Box 2, unpublished document.

Scagel, R.F. et al. *Nonvascular Plants: An Evolutionary Survey*. University of British Columbia: Worth Publications, 1982.

Sharma, H.C. "How Wide Can a Cross Be?" *Euphytica* 1995 vol. 82 no. 1 (1995): 43–64.

Sheffield, E.F. *Canadian University and College Enrolment Projected to 1965: Prepared for a Symposium on "The Expansion of Enrolment, 1955–1965. National Conference of Canadian Universities, Toronto, June 10, 1955* and *University and College Enrolment in the Province of Saskatchewan – Projects to 1961–62* (August 1955).

Sokolov, V.A. "Imprinting in Plants." *Russian Journal of Genetics* vol. 42 no. 9 (2006): 1250–60.

Spafford, Shirley. *No Ordinary Academics: Economics and Political Science at the University of Saskatchewan, 1910–1960*. Toronto: University of Toronto Press, 2000.

Spinks, John. *Two Blades of Grass: An Autobiography*. Saskatoon: Western Producer Prairie Books, 1980.

Stager, A.A. "Federal Government Grants to Canadian Universities, 1951–66." *The Canadian Historical Review* vol. 54 no. 3 (September 1973): 287–97.

Stebbins, G. Leydard. *Ernest Brown Babcock, 1877–1954: A Biographical Memoir*. Washington: National Academy of Sciences, 1958.

Stoicheff, Boris. *Gerhard Herzberg: An Illustrious Life in Science*. Ottawa: NRC Press, 2002.

Swanson, Jean. "Books and Authors – a Splendid Book on the Still Controversial "Medicare." *Saskatoon Star Phoenix*, 13 June 1963.

Taft, Michael. *Inside These Greystone Walls: An Anecdotal History of the University of Saskatchewan*. Saskatoon: University of Saskatchewan, 1984.

"The Biological Conception of Progress," Seventh Meeting of the Saskatchewan Educational Conference held in Regina, 10 November 1945.

Taylor, Malcolm, G. *Financial Aspects of Health Insurance*. Canadian Tax Papers, no. 12, (1957), 28.

Thomson, Dale C. *Louis St. Laurent: Canadian*. New York: St. Martin's Press 1967.

Thompson, Margaret. "A Memoir of Mrs. W.P. Thompson," *Saskatoon History Review*, (November 2011), 27.

Thompson, W.P. "Annual Address to Convocation." *The Sheaf*, 18 September 1953, 1.

– "A Botanical Trip Through German South-West Africa," *The Canadian Field Naturalist* vol. 35 no. 1, (April 1921): 74–5.

– "The Cause and Mode of Evolution." In *Evolution: Its Science and Doctrine: Symposium presented to the Royal Society of Canada in 1959*, edited by Thomas M. Cameron. Toronto: University of Toronto Press, 1960, 72–88.

– "Education and Moral Values." *Canadian Education* vol. 7 no. 1, 30–8.

– *Graduate Education in the Sciences in Canadian Universities*. Toronto: University of Toronto Press, 1963.

– *Medical Care: Programs and Issues*. Toronto: Clarke Irwin, 1964.

– "Morphology and Affinities of *Gnetum*," in *American Journal of Botany* vol. 3 no. 4 (1916): 135–84.

– "Presidential Address," *Proceedings of the National Conference of Canadian Universities*, 1954.

– "Saskatchewan Doctors' Opinions of 'Medicare: A Questionnaire Survey.'" *The Canadian Medical Association Journal* vol. 93 no. 18 (1965): 971–6.

– "Shrivelled Endosperm in Species Crosses in Wheat, its Cytological Causes and Genetical Effects." *Genetics* vol. 15 no. 2 (1930): 99–133.

– "Some Problems in the Cytogenetics of Cereals: A Historical Review." *Transactions of the Royal Society of Canada* vol. 43 (June 1949).

– "A University in Trouble." *Saskatchewan History* vol. 17 no. 3 (Autumn 1964): 81–104.

– *The University of Saskatchewan: A Personal History*. Toronto: University of Toronto Press, 1970.

Thompson, W.P., T.J. Arnason, and R.M. Love. "Some Factors in the Different Chromosome Sets of Common Wheat." *Canadian Journal of Research*. vol. 12 (1935): 335–45.

Thompson, W.P. and H. Haining. "Development of the Embryo of Gnetum." *Botanical Gazette* vol. 70 no. 6 (December 1920): 436–45.

Thompson, W.P. and L. Hollingshead. "Preponderance of *dicoccum*-like Characters and Chromosome Numbers in Hybrids between *Triticum dicoccum* and *Triticum vulgare*." *Journal of Genetics* vol. 17 (January 1927): 283–307.

Thompson, W.P. and J. Jenkins. "Chromosome Conditions in the Second and Third Generations of Pentaploid Wheat Hybrids." *Canadian Journal of Research* vol. 2 (1930): 162–70.

– "Chromosome Homologies in Wheat and Aegilops." *American Journal of Botany* vol. 16 (April 1929): 238–45.

Thompson, W.P. and M.C. Melburn. "Heterotypic Prophases in the Absence of Chromosome Pairing." *Canadian Journal of Research* vol. 1 (1929): 512–27.

Thomson, J.S. *Yesteryears at the University of Saskatchewan: 1937–1949*. Saskatoon: Modern Press, 1969.

Tijo, J.N. and A. Levan. "The Chromosome Number of a Man." *Hereditas* vol. 42 (1956): 1–6.

Tollefson, E.A. *Bitter Medicine: The Saskatchewan Medicare Feud.* Saskatoon: Modern Press, 1963.

– "The Medicare Dispute," in *Politics in Saskatchewan*, edited by Norman Ward and Duff Spafford. Don Mills, ON: Longmans Canada, 1968.

Tudiver, Neil. *Universities for Sale: Resisting Corporate Control over Canadian Higher Education.* Toronto: James Lorimer, 1999.

University Act, Statutes of the Province of Saskatchewan, 3 April 1907.

University of Saskatchewan Archives. "1963: Western College of Veterinary Medicine." In *Deo et Patriae: Events in the History of the University of Saskatchewan*, accessed November 2010, http://scaa.sk.ca/gallery/uofs_events/articles/1963.php.

Vaughan, Frederick. *Aggressive in Pursuit: The Life of Justice Emmett Hall.* Toronto: University of Toronto Press, 2004.

Waiser, Bill. *Saskatchewan: A New History.* Calgary: Fifth House, 2005.

Waite, P.B. *Lord of Point Grey: Larry MacKenzie of U.B.C.* Vancouver: University of British Columbia Press, 1987.

Warnock, John. *Saskatchewan: The Roots of Discontent and Protest.* Montreal: Black Rose Books, 2004.

Wise, S.F. "God's Peculiar Peoples." In *The Shield of Achilles: Aspects of Canada in the Victorian Age*, edited by W.L. Morton. Toronto: McClelland and Stewart, 1968, 36–61.

Woodside, Willson. *The University Question: Who Should Go? Who Should Pay?* Toronto: Ryerson Press, 1958.

Wright, Donald. "Gender and the Professionalization of History in English Canada before 1960." *Canadian Historical Review* vol. 81 no. 1 (March 2000): 29–66.

Zhong, B. et al. "The Position of Gnetales among Seed Plants: Overcoming Pitfalls of Chloroplast Phylogenomics." *Molecular Biology and Evolution* (2010) http://mbe.oxfordjournals.org/content/27/12/2855. Abstract.

Index